CAMBRIDGE STUDIES IN EARLY MODERN HISTORY

Editors

J. H. ELLIOTT   H. G. KOENIGSBERGER

CALVINIST PREACHING AND ICONOCLASM IN THE NETHERLANDS, 1544–1569

CAMBRIDGE STUDIES IN EARLY MODERN HISTORY

Edited by J. H. Elliott and H. G. Koenigsberger

The idea of an 'early modern' period of European history from the fifteenth to the late eighteenth century is now widely accepted among historians. The purpose of the Cambridge Studies in Early Modern History is to publish monographs and studies which will illuminate the character of the period as a whole, and in particular focus attention on a dominant theme within it, the interplay of continuity and change as they are represented by the continuity of medieval ideas, political and social organization, and by the impact of new ideas, new methods and new demands on the traditional structures.

CALVINIST PREACHING AND ICONOCLASM IN THE NETHERLANDS 1544-1569

PHYLLIS MACK CREW
Associate Professor of History, Rutgers University

CAMBRIDGE UNIVERSITY PRESS

Cambridge

London · New York · Melbourne

Published by the Syndics of the Cambridge University Press
The Pitt Building, Trumpington Street, Cambridge CB2 1RP
Bentley House, 200 Euston Road, London NW1 2DB
32 East 57th Street, New York, NY 10022, USA
296 Beaconsfield Parade, Middle Park, Melbourne 3206, Australia

First published 1978

Printed in Great Britain by
Western Printing Services Limited, Bristol

Library of Congress Cataloguing in Publication Data
Crew, Phyllis Mack, 1939–
Calvinist preaching and iconoclasm in the
Netherlands, 1544–1569.
(Cambridge studies in early modern history)
Bibliography: p.
Includes index.
1. Clergy – Netherlands. 2. Calvinism – Netherlands.
3. Preaching – History – Netherlands. 4. Reformation –
Netherlands. I. Title.
BR395.C73   284'.2492   77–77013
ISBN 0 521 21739 3

For David

CONTENTS

Introduction   *page* 1

1   The troubles   5

2   The ministers   39

3   The reformed movement 1544–1565   51

4   Exile   83

5   The consciousness of the reformed clergy   107

6   The ministers and the troubles   140

Appendix A: Ministers active before the troubles   182

Appendix B: Ministers active during the troubles   185

Appendix C: Lay preachers active during the troubles   189

Bibliography   197

Index   213

ACKNOWLEDGEMENTS

Many people have generously helped me in preparing this study. My thanks to the librarians and archivists of the *Bibliothèque royale* and the *Archives générale du royaume* in Brussels, the municipal library of Bruges, the municipal archives of Antwerp and Valenciennes, the British Museum and Guild Hall libraries in London, and the Bodleian Library at Oxford. Special thanks to the staff of the Faculty of Protestant Theology in Brussels for permission to examine their valuable library in the most congenial surroundings. The original research for this study was made possible by a Cornell University graduate fellowship, 1970–1971. The Rutgers University Research Council provided welcome financial assistance during the summers of 1974 and 1976. I am grateful to the editors of Garland Press for permission to quote from the work of Keith Moxey, *Pieter Aertsen, Joachim Beuckelaer and the Rise of Secular Painting in the Context of the Reformation*.

Thanks to teachers, colleagues and friends who encouraged my work. I am grateful to Elizabeth Gleason for introducing me to the study of the Reformation, and to Clive Holmes, David Lagomarsino, Herbert Rowen, Jacob Smit and Donald Weinstein, who read the manuscript in various stages. Emile Lousse, Jan Craeybeckx and Emile Braekman were hospitable and patient in introducing me to research facilities in Brussels. I am grateful to Marcel Backhouse, Alistair Duke, David Lagomarsino and Keith Moxey for sharing unpublished material on the Troubles of 1566, and to Jean Meyhoffer for graciously allowing me to examine his private notes on Protestant ministers in the Netherlands. Special thanks to my editor, Professor John Elliott, for his constructive criticism of the manuscript, and to my thesis adviser, Helmut Koenigsberger. Professor Koenigsberger's enthusiasm and broad intelligence were – and are – an invaluable example for a young historian; I am grateful for his guidance during the early stages of the project and for his continued encouragement of my efforts to transform my Ph.D. thesis into a more coherent form. Finally, my thanks to David Crew, who as colleague, friend and husband helped me, more than anyone else, to do my best.

ABBREVIATIONS

AA	*Antwerpsch archievenblad*
AGR	Archives générale du royaume
BB	*Bibliotheca Belgica*
BCHEW	*Bulletin de la commission pour l'histoire des églises Wallonnes*
BCRH	*Bulletin de la commission royale d'histoire*
BN	*Biographie nationale*
BSHPB	*Bulletin de la société d'histoire du Protestantisme Belge*
BSHPF	*Bulletin de la société d'histoire du Protestantisme Français*
BvGN	*Bijdragen voor de geschiedenis der Nederlanden*
BWK	*Biographisch woordenboek*
BWK Prot.	*Biographisch woordenboek van Protestantische godgeleerden in Nederlanden*
CC	Chambre des comptes
CT	Conseil des troubles
EA	Etats et audiences
KP	*Kerkeraads protocollen der Nederduitsche vluchtelingen-kerk te Londen 1560–1563*, ed. A. A. van Schelven
NAvKG	Nederlandsch archief voor kerkgeschiedenis
NNBW	*Nieuw Nederlandsch biographisch woordenboek*
RHE	*Revue d'histoire écclésiastique*
SHRB	*Sources d'histoire religieuse de la Belgique*
TvG	*Tijdschrift voor geschiedenis*
WMV	*Werken der Marnix-Vereeniging*

The Netherlands in 1566

NORTH

SEA

FRIESLAND

BRENTHE

Emden

OVERYSSEL

GELDERLAND

Amsterdam

UTRECHT

HOLLAND

Culembourg

ZEELAND

UPPER
GELDER-
LAND

Breda

Bois-le-Duc

Bergen
op Zoom

Eindhoven

Ostend

Hulst

Turnhout

Nieuport

Axel

Antwerp

Graveliness

Dunkirk

Furnes

Bruges

Lierre

GERMANY

Calais

Dixmuide

Ghent

Termonde

BRABANT

Roulers

Deinze

Mechelen

LIÈGE

Poperinghe

Ypres

Courtrai

Alost

Audenarde

Louvain

Hasselt

Maastricht

St. Omer

Cassel

Werwick

Menin

Brussels

St. Trond

LIMBURG

Warneton

Armentieres

Renaix

ARTOIS

Lille

Lannoy

Tournai

Enghien

NAMUR

Liège

Béthune

Ochiès

Mons

HAINAUT

Douai

Arras

Valenciennes

Quesnoy

Cambray

LUXEMBOURG

F R A N C E

Metz

INTRODUCTION

In the spring of 1566, some fifty Calvinist preachers made their way to the Netherlands from churches in England, Germany, France and Switzerland.[1] A clandestine Reformed[2] movement had existed there for many years, and when the government issued a decree which limited the activities of the Inquisition against heresy in April, many ministers in exile returned home expecting to witness the beginning of religious toleration. In the early summer they began preaching publicly to huge audiences in the countryside. Then, in August, small bands of Reformers broke into the churches and demolished the images of Catholic worship; within a few days the iconoclasts had destroyed the interiors of over four hundred churches in Flanders alone. Triumphant, the Calvinists moved into the 'purified' churches and began holding formal religious services, but within a few months they found themselves under siege by government troops. When the Duke of Alva arrived from Spain in 1567 to inflict the king's punishment on the heretics, the era of Reformed worship, and Reformed violence, was already over; contemporaries called it the Wonderyear.

Those ministers who did not escape were executed, and when the execution was by fire, the royal official sometimes fastened a small bag of gunpowder to the chest of the victim. When the gunpowder exploded the priests told the assembly that it was the noise made by the Devil escaping from the corpse of the heretic.

This drama of martyrdom is tragic in itself, but it is also significant as a historical problem, because the three figures of the drama – priest, martyr,

---

[1] By 'Netherlands' I mean the provinces of Brabant, Flanders, Hainaut, Liège, Artois. My reasons for limiting this study to the southern provinces are chiefly practical, but there is also some historical justification for this division. Antwerp was the center of the Reformed movement in the south, Emden in the north. The south was partly French-speaking and the Walloon ministers corresponded mainly with churches in France and Geneva, while the north was almost entirely Dutch-speaking, and had closer relations with churches in Germany and England.

[2] I have used the term 'Reformed' interchangeably with 'Calvinist,' as contemporaries did. In chapter 3 I have used the term 'Protestant' in connection with the early evangelical movement in the Netherlands, to distinguish these reformers from those who were explicitly allied with Calvin after 1544.

audience – personify all of the discrete elements of the Reformation on which historians have focused their attention. Observing the drama from a distance, the three figures seem to be irreconcilably opposed and isolated from one another; the priest manipulates the ignorant populace by magical tricks which he himself does not believe; the martyr remains detached and spiritual, certain of his membership in God's Elect; and the passive audience simply watches, acted upon by forces which it does not comprehend. This is the way many historians, observing the Reformed movement from a distance, have chosen to analyze the disparate elements of that movement. They describe the corrupt bureaucracy of the Church and the properties of ecclesiastical magic as opposed to the fanaticism and spirituality of the Calvinist leaders, whom they designate as members of the 'magisterial' Reformation. They have also perceived a dichotomy between the magisterial Reformation, which they describe as organized, intellectual, and political, and the radical Reformation – those movements of social upheaval involving the lower classes of society, which they describe with phrases like 'inchoate,' 'inarticulate,' 'violent,' 'anarchistic.'

I began this study of the Troubles with the intention of describing one group of figures in the drama, the Calvinist ministers who were active in 1566. My assumption was that the ministers who preached in the years before the Dutch Revolt were similar in importance to the Huguenot pastors who fomented the civil wars in France, or to the radical Puritans in England. I was hoping to verify what many historians of the Netherlands had already assumed; that Calvinist ideology and organization created a radical, underground movement in the years before the Troubles, and that this clandestine movement, combined with the factors of economic unrest and political upheaval, led to a popular explosion of hostility against both Church and government in 1566, and ultimately to the Dutch Revolt. But as I became more familiar with the background and character of these ministers, I realized that they simply did not conform to the image which I had provided for them. Far from being a disciplined corps of Calvinist fanatics, the men who preached in the Netherlands were not even certain what it was to be a minister; three years before the Troubles they sent a mission to the church at Emden to inquire whether ordination was necessary to preach the Word of God.[3] The ministers also wondered about the political implications of Cal-

---

[3] Since the standards for distinguishing pastors from lay preachers were so vague during this early period of the Reformation, I have defined as a minister every preacher in 1566 who was involved in the activities of the orthodox Reformed movement in the years before the Troubles – either as a minister or as a member of an established church. Those who had no apparent connections with the movement and who preached during the Troubles are analyzed as lay preachers in chapter 6.

vinist ideology. Several were political radicals, an equal number were conservative, and almost all were obsessed by the importance of defending themselves as members of a legitimate movement in support of the Catholic government.

Thus the ministers who directed the Netherlands Reformed movement did not perceive the doctrines of Calvin as intrinsically revolutionary, and they certainly did not perceive themselves as members of a united revolutionary vanguard. On the contrary, the ministers saw the figures in the drama not as fixed entities, but as alternatives among which a choice had to be made. In exile, they had to decide whether or not they would compromise their religious principles in order to protect their congregations; at home, they had to decide whether or not they should give up the luxury of being 'fanatic Calvinists' in order to ally with the local Catholic nobility; in 1566, they had to decide to what extent they would encourage popular violence for the sake of the Reformed movement. In short, their interest as a historical subject lies in this: that we can observe, in concrete terms, how individuals tried to span the gap between an elitist Reformed movement and a spontaneous popular upheaval, between formalized religion – involving organized consistories, standards of behavior and inflexible doctrine – and a mass movement involving public demonstrations, the leadership of untrained lay preachers, and violence.

But once having questioned the popular conception of the Calvinist clergy as a corps of disciplined fanatics, and of Calvinism itself as a doctrine whose implications were fundamentally radical, we must also consider the broader question of the nature of charismatic leadership. For if the ministers who preached during the Troubles were not as united and purposeful as the Huguenot or Puritan pastors, how can we explain their popularity during the summer of 1566? Certainly the Reformed movement in the Netherlands cannot be viewed as a drama between the ignorant masses and the enlightened few, and we cannot explain the public preaching or the iconoclasm simply by discovering who planned these events; we must ask instead what needs the preaching and iconoclasm fulfilled in both the minister and his audience. My argument is that the ministers were accepted as popular leaders not because of their superior dedication and methods of organization; still less was their success a product of their commitment to a unique and radical ideology. On the contrary, it was the ministers' concern to appear as leaders of a legitimate, politically conservative Reformed movement that attracted their audience to them during the summer of the hedgepreaching. The ministers were regarded by their adherents not as prophets of freedom from the dictates of the Catholic government, but as reformers who were also defenders of the traditional social and political hierarchy.

·   ·   ·

Introduction

The sources for this study fall into two main categories: the writings of the ministers themselves, and the information collected by the Catholic government which persecuted them. A good deal of the ministers' correspondence has been published, along with the consistory records of the refugee churches in London. The ministers' published works – religious tracts, public letters to the magistrates, Confessions and poems – were consulted in manuscript form or in the sixteenth century editions which have survived; the writings of a very few pastors, such as Guy de Brès, have been re-edited by modern scholars. Information about the ministers' activities was also available in the diaries or 'daybooks' of contemporaries who witnessed the Troubles, and in the reports of the Council of Troubles, an agency set up by the Spanish government to seek out and punish heretics. All of these sources are biased to some degree. The official reports were based largely on hearsay, or on information extracted under torture, and almost every account was written either by a partisan of the movement or by the Reformers' enemies. But these diaries, letters and trial records are useful not merely as sources of information about the ministers' personal background; they make it possible to distinguish between the ministers' own perception of their goals and capabilities and their actual impact upon outsiders, and in this context the subjective nature of the literary evidence is a positive advantage to the historian.

I
THE TROUBLES

I cannot write you in ten sheets of paper the strange sight I saw there –
organs and all, destroyed! [. . .] Yet they that thus did, never looked towards
any spoil, but break all in pieces, and let it lie underfoot. . .[and] as I do not
understand they neither said nor did anything to the nuns: but when all was
broken, left it there, and so departed.

> Richard Clough, describing the
> iconoclasm at Antwerp in 1566.

A Protestant crowd corners a baker guarding the holy-wafer box in Saint-
Médard's church in Paris in 1561. 'Messieurs,' he pleads, 'do not touch it
for the honor of Him who dwells here.' 'Does your god of paste protect you
now from the pains of death?' was the Protestant answer before they killed
him.

> Natalie Davis, describing the
> iconoclasm at Paris in 1561.

HEDGEPREACHING

To many contemporary observers, both Reformed and Catholic, the beginning of the public preaching in the spring of 1566 seemed abrupt and somehow awesome. A Catholic burgher wrote in his diary that the preaching
'spread rapidly like the fire which a stormy wind quickly stirs up here and
there in the straw. . .'[1] Everyone had been expecting some kind of apocalyptic
change: the Protestants looked forward to an imminent restoration of the
true faith, while the Catholic clergy worried about the possibility of religious
toleration. And there had recently been signs that the change would occur
very soon. At Ghent the annual *ommegang* or religious procession was can-
celled because of certain portents: the altar of the Virgin which was being
prepared for display had burned down, while another fire had destroyed the
great bridge at Mainz. This, wrote a chronicler, signified the dismemberment
of France and Germany.[2]

[1] M. van Vaernewijck, *Troubles religieux en Flandre et dans les Pays-Bas au XVI*
siècle, trans. H. van Duyse, 1 (Ghent, 1905), p. 26.   [2] *Ibid.*, pp. 64–5.

In retrospect, we can see that contemporaries were wrong to be shocked about the hedgepreaching, for members of the Protestant movement had been continuously active in the Netherlands for nearly half a century. The Lutherans, or 'Martinists,' had circulated forbidden literature since the 1520s; they and the Anabaptists were already holding secret conventicles when the first Calvinist pastor from Geneva arrived at Tournai in 1544. The Calvinists proceeded to form consistories and synods, and had even begun to organize public religious services in Tournai, Valenciennes and West Flanders when the Catholic government forced them underground in 1563. The Calvinists had also established contacts with members of the German and Netherlands nobility. In December, 1565, when a group of Protestant nobles met at Brussels to form a League in support of religious toleration (the famous Compromise), it was a Calvinist pastor, Franciscus Junius, who delivered the opening prayers.[3] Junius also collaborated with the noble Marnix of Thoulouse on a series of pamphlets which, along with ballads, cartoons and songs, inundated the country in the spring of 1566. Propaganda of another sort emanated from the churches themselves, in the sermons of Catholic priests who had become Reformed sympathizers. One priest, Cornelis Huberti, was arrested and tried as a Lutheran in 1565. 'There are many wolves,' Huberti preached, 'who want to divert us from Christianity to idolatry...there are now many who wear the spiritual habit and are hypocrites...Had the whore of Babylon and Antichrist not dominated so long, the lambs should not suffer what they suffer...'[4] Another apostate priest called Kackhoes (Shithouse) by his enemies, became notorious in the neighborhood of Maastricht for his heretical sermons, delivered in the spring of 1566 to an audience of burghers and notables. After reading a biblical text Kackhoes began to fulminate against the Host, calling it 'the baked God' and denying 'that our Lord should enter into bread.'[5]

Finally, in April 1566, a group of nobles called the 'Confederates' presented a public request to the Regent, Margaret of Parma; they demanded that the Inquisition be abolished along with the King's edicts against heresy, and that religious policy be decided at a meeting of the Estates General. Margaret hedged by offering a 'Moderation' which effectively suspended the edicts. Immediately, hundreds of Reformers who had fled the Netherlands in order to escape prosecution by the Inquisition returned home, and the Walloon minister Jean Taffin wrote to Beza that at last the time had come when the true religion might be practiced in freedom, and that Beza himself

[3] M. L. van Deventer, *Het jaar 1566* (The Hague, 1856), pp. 16–17.
[4] Fl. Prims, *Het wonderjaar (1566–1567)*, 2nd ed. (Antwerp, 1941), p. 93.
[5] W. Bax, *Het protestantisme in het bisdom Luik en vooral te Maastricht 1557–1612* (The Hague, 1941), p. 128.

should visit the Netherlands and assist in the triumph of the Reformed cult.[6]

Thus the apocalyptic mood which pervaded the country in the spring of 1566 was largely the creation of the Reformers themselves as well as of factors, like the rise in unemployment and the agitations of the Confederates, which had little to do with religion. But the Calvinist consistories did not initiate the hedgepreaching; in this sense the nocturnal, clandestine services which took place in the countryside of Flanders *were* spontaneous, even awesome. On the night of May 28, a young monk named Carolus Daneel fled his cloister in Ypres and began preaching in the area, attracting a large personal following. The prior of the cloister wrote to Daneel, pleading with him, as a respected member of the Augustinian order, to return, but he received no reply.[7] In June, the magistrates of Ypres informed the Regent that 'lately' meetings of more than one thousand had been held in the open fields by another apostate monk named Antonius Algoet, who had only recently left the cloister.[8] These early hedgepreachers were certainly Reformers in spirit, but they were not formal Calvinists; in fact, the first public meeting outside Antwerp in May was conducted by a former priest whose religious affiliation was described as Lutheran.[9] The Calvinist consistory at Antwerp sanctioned, and attempted to canalize these popular demonstrations only after the fact. At a series of consistory meetings in May and June, it was decided 'to do what the Flemings had been doing for some time, to assemble our community in public and hold our *prêches* openly.'[10] Pastors in exile were summoned home, and the minister Ambroise Wille transmitted the order, which stated that the Confederate nobles had authorized the preaching, to the consistories of Tournai and Valenciennes.

The hedgepreaching started in the industrial districts of Flanders, where large numbers of workers had already responded to Calvinist propaganda. At Ghent the early congregations consisted of 'a group of unsavory-looking people...foreign workers who had come to our city as apprentices...'[11] The

[6] Boer, *Hofpredikers van prins Willem van Oranje. Jean Taffin en Pierre Loyseleur de Villiers*, v (The Hague, 1952), p. 23.

[7] H.-Q. Janssen, *De kerkhervorming in Vlaanderen* (Arnhem, 1868), pp. 276-7. This may not have been the first outdoor service. One chronicler reported a meeting in Ghent as early as April (P. de Jonghe, *Gendsche geschiedenissen*, i (Ghent, 1746), pp. 5-6).

[8] I. L. A. Diegerick, ed., *Documents du XVI⁰ siècle, archives d'Ypres*, i (Bruges, 1874), pp. 152-3.

[9] Prims, *Het wonderjaar*, p. 99. The Calvinists' first formal service at Antwerp was on June 24.

[10] F. Junius, *Francisci Junii theologileidensis vita*, ed. Daniel Gerdes, *Scrinium antiquarium*, i (Groningen, 1749), pp. 46-50.

[11] Van Vaernewijck, *Troubles*, i, p. 21.

ritual of these early meetings was primitive. The preacher at Ghent 'had taken for a pulpit the ladder of a mill. The congregation. . .invited passers-by to join them to hear the "Word of God", as they called it.' The minister, who spoke the dialect of a town in Flanders, was bareheaded and dressed in grey; he held a book from which he occasionally read a text and then delivered a sermon, admonishing sinners and praying for the enlightenment of king and pope. The congregation sat in rows, divided into three groups of about thirty each, and each held a booklet of psalms which sold for a *denier*. Van Vaernewijck had this from his laundress, who found the *prêche* edifying, 'like many people of little sense.'[12]

But van Vaernewijck, whose first response to the *prêches* was indifferent and condescending, soon observed with astonishment that the hedgepreaching had become a mass movement. Estimates of attendance ranged from seven to fourteen thousand auditors; some went as high as twenty-five thousand. Contemporaries were even more astonished by the increasing participation of respectable citizens. Among the men on horseback who were guarding the pastor at Ghent on July 3, commoners noticed the Count of Batembourg: 'Nobody could explain the attitude of these gentlemen,' wrote van Vaernewijck, 'for, among the thousands of people who streamed to the *prêches*, one saw only those of low extraction, those who had nothing to lose.'[13] But by July even people with a great deal to lose had joined the congregations: women with golden necklaces, city notables, even members of the Council of Flanders. At Tournai the magistrates reported that at one meeting there were over a hundred men on horseback, 'as many gentlemen, bourgeois and merchants as peasants.'[14] What seemed to have been a popular movement emanating from the lower classes, appealing as much to a desire for charity as the desire for prayer, soon encompassed all elements of society. Originally the magistrates hesitated to interrupt the meetings because of the enthusiasm of the Calvinists, but by mid-summer many of these same magistrates had joined the Reformed congregations – and all of them carried weapons.

Although armed preaching was everywhere carried on since July, there had been few actual incidents of violence; people marched to and from the *prêche* in battle formation, but quietly. Certain ministers, however, became notorious for actions which the Catholics regarded as provocative. At Ypres, two preachers (Antoine Algoet and Jacques de Buzère) entered the city from opposite sides, Algoet accompanied by fifty men, Buzère by two thousand. The two groups marched through the city singing psalms, and then left with-

[12] *Ibid.*, p. 21.
[13] *Ibid.*, p. 26.
[14] A. Hocquet, *Tournai et le Tournaisis au XVI* siècle au point de vue politique et social* (Brussels, 1906), p. 318.

out incident.[15] At Tournai, Ambroise Wille boasted in a sermon that if he were killed, fifty thousand men were ready to avenge his death; he also announced that in two weeks he hoped to have the power and means to preach inside the city.[16] At Ghent, Herman Moded held a secret meeting at which he was said to have recruited troops.[17] Still another incident was reported by Richard Clough, an Englishman living at Antwerp.[18]

As on Saturday last, was a proclamation...that no man should go to the sermons upon pain of hanging; whereupon on Sunday...went out of the town...above sixteen thousand persons, all with their weapons in battle array; and so, after the sermon [they] returned to the town, and went to the high bailiff's house (who had taken one preacher prisoner two or three days before) and commanded him to deliver the prisoner; which he refused. Whereupon they went to the prison and brake it, and delivered the preacher; and so, everyone departed.

Elsewhere the Calvinists, who had been unsuccessfully requesting permission to preach inside the city walls, entered the cities by force. At Bois-le-Duc ('s-Hertogenbosch) Cornelis Walraeven preached outside the city until mid-August, when he led the congregation through a gate and took up lodgings in the town.[19] Even more ominous was a meeting of the ministers and the Confederates at St Trond (St Truiden) in July, when the Protestant nobles agreed to protect the Reformed church in return for funds donated by the consistories – money which would be used to raise German troops in case the April Request was rejected by Philip.[20]

Another incident which occurred on August 10 was less radical, but perhaps even more insolent. Four ministers who had traveled from Ghent to Bruges to hold services took advantage of a rainstorm to preach inside a church. The magistrates objected and the ministers withdrew and preached in the cemetery.[21] This 'invasion' of a church adumbrated the type of violence which was to occur during the following weeks. The next day Clough wrote, 'as far as I can learn, these matters will break out, and that out of hand... God be merciful unto them, and to us all. For and if they do once begin, it

[15] Diegerick, *Documents*, I, pp. 53–5.
[16] Hocquet, *Tournai*, p. 318. Taken from a report of the magistrates, who may have exaggerated Wille's boasts.
[17] C. Blenk, 'Hagepreek en beeldenstorm in 1566. Een historische analyse,' *Hagepreek en Beeldenstorm* (1966), p. 23.
[18] J. W. Burgon, *The Life and Times of Thomas Gresham*, II (London, 1839), p. 132. Letter to Gresham, July, 1566.
[19] BWK Prot., II, p. 485.
[20] C. Paillard, *Huit mois de la vie d'un peuple* (Brussels, 1877), pp. 165–73. The ministers were not admitted to the meetings; their requests were submitted in writing. They agreed to keep the peace and do nothing against the king or the local magistrates; in turn they were promised protection by the Confederates.
[21] H.-Q. Janssen, *De kerkhervorming te Brugge* (Rotterdam, 1856), p. 49.

will be a bloodie time; for it is marvelous to see how the common people are bent against the papists.'[22]

ICONOCLASM

In the end it happened that some of the baser sort, meaning to show an inconsiderate zeal unto their religion. . .advanced and encouraged each other to beat down images and crosses set up in the highways. Then they went to chapels and so to churches and monasteries in the country, and in the end to towns. . .so as the insolencie of these base people, and of some women and children, exceeding all temper and modestie, broke down and beat down all images, crucifixes, altars, tables. . .and generally that which was displeasing unto their eyes.[23]

The image-breaking of 1566, like the hedgepreaching which preceeded it, was not the first such event in recent memory. Many Netherlands preachers had originally come from France, where iconoclasm had occurred in 1561. In the Netherlands itself, the placard of 1550 already mentioned those who broke images and statues, and in 1562 the Council wrote to Margaret complaining that some gentlemen passing through on their way to France had beaten down roadside crucifixes and icons with their swords. In May, 1566, during a Mass at Audenarde, a young bourgeois named Hans Tuscaens suddenly grabbed the Host from the priest, crying that it was merely bread and that the worship of men was idolatry.[24] In July, the bailiff of Furnes testified in a report to Margaret about the plundering of churches and cloisters in the area.[25] In fact, hostility to images was apparently endemic in the popular culture of the time. Van Vaernewijck described a procession at which a statue of St Anthony was carried through the streets; it became the custom to treat the statue as an object of mockery, tossing it back and forth until it was lost in the sand.[26]

The image-breaking of 1566 probably shocked contemporaries less because it was sacrilegious than because the movement was so explosive and so thorough. In less than two weeks, acts of iconoclasm were committed in

[22] Burgon, *The Life and Times*, p. 137. Letter of Clough to Gresham, August 11. At Tournai a priest, hearing a clapping sound outside the church, fell as though dead, thinking that the Confederates, who now called themselves the Beggars, were attacking him. It turned out to be a boy who was beating two bladders against the walls of the church to dry them out; he had been using them as water wings. (Pasquier de la Barre, *Mémoires*, ed. Alex. Pinchart, 1 (Brussels, 1859), pp. 108–9).

[23] J. F. Petit, *A General History of the Netherlands* (London, 1609), p. 400.

[24] J. Russe, 'Le procès et le martyre de Hans Tuscaens à Audenarde en 1566,' BSHPB (1953), pp. 90–122.

[25] Blenk, 'Hagepreek. . .', p. 28.

[26] Van Vaernewijck, *Troubles*, 1, pp. 65–6.

almost all of the seventeen provinces.[27] It started on August 10, in the *Westkwartier* of Flanders close to the French border, where the central government was remote and where the first hedgepreachers had been active. On that day, following a sermon by the Flemish preacher Sebastien Matte, the congregation at Steenvoorde broke into a chapel and sacked it. During the next few days, bands of iconoclasts under the direction of Matte and another preacher, Jacques de Buzère, attacked other churches in the neighborhood.[28] On the 15th they arrived at Ypres, where Bishop Martin Rythovius had been trying to forestall the violence by persuading Egmont, the governor of the province, to remain in the city. Egmont left after dinner on the 14th; two days later the churches and cloisters in Ypres and the surrounding villages had all been sacked, including an important center of pilgrimage, the parish church at Beveren. When asked who had given them the authority to commit such deeds the iconoclasts answered that it was God – and the Count of Egmont.[29] The iconoclasts proceeded to other towns and villages in Flanders, often assisted by local Reformers. Audenarde was attacked on the 18th, Antwerp on the 20th, Ghent and Bois-le-Duc on the 22nd, Tournai on the 23rd and Valenciennes on the 24th.

In Antwerp, sometime before the 20th of August, the pastor Herman Moded had preached against idolatry.[30] On the 15th, the feast of the Assumption, a statue of the Virgin was paraded through the streets and then returned to the chapel; the same day William of Orange, who had come to Antwerp in July to maintain law and order, left for Brussels to attend a meeting of the Golden Fleece. On the 19th a group of youths entered the chapel and began to mock the Virgin. One who was playing near the pulpit climbed up and began making the gestures of a priest, until he was thrown down by a young sailor who was later wounded by the crowd. Somehow the mob was dispatched, only to return on the following day. The Margrave again dispersed the people and fled to the City Hall, leaving one door of the church open through which the people returned. They began the work

[27] Actually the iconoclasm was not as thorough as it seemed to contemporaries; it did not occur in Brussels, Artois, Namur, Luxembourg, Limbourg and the northern part of Hainaut (Paillard, *Huit mois*, p. 226).

[28] M. Backhouse, 'Beeldenstorm en bosgeuzen in het Westkwartier (1566–1568),' *Handelingen van de koniklijke geschied-en oudheidkundige kring van Kortrijk*, n.s. xxxviii (1971) p. 78.

[29] J. van Vloten, *Nederlands opstand tegen Spanje* (Haarlem, 1856), p. 91.

[30] One chronicler says that Moded preached on the 20th in the cathedral, immediately before the iconoclasm (F. G. Ullens, *Antwerpsch chronykje* (Leyden, 1743), p. 87). Wesembeke maintained that he preached some time before the violence (*Mémoires*, ed. C. Rahlenbeck (Brussels, 1859)). The following account is by Wesembeke, a local official who negotiated with the ministers, and who later wrote propaganda for William of Orange (pp. 280–7).

with psalm-singing; then they paraded in vestments, drank toasts to the Confederates with sacramental wine and smeared their shoes with sacred oil. With all this, a group of twenty to thirty men and boys, salaried, it was said, by one Jehan le Maistre, succeeded in destroying the interiors of thirty churches in the next two days, while the citizen guard stood in the market-place, forbidden to interfere.[31] Richard Clough witnessed these events:[32]

I went into the church with ten thousand others. It looked like a hell, as if heaven and earth had gone together, with falling of images and beating down of costly works, so that in fine I cannot write you in ten sheets of paper the strange sight I saw there, organs and all, destroyed! [It was] the costliest church in Europe; and they have so spoiled it, that they have not left a place to sit on in the church.

The next day Herman Moded preached in the same cathedral against idolatry.

On the 22nd the iconoclasm reached Ghent. Under the direction of Lievyn Onghena, an important local Reformer, the iconoclasts divided into small groups and sacked every church and cloister in the city.[33] Images were not merely destroyed – they were tortured; the eyes and faces of the portraits were mutilated or the heads cut off, as at an execution. At one church there was a portal with statues of Christ and the Apostles; all the statues, including God's, were still there after the iconoclasm, without the heads.[34] At the church of St Nicholas the mob maligned a famous statue of the Holy Family: 'Come down Mariette, you have been in childbed long enough...' and then knocked it down.[35] Through the night and the following morning the iconoclasts wandered through the streets of the city and into the *faubourgs*, carrying torches and singing psalms. By Friday morning, when the High Bailiff ordered them to leave the city, seven parish churches, one collegial church, twenty-five cloisters, ten almshouses and seven chapels had been sacked. The image-breakers then divided into three groups and dispersed to villages in the countryside, where they continued to 'purify' the churches.[36]

REBELLION

No one knew whether the ministers had initiated the image-breaking or had merely exerted their influence on a spontaneous popular uprising; still less could anyone know whether they had acted as individuals or as representa-

[31] M. Dierickx, 'Beeldenstorm in de Nederlanden in 1566,' *Streven*, XIX (1966), p. 1044.
[32] Burgon, *The Life and Times*, p. 139.
[33] Van Vaernewijck, *Troubles*, I, p. 41.
[34] *Ibid.*, pp. 126–7, 138.
[35] *Ibid.*, pp. 102–3.
[36] Dierickx, 'Beeldenstorm,' p. 1045.

tives of the consistories. But these questions of blame proved to be im-
material as time went on, for it was an indisputable fact that the Reformers
hoped to make good use of the image-breakers' success by establishing
Calvinism as an officially recognized cult. They behaved, in other words, as
if they had planned things that way. Several ministers, having condemned
the iconoclasm, demanded amnesty for the iconoclasts. In Ghent, Moded and
Carpentier requested that those who had 'only' broken images be set free,
and a week later the ministers again appeared at the City Hall to request the
use of churches in the town; in Tournai the ministers went so far as to demand that the city pay for the new Reformed temples. The Reformers also
flaunted their alliance with members of the nobility: in Valenciennes, Peregrine de la Grange asserted that religious freedom had been assured them
in an agreement with the nobles, and that Margaret was therefore not free
to oppose their requests.[37] The atmosphere was clearly one of triumph for
the Reformers, and attendance at the *prêches* was greater than ever.

Indeed, once the Reformers had established the right to hold public
religious services, the question of whom to blame for the iconoclasm was
superseded by the more immediate one of intentions: Would the Calvinists be
satisfied with limited religious toleration, or would they insist on establishing
control over social and political life as well? The concrete issue over which
this question would be decided was the Accord published by Margaret on
August 23. Safety was guaranteed to Reformers who attended services in
locations where they had hitherto taken place, provided they were peaceable
and did nothing to hinder the Catholic cult.[38] Margaret interpreted this to
mean that only preaching would be allowed, and that it would take place
only outside the city walls, while the Calvinists assumed that the right to
celebrate their own cult implied permission to conduct rites and sacraments.
This difference was crucial: as long as the Reform was limited to preaching,
none of the social and spiritual functions of the Catholic clergy would be
usurped. But if the Reformers carried on communion, marriages, burials,
education, dispensation of charity, etc., and if they did this inside public
buildings, clearly the authority of the ministers would intrude on that of the
clergy and even of the magistrates. Indeed, according to the Genevan ideal,
the members of the consistory *were* the magistrates. But the implications of
full toleration were much more serious than this, for if the Calvinists began
to dispense the social and spiritual functions which they considered essential
to the faith, might not the logical next step be to institute cities of God in
imitation of Geneva? If this were so, then the implication of full toleration
for the Calvinists was the total expulsion of the Catholics.

[37] Van Deventer, *Het jaar 1566*, p. 42.
[38] Paillard, *Huit mois*, p. 385.

This question of ultimate goals was not yet apparent in August, and Reformers in many towns and villages optimistically presented requests for religious toleration to the local magistrates. Often they operated from a position of apparent strength, since they were already installed in churches which they had taken over after the iconoclasm, while the Catholic cult had often ceased to function altogether. In Bois-le-Duc, for example, a Reformed minister preached in the church the day after the iconoclasm, baptizing children in front of the pulpit.[39] Thereafter, four regular ministers preached twice weekly, each in a different church; from August 22 until September 9, no Catholic services were held in the city. At Antwerp, Herman Moded and Jean Taffin preached in the cathedral the day after the iconoclasm on the request of the magistrates, who wanted them to dissuade the people from further violence. The preachers then submitted a statement to the officials in which they protested their ignorance of the iconoclasm and their willingness to aid the government in bringing pillagers to justice; they also asked the magistrates not to think ill of them if they continued to preach in the churches, assuring them that no violence would occur. The magistrates, to the Reformers' surprise, agreed.[40] Typically, the accords which were finally concluded by these and other cities stipulated that the ministers were to be natives, take a loyalty oath, preach outside the cities (with permission to build their own temples), respect the Catholics, and guarantee religious peace. When Margaret forbade preaching in the churches on October 15, Reformers in most cities had already started building their own temples.

The Calvinists also penetrated into cities where there had been no iconoclasm. There had been no violence at Bruges, and no Reformed services were held until mid-September. By then Jan Munt was established as permanent minister and on his request the pastor Junius also came for a few days to preach in French and advise the Reformers how to treat with Egmont. Encouraged by these negotiations, by which they were granted the right to build a temple and to lodge the minister in the city, the Reformers announced the wedding of one Michel de Royere, a former priest. This was the first time a priest had been publicly married, and the Catholic friar, Brother Cornelis, was scandalized: 'I am no prophet. . .but I assure you that the king, after he hears of these outrages, will come with his Spaniards and smite the

---

[39] W. Meindersma, 'Over het protestantisme in westelijk Brabant,' NAvKG VIII (1911), pp. 384–5.

[40] L. van der Essen, 'Episodes de l'histoire religieuse et commerciale d'Anvers dans la seconde moitié du XVIᵉ siècle. Rapport secret de Geronimo de Curiel, facteur du roi d'Espagne à Anvers, sur les marchands hérétiques ou suspects de cette ville (1566),' BCRH LXXX (1911), pp. 160–1.

people from the land. . .and deliver them into slavery, as Nebudchadnezzar did to the children of Israel.'[41]

There were many, including Orange, who suspected that the Calvinists would not be content with this sort of toleration, but would eventually try to extirpate the Catholics and establish control over the cities as well as the churches, as they had in Geneva. In cities where the Reformers were strong, this attempt to acquire ultimate power already seemed to be materializing. At Bois-le-Duc one witness testified that the consistory had elected elders who were expected to become magistrates; another overheard the Calvinists say, 'One day, we shall have another sheriff's seat here.' Still another stated that the Reformers took over the rents from the cloisters, another that they planned to summon a Confederate noble from Antwerp to aid them in throwing out the papists.[42] In Ypres, when one of the preachers (Jacques de Buzère, who led the iconoclasm) read the Reformers' request for one or two churches in the city, he told them to request *all* the churches in the city.[43] Van Vaernewijck reported rumors that Ghent and Flanders were getting a new form of justice; the Reformers would form a tribunal, abolish bribery and reconcile parties. A Catholic spy reported that the Calvinists intended to sack the city of Lille, and for this purpose they had organized a chain of cities in Artois and French Flanders which communicated by the ringing of bells.[44] Another rumor told of a plot to murder the members of the Council of Flanders by throwing them out of a window.

In Valenciennes the superintendents of charity reported that the Reformers had collected money during *prêches* without reporting it, and declared that the funds must be distributed in the presence of the deacons. The ministers also insisted on entering the hospital to minister to the sick, although they had been prohibited from this by the magistrates.[45] Finally, the ministers openly violated the Accord, prohibiting the use of churches, by announcing that

---

[41] Broer Cornelis Adriaensz, *Historie van Br. Cornelis Adriaensz van Dordrecht, minnebroeder tot Brugge* (n.p., 1628), p. 73. Cornelis later disavowed the sermons; it is still unclear whether they were originally composed by Cornelis himself, or by another witness (B. de Troeyer, *Bio-Bibliographia Franciscana Neerlandica Saeculi XVI*, I (Nieuwkoop, 1969), p. 269.

[42] Prosper Cuypers van Velthoven, ed., *Documents pour servir à l'histoire des troubles religieux du XVIᵉ siècle dans le Brabant septentrional, Bois-le-Duc (1566–1570)*, I (Brussels, 1858), pp. 351, 259–60, 364.

[43] Diegerick, *Documents*, II, p. 128.

[44] 'La chainture des gheustz du jour Saint-Andrieu 1566, de laquelle chainture lesdicts gheutsz se vantoient de chaindre la ville de ville,' Gachard, *La Bibliotheque Nationale à Paris*, I, pp. 388–93.

[45] Deliberation of the *conseil particulier*, October 9, printed in Ch. Paillard, 'Papiers d'état et documents inédits pour servir à l'histoire de Valenciennes pendant les années 1566 et 1567,' *Mémoires historiques sur l'arrondissement de Valenciennes*, VI (Valenciennes, 1878), pp. 91–2.

Communion would be distributed in church; it was also reported that one Reformer, Michel Herlin, had more than one hundred sixty troops at his disposal. Meanwhile the Reformers had repeatedly failed to turn up for meetings with Margaret's representative, Noircarmes, to determine places of worship; Noircarmes reasoned that if the Reformers refused to appear, it meant that they refused to preach outside the city walls.[46] Throughout these negotiations, the local magistrates had been consistently intimidated in their relations with the Calvinists. Instead of negotiating on an equal basis the Reformers would appear before the magistrates, hear proposals, deliberate, and then deliver their decision through one of the ministers; and although the consistories were supposed to discuss only religious matters, 'nevertheless nothing took place in the city council on the matter of the Troubles without their advice and consent.'[47]

Not only did the Reformers seem to be taking over the cities by infiltrating official posts and usurping municipal functions; before the winter they had actually tried to take over three cities by violence. On November 3 the Calvinists at Maastricht occupied and barricaded the marketplace and committed iconoclasm under the direction of their ministers. The magistrates managed to expel them from the market and a policy of co-existence was accepted, but the Reformers remained in control of the church. At Furnes the minister Gilles Dumont wrote to the magistrate to request the release of an iconoclast. The magistrate, fearing repercussions from Brussels, refused; Dumont and several other ministers then gathered some thousands of people at a nearby town from which they planned to storm the city and release the prisoner. The assault on October 8 failed, and the Reformers retired to Hondschoote.[48] At Hasselt the pastor Herman Moded preached on the marketplace on December 5. When he was ordered to retire, armed Reformers attacked the officials, obtained the keys to the city and began to enroll troops. The Bishop of Liège tried to negotiate with the magistrates, who declared themselves powerless against the armed Calvinists. On January 19 Moded and two other preachers directed the pillage of all the churches, and a few days later all the inhabitants were declared enemies of the Prince.[49]

Clearly, many of the reports of the aggressive activities of the Reformers could be interpreted as slander, as misinformation, or as the radical acts of individual ministers, but not as proof that the Calvinists had formulated a coherent policy of usurping the functions of local authority. Indeed, all of the

---

[46] *Ibid.*, pp. 179, 183–4. Letter of Noircarmes to Margaret, November 22.
[47] Report of the magistrates, printed in L. van Langeraad, *Guido de Bray, zijn leven en werken* (Zierikzee, 1884), p. xliv.
[48] P. Heinderycx, *Jaerboeken van Veurne en Veurnambacht* (Veurne, 1855), pp. 32–57.
[49] J. Daris, *Histoire du diocèse et de la principauté de Liège* (Liège, 1884), pp. 400–5.

accusations against the political ambitions of the Calvinists as a group might be discounted as rumor, were it not for certain other evidence that the Calvinists really did intend to press their demands for full toleration – if necessary by the use of force. In early October a synod was held in Ghent at which the Reformers voted to raise three million guilders and offer them to Philip in return for religious freedom. A great deal of money was duly collected and forwarded to the care of Marcus Perez, a Calvinist merchant in Antwerp; a copy of the printed request, with the signatures of nobles who had made contributions, was circulated in Flanders as part of the collection campaign. Ultimately the funds were used not to improve Philip's disposition but to raise troops in Germany for the defence of the Reformers against the king.[50]

The question whether or not the Reformers had always planned to use the money to buy troops, or whether they were sincere in their attempts to buy religious peace, has never been answered.[51] But Gilles le Clercq, one of the authors of the Request, had appeared in Armentières in August, 1566 and was said to be visiting different cities in order to collect money; he had received a letter from Louis of Nassau, instructing him to collect funds for troops to be raised in Germany, as had been agreed at St Trond in July. Meanwhile Herman Moded conducted a meeting at Ghent (August 16) at which he solicited the sum of seventy-two thousand guilders for payment of troops who would protect the Reformers. Possibly this campaign of armed resistance to Philip was the genesis of the October Request; in that case the Reformers' pleas for peaceful toleration might have been a ruse from the start. At any rate, the minister Ambroise Wille wrote to Guy de Brès at Valenciennes on September 20 that a defensive league of all the Reformed churches in the area had been formed; if one of them were in danger, an army of twenty thousand men could be raised in twenty-four hours.[52]

Whatever their ultimate plans for the three million guilders, the Reformed delegates at Ghent did agree to press their demands to the local magistrates more aggressively. The consistory of Valenciennes received a letter from Gilles le Clercq telling them not to hasten negotiations with Noircarmes since the ministers were gathered at Ghent to devise a common plan.[53] But this

[50] J. Scheerder, 'Eenige nieuwe bijzonderheden betreffende het 3.000.000 goudguldens rekwest (1566),' *Miscellanea van der Essen* (Brussels, 1947).

[51] The arguments of several historians are summarized in Scheerder's article. Of the ten ministers who organized the Request, eight participated in military campaigns and six committed iconoclasm. The Lutherans also signed the accord, but disavowed any alliance with the Calvinists for purposes of violence (van der Essen, 'Episodes,' p. 200).

[52] Paillard, *Mémoires*, vi, p. 54.

[53] Moded announced at the synod that those of Ghent repented signing the accord, and warned others to be well-advised before signing any capitulation. (van Langeraad, *Guido de Bray*, p. liii).

new intransigence on the part of the Reformers was matched by that of the Regent, who had received money to recruit troops. The situation was therefore polarized: the Reformers renewed their demands for public sacraments, and Margaret countered by attempting to introduce garrisons into the cities; by winter, several cities found themselves under siege, declared by the government to be rebels.

The immediate cause of this rebellion was the Reformers' decision to celebrate Communion in one of the churches of Valenciennes, and Margaret's subsequent order that a garrison enter the city. When the ministers agreed to postpone the Communion the people rioted, declaring that they would sack the church if they were kept out of it. In the eyes of Noircarmes and the magistrates, the city had become polarized between the bourgeois notables, who were willing to accept the garrison, and the ministers and consistory who, with the populace, were determined to resist it. It was the ministers' fault that the Reformers vacillated in their negotiations, Noircarmes wrote to Margaret: 'I am convinced...that the ministers, who pretend to be gods and lords in Valenciennes (as Calvin did in Geneva), will never accept that the king should be stronger there.'[54] Finally, on December 14, the people of Valenciennes were declared rebels and the city was put under siege.

Two days later the ministers from towns in West Flanders met at Nieuwkerke under the charge of Pieter Dathenus and voted to levy troops to come to the aid of Valenciennes. Two captains were chosen to recruit soldiers and a campaign to collect funds was organized. The first army, consisting of a few hundred ill-equipped soldiers under Jean Denys, marched to Wattrelos, while the second army, led by a minister, Corneille de Lesenne, went to Tournai and then to Lannoy; their armed force amounted to about three thousand. De Lesenne maintained morale by promising the imminent arrival of noble reinforcements; at one point he opened a letter from a messenger and announced: 'Courage, courage, the lord of Escoubecque is only three leagues from here.'[55] But no help came, and on December 28 both armies were cut down by Noircarmes and the Seigneur de Rassenghien. Most of the ministers in Flanders fled to Antwerp or to Amsterdam to join the Confederate Brederode. On January 1, when the Regent's troops arrived at Tournai, the garrison was accepted by the ministers without a murmur.[56]

Tournai succumbed, but Valenciennes was incited to hold public catechism and Communion on January 5 in defiance of the surrounding troops. The Calvinists made forays into the countryside to get supplies and harass the

[54] Paillard, *Mémoires*, VI, p. 290.
[55] Ed. de Coussemaker, *Troubles religieux du XVIᵉ siècle dans la Flandre maritime, 1560–1570*, IV (Bruges, 1876), pp. 18–19, 84.
[56] Pasquier de la Barre, *Mémoires de Soldoyer*, p. 256.

enemy; they also decided to expel numbers of Catholics from the city. On January 10 a Remonstrance was addressed to the Confederate nobles, to be presented in the Council of State.[57] The paper rebutted the charges against the Reformers and maintained their loyalty to the king, except in matters of conscience. Comparing themselves to the Jews persecuted by the Romans, they professed their readiness to negotiate on the basis of religious toleration and their eagerness to be massacred if they were denied their religion. Throughout the winter the ministers continued to believe that the Confederates with whom they had negotiated at St Trond would come to the aid of the city.[58] The consistory claimed to have received letters from Antwerp with good news and promises; meanwhile the Reformers were enjoined to pray for Brederode in church while they waited for his appearance outside the gates.[59]

Not only did the siege of Valenciennes trigger similar revolts in other cities; it forced the Reformers to take overt and unified action against the Regent. On December 15 Maastricht, whose ministers had barricaded the marketplace a few weeks before, refused to admit government troops.[60] On February 18 Cornelis van Bombergen, a Confederate noble, appeared at Bois-le-Duc for the declared purpose of forcibly obtaining religious equality.[61] Van Bombergen immediately established himself as master of the city, arresting recalcitrant magistrates and occupying the City Hall. Meanwhile Brederode assumed nominal leadership of the entire Reformed rebellion, following a decision taken by a synod held in Antwerp.[62]

The Reformed rebellion – in the winter of 1566-7 five cities in the South Netherlands were barricaded – lasted effectively until March, 1567, when the forces of Marnix of Thoulouse were defeated at Austerweel, near Antwerp. Inside the city the Calvinists rioted, demanding that the Catholic clergy be expelled and that they be given the keys to the city. When Orange refused, they attempted to join with the Lutherans against the papists, but the Lutherans sided with Orange, who succeeded in pacifying the city with their support. With this defeat the Reformers had lost all their power. All of the cities under siege capitulated; their populations either emigrated or

---

[57] *Remonstrance et supplication de ceus de l'église réformée de la ville de Valencenes, Decembre, 1566* (1567).
[58] Ch. Paillard, 'Interrogatoires politiques de Guy de Brès,' BSHPF xxviii (1879), pp. 59-67.
[59] van Langeraad, *Guido de Bray*, pp. lxxviii, lxxxi.
[60] Daris, *Histoire*, p. 396. The town of Maeseyck was also put under siege.
[61] G. H. Dumont, *La vie aventureuse d'Antoine van Bomberghen* (Antwerp, 1952), pp. 89-93.
[62] The synod voted to support an armed uprising and to offer command to Orange and, if he refused (which he did), to Hornes or Brederode.

endured humiliation or execution. At Valenciennes, the ministers argued over the length of delay they should demand, to give the Reformers time to flee the city before it was taken, while in Antwerp the pastor Isbrand Balck preached the last sermon held by the Reformers before the ministers left the city:[63]

Christ said that just as the birds under heaven live under His shadow, so we poor men, who with Christ are reborn through the Evangile, fly as birds over all the world, finding their shelter in the Evangile...We fear no stings or shocks, for our victory is our belief, which no one can take from us.

Although there had been widespread destruction of church property during the iconoclasm and the military campaigns which followed, surprisingly few people were physically attacked. But in the autumn of 1567 a group of Reformers, including the minister Jan Michiels, arrived from England for the purpose of breaking open prisons, pillaging the churches and houses of the rich, and murdering priests. These were not vagabonds; they had been sent from Sandwich and Norwich to prepare for a large-scale military invasion of the Netherlands, and they were assisted by members of Calvinist consistories in Flanders and by a young nobleman, Jehan van Huele.[64] In November, 1567, they attacked a priest of Houtkerke, cutting off his ears and then killing him. They also murdered the soldiers of the bailiff of Bergues and several other priests. The Reformers were captured and executed in 1568; their acts of violence were the last attempts to propagate the Reform in the Netherlands before the Calvinists were silenced by the Duke of Alva and his Blood Council.

EXPLANATIONS

Because the image-breaking was so explosive and so thorough, many contemporaries were certain that a conspiracy was involved; whose conspiracy they were not sure, since the act was universally repudiated. The Catholic royal administrator Viglius thought that the Confederate nobles meeting at St Trond had proposed to terrorize the Catholics by inciting the mob to break images. The historian Strada thought that Louis of Nassau was the main organizer; the preachers told him all their designs. The Spanish nobleman Bernardino de Mendoza, who came to the Netherlands with Alva in

---

[63] *Leerrede over Marcus 4, door Isbrandus Balckius*, ed. B. Glasius (Dordrecht, 1858).
[64] Backhouse, 'Beeldenstorm.' The author analyzes the trial of one of the Reformers who came from England, Jehan Camerlinck; he testified that the group was advised by consistory members at Bruges and Armentières. One of the party, Pieter Waels, had been a deacon in Norwich. Their object was to bring a preacher with them to preach and to cause trouble in the land.

1567, wrote in his memoirs that the event was planned by the representatives of the consistories at the same meeting at St Trond, where twelve men were designated to prepare the people for revolt in each province. Motley tells us that 'it was asserted by Catholics that the Confederates and other opulent Protestants had organized this company of profligates for the meagre pittance of ten stivers a day.' Pontus Payen, an ardent Catholic royalist, wrote that the Calvinists who stayed home, letting the rabble do what they had advised in the consistory, feigned disapproval, but among themselves they rejoiced. It was also believed by many that the Catholics had themselves encouraged the whole outrage in order to bring odium upon the Reformers.

In short, the Catholics thought that the preachers wanted to take over the churches, while the Calvinists believed that the Catholics wanted them to dig their own graves. No one was sure exactly what had taken place at St Trond except that the preachers had been present and had had dealings with the Confederates. Everyone suspected the French; Condé and Coligny had made overtures to the Confederates and French preachers were thought to be everywhere. Mansfeld told Margaret that the agitators came from France, where the Huguenots sought to weaken the Netherlands by the image-breaking in order to take over the cities. Egmont wrote to Philip that he had intelligence of the heretics' contacts in other countries; he did not think that they were planning a revolution, but that they did intend to take possession of certain cities.

There were certainly grounds for believing all of these rumors, but the most credible villains were the ministers. At a *prêche* near Lannoy, Ambroise Wille inveighed against the image-breakers: without the authority of the magistrate they might only destroy the idols in their own hearts. The iconoclasts who were present answered that their own preacher, Corneille de Lesenne, had given them their commission to break images.[65] At Tournai, Wille himself arranged for the payment of the iconoclasts and, with two other pastors, he supervised the work to see that nothing was pillaged.[66] At Bois-le-Duc, when one of the iconoclasts was asked where he received his commission a few days after the event, he pointed to a Reformed preacher, Cornelis Walraeven, who was then baptizing a child in the purified church.[67]

[65] Pasquier de la Barre, *Mémoires*, I, p. 132.
[66] Desilve, *Le protestantisme dans la seigneurie de Saint-Amand de 1562 à 1584*, (Valenciennes 1910), p. 58. Wille wrote to the pastor of Valenciennes, Guy de Brès, on August 29: 'Quant au récompensement de ceulx quy onc travaillé à abattre les imaiges, nous avons prins ceste couleur, que ce n'est point pour cela qu'ilz sont aydez et assistez (s'aultant que la chose est trop odieuse au Magistrat): ains disons que c'est à cause qu'ilz ont esté fort travaillé du guet et d'avoir esté tant de temps sans besoigne.'
[67] Cuypers van Velthoven, *Documents*, p. 460.

But commentators on the Troubles of 1566 have always realized that it was not enough to hunt for conspirators, because the violence was not contingent on the character and ambitions of the individuals who committed it. These people viewed the events of 1566 as one symptom of more fundamental disturbances in the society as a whole; they blamed the agitations of the preachers or the political machinations of the nobility, but in doing so they made no claim to understand the significance of the iconoclasm or the events which followed:

...men say that the iconoclasm is the fruit of our preaching and the cause of all the nation's troubles. That is as much as to say that the prophet Elias was the cause of the destruction and uproar in Israel; whereupon the Prophet. . .answered: *I* trouble Israel not, but *you* and your father's house, when you forsook the Lord and followed Baal.[68]

In their attempts to understand the Troubles in this fundamental sense, contemporaries focused on two elements: the economic crisis, and the inherent truth and purity of the Reformed faith (or, conversely, the cruel fanaticism of the Calvinists). In both cases, conditions were exacerbated by the people's hatred of the Catholic clergy, either as representative of an exploitative and decadent social class, or as idolators and inquisitors. Van Vaernewijck was convinced that the people would behave peaceably if they could pay reasonable prices for grain; it was their hostility to the rich that had caused them to attack statues, and the magistrates feared that they would go from images to people, 'for the mob is blind and knows not what it does.'[69] The importance of the economic factor was verified by the fact that many of the iconoclasts were vagabonds and indigent workers. At Ghent the magistrates tried to prevent further violence by forbidding all workers who were not citizens of Ghent to leave the city.[70] A magistrate of Tournai, Pasquier de la Barre, also cited the poverty of the inhabitants as an explanation for the Troubles; being himself a Calvinist sympathizer, later accused of opening up a church to the iconoclasts, he had good reason to skirt the 'superficial' question of who had organized it. The Calvinists in general were quite willing to attribute the excesses of the iconoclasts to economic hardship, but they did not intend to forego the credit for inspiring the entire Reformed movement. In September the ministers of Ghent learned that Egmont had been told that only people from the lower classes attended the *prêches;* to convince him of the social and spiritual status of the movement, they invited the congregation to attend a service in Egmont's courtyard, dressed in their finest clothes.[71]

---

[68] Herman Moded, *Apologie* (1567), printed in Brutel de la Rivière, *Het leven van Hermannus Moded* (Haarlem, 1879).

[69] van Vaernewijck, I, pp. 88–9, 165, 167.

[70] *Ibid.*, pp. 177–8.   [71] *Ibid.*, p. 200.

If the restlessness of the people could be attributed to economic discontent, their specific hostility to images could be attributed to their hatred of the wealthy clergy. Van Vaernewijck explained the sack of the most important centers of pilgrimage by saying that those were the richest churches.[72] When the iconoclasts at Ghent destroyed the books which they found in the cloisters, they asserted that the clergy had already confiscated *their* books. When they were reminded that the king had decreed the persecution, they replied that the papists influenced the king. This hostility to the clergy had reached such a pitch that many committed iconoclasm in the belief that the priests were sorcerers and murderers. It was whispered that the hangman was regularly summoned to the cloister of the Dominicans where he decapitated people who were brought there in secret; many also spoke of torture instruments, secret jails and other horrors which existed in the monasteries.[73]

The partisans of the 'economic' theory had asserted that the image-breakers were simple, lower-class people. The Calvinists themselves used the same information to advance a quite different explanation for the Troubles. How, they asked, could ordinary people, without authority or arms, accomplish such a thing? It must have been the hand of God. The Catholics *were* pagans and the people, inspired by the forcefulness and truth of the Calvinist sermons, accepted the imperative need to purify the churches. An Apology written in 1566 identified the Netherlanders with the Jews: 'how many times has the Lord commanded the children of Israel to destroy all idolatry?...How many times have they again been reconciled, and appeased their sorrows, by the sole breaking of images?'[74] Another Protestant polemic accused the Catholics of destroying 'the very marrow' of Christian doctrine by worshipping pagan idols:[75]

And to finish the game...they have, against the express commandment of God, erected an infinity of beautiful images, paintings and statues, gilded...like whores ...Finally, to sustain such an enormity by force, they have burned the true and living images of God, living men, in order to make sacrifices to their images and dead idols.

Herman Moded preached that men should expel idols not only from their hearts, but from before their eyes, while a Lutheran preacher at Antwerp admonished, 'We must believe in God alone...thou shalt have no other gods before me, said Moses...'[76] The ministers repudiated the iconoclasm after

[72] *Ibid.*, p. 75.   [73] *Ibid.*, pp. 156–7.
[74] Philippe Marnix de St Aldegonde, *Vraye narration et apologie des choses passées au Pays-Bas, touchant le fait de la religion en l'an 1566* (n.p., 1567), n.p.
[75] *Recueil des choses advenues en Anvers, touchant le fait de la religion, en l'an 1566* (n.p., n.d.).
[76] Van Vloten, *Nederlands Opstand*, pp. 82–3.

the fact, but behaved as though it were an act of God which gave them entrance to the churches; when Moded heard the church bells rung for the first time since the image-breaking he announced to his congregation, 'Listen, the whore of Babylon has resumed her song:' Moded compared the Church to a snail whose body had been crushed and who would gradually heal itself; if only the shell had been crushed as well (i.e., the church buildings and convents), then the Roman whore might have been permanently destroyed.[77] Another minister, Guy de Brès, transmitted the story of one iconoclast to Jean Crespin for his martyrology, which treated only of heroes.[78]

A third explanation for the Troubles, one which was only implied by contemporaries, was that to the ordinary layman, whether participant or witness to the destruction, image-breaking was less the expression of a religious principle than an act of magic – or rather, an act which would test the claims of the ministers against the magical efficacy of the Church's ornaments and rituals. The popular attitude toward images had always been ambivalent. People would regularly attend ceremonies honoring particular statues and relics, and simultaneously use the images as toys; at Ghent a statue of St Anthony, carried in solemn procession, was also used by the participants in a game of catch.[79] On the other hand, most people had exaggerated ideas about the magic which the priests were able to perform. Van Vaernewijck

[77] Van Vaernewijck, *Troubles*, I, p. 199.

[78] Russe, 'Hans Tuscaens', p. 96. Van Vaernewijck, writing at the height of the movement, seemed to have been affected, perhaps unsettled, by this aspect of Reformed doctrine more than any other. Referring to an annual feast day when the image of St Anthony was carried in procession, he admitted; 'To tell the truth, it is only a block of wood which has been sculpted as a bearded man to resemble St Anthony; I repeat, this is not a relic of a saint, but a piece of painted wood.' (I, p. 65). At Ghent many believed that it was outrageous to execute iconoclasts; 'Some people wondered whether it was admissible to punish someone for these miserable statues of wood or stone, which are only dolls and toys.' (I, p. 225).

[79] Professor Jan Craeybeckx has reminded me that in Flanders today, it is common for people to spit on or otherwise abuse statues of saints when their luck has gone badly. This ambiguous relationship to holy images – treating them as play-objects or objects of aggression, as well as of worship – has been observed in studies of other, more primitive cultures. Claude Lévi-Strauss discusses a hamlet in South America where the children played with little wooden figures, some of which were carefully preserved. 'Were these toys? Or likenesses of the gods? Or ancestor-figures? It was impossible to say, so contradictory were the uses to which they were put; and all the more so as one and the same statue would sometimes serve one purpose, now the other.' (*Tristes Tropiques*, trans. John Russell (New York, 1971), pp. 155–6). The historian G. G. Coulton also remarks on this; people in the Middle Ages did not venerate their cathedrals as we do. Churches were often destroyed for military reasons; Charles V destroyed an important church to build a fortress. (*Art and the Reformation*, (Cambridge, 1953), pp. 433, 437).

recounted the sermon of one priest, delivered after the iconoclasm, on the sacrament of baptism. The priest counseled his audience not to think that the mother carries the demon in her stomach for nine months, as if she were possessed. Apparently this idea had so impressed some pregnant women that they became sick, for the priest carefully explained that baptism counteracts a spiritual state of being – not a creature.[80] Many people also believed that the priests used magic powders and strange objects to ward off the devil. Under one altar the iconoclasts discovered a number of vases filled with powders, raisins and other singular objects which they took to be the equipment of sorcerers. This explained the numerous signs of the cross made by the priest, in case the demon was nearby and could not be intimidated by a single sign.[81]

I shudder to report certain allegations which they have circulated, namely that the mass is a magical incantation by which the papists. . .believe God descends from Heaven into their hands and, fearing that the devil will carry them away by some perversity, they make many signs of the cross.

Van Vaernewijck himself admitted that the priests had been censured for simulating miracles in order to increase their revenues.[82]

The iconoclasm must have given immense vicarious satisfaction to those who were convinced that the priests were evil magicians. The new ministers, they must have felt, had finally proved their superiority by demolishing the appurtenances of the Catholic stronghold without being destroyed in a burst of heavenly lightning.[83] This was, after all, the method used by medieval jurists to verify evidence; since God always protected the innocent, it made eminent sense to subject the accused to torture or trial by ordeal in order to elicit the truth. Just so did the iconoclasts deal with the images; not only did they break them to pieces, they selectively 'tortured' them by breaking off noses, heads,

---

[80] Van Vaernewijck, *Troubles*, I, p. 191.

[81] *Ibid.*, p. 154.

[82] *Ibid.*, II, p. 121. In later iconoclastic movements, the Calvinists discovered artifices to make images of saints seem alive; holes were drilled in their eyes to make them cry. (P. Beuzart, 'La Culte des images et la réforme dans les Pays-Bas,' BSHPB, x (1913), p. 17).

[83] In fact this almost happened in Hasselt, where a minister and his followers were engaged in knocking down a huge crucifix in the center of the church. At midnight, without a breath of wind, all of their torches suddenly went out, terrifying the people. One witness said that the preacher made the crowd promise not to tell the papists what had happened; another that he told the people to be calm, that he had seen other similar incidents. (A. Hansay, *Le sac d'église de Saint-Quentin à Hasselt, le Janvier 1567* (Hasselt, 1932), pp. 1–9). Van Vaernewijck included an astronomy lecture in his diary in order to prove that an eclipse which occurred during the iconoclasm was a natural phenomenon, not a miracle – God hiding His face as the truth is obscured (I, p. 435).

etc. 'They hammer away mainly at the faces.'[84] The iconoclasts also treated the images as filth, as polluting elements which were to be given a function more according to their nature; in the villages of East Flanders, one image-breaker stole a mass book and used the pages to wrap herbs and powders, while another took home a religious triptych which he used as a pig trough.[85]

In short, while acts of iconoclasm may have been triggered by hostility toward the clergy as a privileged social group, or by persecution by the authorities, or by hunger, the specific goal of breaking images was to disprove the Church's spiritual authority; it was more satisfying to urinate in the Communion wine-cup than to pawn it. At Ghent the iconoclasts hurled a statue of St Maurice into the river and watched it sink, crying, 'Look, look, this is a miracle! Although completely armed, this saint still knows how to swim!'[86] And the Protestants who murdered the baker in St Médard's church in Paris ridiculed their victim: 'Does your god of paste protect you now from the pains of death?' In breaking down images and attacking members of the Catholic church, the iconoclasts in both countries were demonstrating in the most irrefutable and dramatic way possible that churches or statues of saints were not beloved of God, since God had not chosen to save them from destruction. And for those who were not avowed Calvinists, the violence of the image-breakers must have expressed their own feelings of disequilibrium or anxiety about the real source of religious truth, an anxiety which must have been intensified when the symbols of the Catholic 'gods' were tested and found to be nothing more than pieces of painted wood.

These changes, so radical and so sudden, terrified many people, to the point where they cried out, 'And the air doesn't change!' finding it unbearable that

[84] Van Vaernewijck noticed outside one church 'un monceau où l'on distinguait nombre de testes que l'on eut dit tranchées de la main du boureau.' (II, p. 138). This imitation of judicial punishments was reflected after the iconoclasm too; at Egmont's chateau the people hung images of saints from the gibbets erected to execute iconoclasts. (Kervyn de Lettenhove, *Les huguenots et les gueux*, I (Bruges, 1883), p. 366).

[85] J. Decavele, 'De reformatorische beweging to Axel en Hulst, 1556–1566' (BVGN XXII (1968–9), p. 17). In England the ritual was the same; people fed holy bread to dogs, etc. (K Thomas, *Religion and the Decline of Magic* (New York, 1971), p. 75). Natalie Davis speaks at length about the function of iconoclasm as a means of ridding the community from polluting elements' ('The Rites of Violence: Religious Riot in Sixteenth Century France,' *Past and Present*, LIX (May, 1973), pp. 57–60).

[86] Van Vaernewijck, *Troubles*, II, p. 117. A priest in Culembourg took the Host and roasted it, saying, 'Vous voyez que le Dieu de pain, et sur lequel on vous a tant prêché, n'a ni chair, ni sang, qu'il n'est...rien.' (Gachard, ed., *Correspondance de Philippe II sur les affaires des Pays-Bas*, II (Brussels, 1848), p. 480; letter of Tomas Armenteros to Antonio Perez, November 17, 1566). In England, near Dovercourt in Essex, a famous rood with miraculous powers was removed and carried a quarter of a mile, 'without any resistance of the said idol...' and then burned. (J. Oxley, *The Reformation in Essex* (Manchester, 1965), pp. 89–90).

God had not seen fit to show signs of His anger. . .Others became sick; men and women passed the nights sighing and weeping, wringing their hands.[87]

At the same time the iconoclasm verified the superiority of the Reformers' miraculous powers, since the ministers were able to commit such scandalous actions against the Church and remain unpunished; in the autumn of 1566 one worshipper pulled the grass from where the minister Junius had been standing and took it home as a relic.[88]

It would be foolish to deny the importance of any of these explanations of the Troubles; all of them were perceived, at least implicitly, by contemporaries, and all of them have been accepted and amplified by modern historians. The hedgepreaching *did* contain elements of class hatred; one pamphlet insulted the priests for turning ecclesiastical institutions into boutiques for selling grace. A popular song went: 'You dress these wooden blocks in velvet suits. . .and let God's children go naked.'[89] The iconoclasm *did* begin in West Flanders, an industrial center with a large concentration of unskilled workers, many of whom were unemployed, all of whom suffered from increasing grain prices. At Ghent there had been a grain riot on August 21, the day before the iconoclasm, in which a crowd of women attempted to stone a wealthy merchant. During the violence at a cloister in Ypres, one witness overheard an image-breaker say to the leader of the group, 'We have no bread,' whereupon the man ordered the monks to bake some, saying, 'They have wrecked well; they must eat well.'[90] Contemporaries feared the consequences of this economic insecurity; modern historians dwell on it.[91]

[87] Van Vaernewijck, *Troubles*, I, p. 163.

[88] Frances Yates has observed that perhaps the revival of magic in the Renaissance made the Reformers suspicious of all art and philosophy as tinged with magic, and that this influenced the iconoclasts (*Giordano Bruno and the Hermetic Tradition* (Chicago, 1964), p. 167). This may well have been true for the Calvinist ministers, but in the minds of the ordinary laymen who witnessed the image-breaking, the minister who successfully broke images must have assumed a magical quality of his own. Certainly, many contemporaries felt that a miracle was required; Broer Cornelis scoffed: 'Bah, I would like to ask these men, what miracles or wonders they can do to prove that they were really sent by God to preach the new belief. . .' (*Historie*, p. 40).

[89] Van Vloten, *Nederlands Opstand*, p. 83.

[90] G. Des Marez, 'Documents relatifs aux excès commis à Ypres par les iconoclastes (le 15 et le 16 Août),' BCRH 5th ser. VII (1897), p. 576.

[91] H. van der Wee observed that grain prices were 36% higher than before and that the standard of living was 8% lower than in the previous decade (*The Growth of the Antwerp Market and the European Economy*, II (The Hague, 1963)); M. Delmotte compared the biographies of iconoclasts to those who attended the hedgepreaching. Since the first group came from the lower classes and the second from all segments of society, he concludes that image-breaking and the Reformation were two different movements ('Het Calvinisme in de verschillende bevolkingslagen te Gent (1566–7),'

It is also true that many iconoclasts were inspired by religious ideals. Certainly violence, directed against the inanimate symbols of the Church and, on occasion, against the living defenders of the Church, was a universal element in the Reformed movement. Protestants everywhere were concerned with matters of legality, but what they prayed for was a regenerated social order, a godly society whose leaders would be able to convert, or expel, the ungodly papists. Often the first step toward this social regeneration was the destruction of idolatry and the purification of church buildings in order to transform them into preaching churches. Sometimes the iconoclasts were government officials upholding the law, as in Zurich; elsewhere they were lawbreakers with no apparent connections to the established Reformed leadership, as in the Netherlands. But whatever the position of individual Reformers regarding the legality of religious violence, the destruction of religious art was a clear expression of the spiritual goals of the movement.

The Christian humanists had always spoken out against the use of images. Thomas More banished them from his Utopia, and elsewhere he rejected the argument that the educated believer can distinguish between the concrete image and the reality it represents.[92] Erasmus maintained that it would be wise to limit the use of images to depictions of the crucified Christ.[93] And Folly spoke against idol-woship, because it would

but hinder the worship of me, since by the stupid and dull those figures are worshipped instead of the saints themselves. And it would come about with me exactly as it usually does with the saints. They are thrown out of doors by their substitutes.

The magisterial Reformers also attacked idol-worship. Calvin denied that images were the books of the illiterate; since God's majesty is invisible to the naked eye, whatever images teach man about God must be frivolous and

TvG LXXVI (1963), pp. 145–76. E. Kuttner called 1566 'the hunger year,' a stage in a progressive bourgeois revolution, with the 'Weaver-city' of Valenciennes as a second Geneva, supported by a proletarian army (*Het hongerjaar, 1566* (Amsterdam, 1940)). H. Pirenne correlated the spread of the iconoclasm in Flanders with that of the industrial proletariat of Flemish putting-out workers, ('Une crise industrielle au XVIᵉ siècle: la draperie urbaine et la nouvelle draperie de Flandre,' *Histoire économique de l'occident médiéval* (Paris, 1951), pp. 624–41). Coornaert spoke of the 'violently revolutionary' attitudes of the Hondschoote proletariat during the summer of 1566 (*Un centre industriel d'autrefois: la draperie-sayetterie d'Hondschoote: XIVᵉ– XVIIIᵉ siècles* (Paris, 1930).

[92] 'Dialogue Concerning Heresies,' quoted in E. L. Surtz, *The Praise of Wisdom. A Commentary on the Religious and Moral Problems and Backgrounds of St. Thomas More's 'Utopia'* (Chicago, 1957), p. 194.

[93] *Ibid.*, p. 194. On the influence of humanism on the iconoclasm in England see L. J. Trinterud, ed., *Elizabethan Puritanism* (New York, 1971), pp. 268–9; on Zurich, see C. Garside, *Zwingli and the Arts* (New Haven, Conn., 1966), p. 98.

false.[94] He concluded that only those things which are visibly apparent should be represented – histories or natural phenomena – and that the function of art is simply to provide instruction or pleasure; it is not a vehicle for worship.[95] Quoting Horace, Calvin ridiculed the notion of praying to a statue: 'Formerly I was the trunk of a wild fig tree, a useless log; when the artificer, after hesitating whether he would make me a stool or a deity, at length determined that I should be a god.'[96]

The Netherlands Reformers shared these beliefs, and expressed them not only in religious treatises, but in plays, poems and songs. Thus a Flemish poet, writing around 1540, ridiculed the impotence of the statues in churches:[97]

> [The images] stand in the temple like house beams
> Rusted, dusty, covered with spider webs,
> Dirtied by birds, by cats, by mice.
> And in addition you must also acknowledge
> That they neither smell nor taste
> Nor have any sense of life; that is true.
> Those who love them, must be despised
> And they should not even be regarded as Christians.
> They can neither walk nor stand –
> And I lament about this –
> Even if thieves come to rob them.
> They are incapable of avenging themselves
> Or to do any works in order that we should believe in them;
> . . .it is all fantasy anyway!

Another popular author, writing in 1554, gave his readers a specific program for destroying idolatry in the Netherlands:[98]

Only as many churches should be preserved as are necessary for preaching, baptizing and administering the Eucharist. The authorities should throw the unnecessary idols' nests to the ground, and give the stone to the poor or lay it to the common profit. The preaching churches should be purified of all altars, gross images and other heathen ornaments and then properly decorated.

In 1566, an image-breaker at Ypres was approached by a Catholic who told

---

94 Calvin, *Institutes*, tr. John Allen, 1 (Philadelphia, 1936), Bk. 1, Ch. XI, p. 119.

95 K. Moxey, *Pieter Aertzen, Joachim Beuckelaer and the Rise of Secular Painting in the Context of the Reformation* (New York and London, 1977), pp. 158–9.

96 *Institutes*, p. 118. But he and Beza reprimanded the iconoclasts in France, ('Calvin et les briseurs d'images,' BSHPF xiv (1865), pp. 127–31; *Histoire Ecclésiastique*, 1 (Geneva, 1963), p. 798, Colloquy at the Sorbonne).

97 *Christelijcke en schriftuerlijcke referijnen*, quoted in Moxey, p. 33.

98 Jan Gerritsz Verstege (Velvanus), *Den leken wechwijser* (Strasbourg, 1554), quoted in Moxey, pp. 170–71.

him to spare the organ: 'No! no!' the man answered, 'It must all be broken! We have had too much to do with idolatry.'[99] And in Antwerp the iconoclasts carried hammers to the cathedral the day after the violence began, in order to destroy the choir and simplify the church for preaching.[100]

The image-breakers were also directly influenced by the activities of the Calvinist ministers. Gaspar van der Heyden was sent by the Antwerp consistory to preach at Axel and Hulst; he stayed for only a few days, during which the iconoclasm took place. Joris Wybo was sent from Antwerp to Lierre (Liers) on a visit which lasted from August 18 until August 23; the iconoclasm, done by men from Antwerp, occurred on the 21st, and Wybo preached immediately afterward. The church of Bois-le-Duc, where the consistory led the iconoclasm, was in continual touch with that of Antwerp. At Ghent the iconoclasm was conducted by Lievyn Onghena, who had recently traveled with Herman Moded, then pastor at Antwerp.[101] Whether or not these pastors encouraged the iconoclasm as the policy of the Antwerp consistory, they undoubtedly intended to put a Calvinist stamp on the local Reformed communities, should any opportunity occur to inflict religious toleration on the local magistrates.[102] At any rate, Bois-le-Duc, Ghent, Ypres, Bruges and Limbourg all received visits from important Reformers from Antwerp in the weeks following the iconoclasm, and during the autumn and winter several ministers participated in military operations against the government.[103]

[99] Des Marez, 'Documents,' p. 565.

[100] Moxey, p. 55.

[101] On van der Heyden: van Vloten, 'Losse aanteekeningen betrekkelijk den vrijheidsoorlog: Axel en Hulst,' *Bijdragen tot de oudheidkunde en geschiedenis inzonderheid van zeeuwsch-Vlaanderen*, II, pp. 307–14. On Wybo: R. van Roosbroeck, *Het wonderjaar te Antwerpen, 1566–1567* (Antwerp, 1930), pp. 82–3. On Bois-le-Duc: Cuypers van Velthoven, *Documents*, pp. 304, 309. On Ghent: A. C. de Schrevel, *Histoire du séminaire de Bruges*, I (Bruges, 1895), p. 244.

[102] This second explanation seems the most credible for several reasons: first, Wybo and van der Heyden were sent in response to requests by local Reformers for a resident pastor. Second, the pastors who committed the first acts of iconoclasm, Matte and de Buzère, were not, to my knowledge, in touch with Antwerp during the early summer: they had just arrived from England. (Matte traveled 1,620 km. in the first week of the iconoclasm, leading a group from the Hondschoote Reformed community, which had been in touch with churches in England before the Troubles. Backhouse p. 157.)

[103] For modern versions of the 'Calvinist' theory of the Troubles, see J. Motley, *The Rise of the Dutch Republic*, 3 vols. (New York, 1855). Also see R. Kingdon, 'The Political Resistance of the Calvinists in France and the Low Countries,' *Church History*, XXVII (1958). The process by which Calvinist theology inspired its adherents to radical political action is analyzed by M. Walzer, *The Revolution of the Saints* (Cambridge, Mass., 1965).

It should be possible to explain the significance of the Troubles in terms of one of these theories – or by a synthesis of all of them. We might say that the people were aroused and amenable to violent action because they were uprooted and because they were poor, and this tendency toward social upheaval became fused with Reformed ideology. Here is Pieter Geyl on the iconoclasm:[104]

The movement started…in the area where the new cloth manufacture had created an industrial proletariat…whose religious ecstasy was nearly allied to social unrest…it was a truly Calvinistic work, fierce and honest…striving to purge the land for God's elect from the devilish ornaments of idolatry, and to pull down at one blow a past of a thousand years.

Contemporaries said this too; van Vaernewijck's observations on both the economic situation and the force of Reformed preaching have been cited throughout the body of our narration. The 'Recueil,' a pamphlet from which I have already quoted, contains ample evidence of all three explanations; the anonymous writer fulminates against the wealth of the Catholic clergy, denounces Catholic ritual as magical superstition, and exalts the purity and zeal of the Calvinist ministers. Or, borrowing from the work of historians of other religious movements, we might combine the insights of the economic and the anthropological theories. Thus one historian of image-worship in Florence discusses the contemporary perception of worship *vs.* idolatry. 'Idolatry was something other than "image worship." If the miracles were fraudulent, then the image became an idol. The only iconoclasm conceivable among these people was against images which failed.'[105] Perhaps this distinction can also be applied to the iconoclasm in the Netherlands; perhaps people had begun to feel as a result of economic hardship that their saints had failed them and, as mere idols, deserved annihilation.

But while each of these theories tells us a great deal about the positive causes of the violence in 1566, none of them successfully answers a question which puzzled contemporaries greatly: given the fact that religious violence was of immense significance to so many different people – for so many different reasons – why was there so little of it? If the Troubles are to be understood in terms of economic frustration, why was there so little stolen, either from the churches or from private houses? At the Dominican cloister in Ghent the image-breakers destroyed so many books that the street was soon covered with printed sheets, but when bystanders attempted to recover these and carry them away certain others stopped them, saying that it was

---

[104] Pieter Geyl, *The Revolt of the Netherlands* (London, 1966), pp. 92–3.
[105] R. Trexler, 'Florentine Religious Experience: The Sacred Image,' *Studies in the Renaissance*, XIX (1972), pp. 7–41.

forbidden to steal.[106] In other towns the gold and silver images were delivered to a head officer by weight:[107]

And coming to a town in Flanders where they so spoiled, one of their company did hide away the value of four or five shillings; whereupon they took him, and caused a pair of gallows to be made and hanged him on the market place; and said they came not to steal.

At Tournai, after the ornaments were inventoried and put in boxes they were taken to the magistrate and stored with him; one key was given to the magistrate and one kept by the ministers. The wine was sold by people commissioned by the city.[108] At Bois-le-Duc, after the first night of iconoclasm, the broken ornaments were carried to the city hall for safe-keeping while the image-breaking continued.[109] Morillon, always ready to slander the Reformers, wrote to Granvelle, 'They have taken nothing, consigning gold and silver to leaders to inventory, swearing that they would convert it all into money to use for the poor.'[110]

Another aspect of the iconoclasm which surprised contemporaries was the absence of physical violence against the hated Catholic clergy. The day after the iconoclasm began in West Flanders Clough had written, 'For and if they do once begin, it will be a bloodie time.' But there was no 'bloodie time.' The violence, with rare exceptions, was perpetrated solely against images; there was almost no violence done to people. At Valenciennes a Catholic wrote,

[106] Van Vaernewijck, *Troubles*, 1, p. 106. At Ghent the iconoclasts discovered a casket filled with money. Some wanted to steal it; others said it should be taken to the bailiff – which was done. They later stated that they had taken a little, 'pour solder les gens qui veillent à ce que l'on ne dérobe rien et respecte les personnes.' (*Ibid.*, pp. 73–4).

[107] Burgon, *Life of Gresham*, p. 140.

[108] Pasquier de la Barre, *Mémoires*, 1, p. 138.

[109] Cuypers van Velthoven, *Documents*, pp. 320–1.

[110] Some looting did occur; Wesembeke mentioned an admonition of the Antwerp magistrates to return stolen goods. In general, historians sympathetic to the Reformers, like Beuzart, minimize this, saying that some rabble got in with the 'pure' Calvinists. De Moreau, a Catholic, mentioned looting, but admitted it was surprisingly slight. Delmotte mentions looting 'here and there'; he also notes that the image-breakers did not plunder the grain market although there was a grain riot there two days earlier (p. 162). At Axel and Hulst the workers were passive; there was no talk of getting money from the rich and the wealthy abbeys were not attacked (Decavele, p. 32). At Valenciennes a Catholic witness wrote that the abbot of St Jean's church offered a great sum of money to save a rood screen and organs but the Calvinists refused and the organs were smashed (G. Clark, *An Urban Study during the Revolt of the Netherlands: Valenciennes 1540–1570*, Thesis, Columbia University, 1972, pp. 313–14). Backhouse emphasizes that looting occurred in Flanders, but admits that in Ghent, Antwerp, and also in W. Flanders, goods were returned to the magistrates (pp. 86–8).

Certain chroniclers have greatly mistaken the character of this image-breaking. It has been said that the Calvinists killed a hundred priests in the city, cutting some of them to pieces, and burning others over a slow fire. I remember very well everything which happened on that abominable day, and I can affirm that not a single priest was injured.

The historian Petit thought that this was a great wonder above all the rest, 'considering that it was done in the night time, and so many stones, wood and other stuff broken and rent in pieces.'[111] Personal attacks against the clergy were plentiful, but the attacks were verbal, not physical. At Ghent, for instance, an elderly priest, 'fort riche,' tried to intervene during the icono-clasm, but the Reformers ridiculed him so viciously that the priest retreated outside the church, where he sat 'a man deprived of his senses, no longer recognizing anyone.'[112] Compare this to the iconoclasm in France, where violence against images was accompanied by atrocities not only against the Catholic clergy, but against innocent bystanders.[113] The quotations which introduce this chapter both describe similar activities: the desecration of the symbols of Catholic worship. But the incident in France culminated in a murder, while that in the Netherlands ended in quiet departure. In short, the violence in the Netherlands was both more limited and more refined than elsewhere; in France the violence was more obscene.

This absence of personal or random violence is especially curious because of the degree of anti-clerical and iconoclastic activity in the years before 1566, and because the iconoclasm came after almost three months of public preach-ing in which the ministers had spoken against idolatry and the evils of the Roman clergy. It becomes even more curious when we compare the Troubles of 1566 to the behavior of the Reformers only six years later. In 1572, when the Beggar chiefs entered a city, they guaranteed the lives and goods of

[111] Petit, *A General History*, p. 402.
[112] Van Vaernewijck, *Troubles*, II, p. 104. At Richebourg, the preacher Julien threatened a priest – and then left the church with his followers (van Vloten, p. 86). At Antwerp, a Lutheran preacher was defeated in a public debate by a priest; the crowd threatened to kill the priest, but nothing happened (G. Bertrijn, *Chronyck der stadt Antwerpen* (Antwerp, 1879, pp. 123–4). At Valenciennes a Catholic witness wrote about the horrible insults endured by the priests during the iconoclasm, but he does not say that the Catholics were hurt (Mss. Valenciennes No. 689, ff. 9–10).
[113] Claude de Sainctes, a Catholic, wrote that the Calvinists found a priest and cut his garments, while elsewhere the mob led an old monk through a town naked and then killed him, tied him to a tree and molested his corpse (*Discours sur le saccage-ment des églises catholiques* (Paris, 1563, pp. 371–2, 382). The best modern account is by Natalie Davis ('Rites of Violence'); she notes that Catholics probably killed more people than Calvinists, but she also cites numerous cases of Calvinists murdering Catholic priests and desecrating bones in the churches. Van Vaernewijck was shocked by accounts of atrocities in France – opening the stomachs of victims, filling them with grain and letting horses eat from them (I, p. 325).

ecclesiastics. 'But no sooner was the Beggar chief inside than the agreement
...was violated, churches and monasteries were plundered, and priests murdered. Next there came...the expulsion of magistrates who were considered
too favourable to Catholicism.'[114] The absence of personal violence seems even
stranger when we realize that in many cases the iconoclasts were drunk;
numerous contemporary accounts speak of people breaking into wine and
beer cellars in the cloisters and wading up to their ankles in drink. At Ghent
the image-breakers at the Dominican cloister got drunk on wine and beer:[115]

The darkness and the wine gave these evildoers courage: the scoundrels also became
undisciplined. [The leaders]...wanted to prevent certain outrages, particularly
the squandering of the wine cellars; but the populace overwhelmed them, ignor-
ing their injunctions. The wine dulled their senses and made them deaf.

Even so, they killed no priests. The Catholic clergy was not run out of town,
and Catholic worship was resumed a few weeks afterward.

Finally, and perhaps most important, contemporaries were astonished by
the fact that the image-breaking was accomplished by so few people. Clough's
letter of August 21 described the events at Antwerp:[116]

...being done after such order and with so few folks, that it is to be marveled at,
and not so much to be wondered at of the doing, but that so few people durst or
could do so much; for then when they entered into some of the houses of religion,
I could not perceive in some churches above ten or twelve that spoiled – all being
boys and rascals, but there were many in the church lookers-on...This thing
was done so quiet and so still, as if there had been nothing ado in the churches;
all men standing before their doors in harness, looking upon these fellows passing
from church, which as they passed through the streets, required all men to be
quiet.

Margaret wrote that not more than a hundred were involved. The historian
Strada stated that if they had not each one hundred arms it would be right
to think, as many did, that demons possessed them. Wesembeke wrote, 'All
was done with such incredible speed, that before it was day there was in the
whole city no church, no chapel, no monastery, which they had not totally
demolished and destroyed.' Van Vaernewijck spoke of 'about fifteen young
people, poorly dressed, who appeared to be strangers to the city' who tore
down the images at the Dominican convent.[117] Again, compare this to the

---

[114] Geyl, *The Revolt*, p. 128.

[115] Van Vaernewijck, *Troubles*, II, p. 120. At Axel and Hulst the iconoclasts got drunk
too (Decavele, p. 17). At Ypres witnesses described the drunkenness of the image-
breakers (Des Marez, pp. 95–127).

[116] Burgon, *Life of Gresham*, pp. 137–9.

[117] Van Vaernewijck, *Troubles*, II, p. 114. A recent article on Antwerp cites 20–30
men and youths, hired for 3–7 stuivers, who broke images in one church (Dierickx,
p. 1044). At Axel, 30 men broke images; at Hulst the list also included 30 names

34

cases of Basel and Wittenberg, where the iconoclasm was committed by the mass of the population, and to France, where contemporaries referred to the crowds of image-breakers who terrorized the Catholic populace.[118]

This curious passivity on the part of the general population was matched by that of the magistrates, who behaved, throughout the iconoclasm, as though they were paralyzed. After the sack of the Antwerp church a messenger was dispatched to the city hall, but the magistrates, thinking that the troops might not be loyal, did nothing, and the mobs were even more audacious the following day. When the iconoclasts arrived at Courtrai (Kortrijk), the city had already been abandoned for five or six days. Crespin thought that God caused the magistrates to be terrified so that it required only one man to break all the images in Lierre. Elsewhere two poor men asked at the gate of a town to see if the images were broken; they were taken to the churches and told to break what was left. At Ghent, three or four days before the event, the magistrates heard a rumor that an 'army from the West' was approaching and would penetrate the city in small groups, but took no precautions.

This passivity on the part of the local magistrates seemed all the more surprising because in the few cities where the officials made some attempt to resist the iconoclasts, they succeeded without difficulty. At Malines (Mechelen) a group of image-breakers demanded the keys to a church. The sacristan fetched a magistrate, who demanded to see their mandate to commit iconoclasm or he would attack them with a hundred gendarmes; the iconoclasts disappeared. At Bruges a watch was set at the gates and in front of the churches, the ornaments were removed and a curfew was put in force; there was no iconoclasm at Bruges, although several massive *prêches* had taken

(Decavele, pp. 15–17). The same holds true for Ghent (Delmotte, p. 159). At Tournai the image-breakers were hired (Dierickx, p. 1046), as they were at Turnhout and Mechelen (*Ibid.*, pp. 1046–7). At Dixmude a preacher arrived with 11 people to break images (Justification of the magistrate, van Vloten, p. 174). At Ypres, witnesses spoke of 10–12 (Des Marez). The total number of image-breakers in Flanders was even smaller than it appeared, because a single group, largely from Hondschoote, traveled to different towns and villages (Backhouse, pp. 91–4).

[118] On Basel, see G. Williams, *The Radical Reformation* (Philadelphia, 1962), p. 196. On Wittenberg, see C. Garside, *Zwingli*, p. 127. On France, see Davis, 'Rites of Violence' in which the author refers to crowds of image-breakers, but does not analyze the exact numbers. A Protestant account of the iconoclasm in Paris states that a crowd of about 12,000–13,000 tried to force the doors of the church of St Médard ('Histoire véritable,' printed in L. Cimber and F. Danjou, ed. *Archives curieuses de l'histoire de France*, IV, (1834–40), pp. 52–55). Another account says that 3–4,000 controlled the neighboring streets while the crowd went 'en grand numbre' into the church (relation of Bruslart, quoted from the *Mémoires de Condé*, I (1743), in *Archives Curieuses*, IV, p. 57, n.1).

place there. [119] At Marchiennes, a village near Tournai, a group of iconoclasts was quickly routed by a mercenary soldier, Fery de Guyon.[120]

All of this should make us somewhat sceptical of accepting the 'economic' theory as a complete explanation of the Troubles. It makes little sense to describe the mentality of the people as frustrated and hostile, and then to describe their behavior during the iconoclasm as passive, but in fact the vast majority of the people *were* passive during the Troubles. If we attempt to explain the iconoclasm in terms of social conflict, how explain the fact that neither the workers nor the ruling magistrates appeared willing to participate in this conflict? On the other hand, if we describe the Troubles as the action of a dedicated minority, an army of Calvinist ministers and their adherents, we are then faced with the problem of determining exactly what role the ministers played during these events. It is certainly true that the iconoclasm and military campaigns were in some sense led by the Reformed ministers, but in what sense? From the beginning of the hedgepreaching the ministers had sometimes acted as prophets, sometimes as secondary members of the consistories, sometimes as envoys to the nobility and the local magistrates. But it was rarely clear at which moments they were acting as individuals, on their own initiative, and when they were effecting policies which had been formulated in the consistories. Some ministers, like Daneel, were lay preachers who traveled with a personal following. Others, like Herman Moded, were directly patronized by the Calvinist nobility. Still others, like Gaspar van der Heyden, were formally instructed by the Antwerp consistory to preach in other cities, and remained in close touch with the central church. In Bois-le-Duc the ministers were totally subject to the authority of the local consistory, which dictated what they might preach.

The role of the preachers in the iconoclasm was no less confusing. In some cities, particularly in West Flanders, it was apparently led by ministers and their personal retainers, in others (like Ghent) by the local consistory, in still others by people whose affiliations with the Reformed movement were unknown.[121] During the sieges, the ministers played different roles in different

---

[119] Janssen, *Bruges*, pp. 53–4. Van Vaernewijck noted that Ghent had lost her walls and artillery; still, he says, the magistrates could have taken some precautions (II, p. 97).

[120] A. L. P. de Robaulx de Soumoy, ed., *Mémoires de Fery de Guyon, écuyer* (Brussels, 1858), Ch. XXXI.

[121] e.g., the minister Jean Leseur testified that when he was at Prémont, news arrived of the iconoclasm in Valenciennes. Another minister said, 'We must do the same in your city.' The group then went to Cateau, to the house of a Reformer, where an argument ensued whether or not to break images; the group from Prémont then left for the church; on the way out Leseur saw a statuette on the mantel and smashed it (interrogation of Leseur, printed in Desilve, pp. 229–31).

cities. In Valenciennes, they dominated the consistory and effectively ruled the city; in Bois-le-Duc they were not even visible during the siege, although they were present in the town; in Tournai, the minister Marmier exhorted the people to accept a garrison and then escaped from the city on horseback.[122]

If the historian wishes to prove that events were determined by a specific ideology and type of organization, then this question of leadership becomes crucial. If the ministers acted according to policies which were formulated in the Calvinist consistories, or in Geneva, then one might infer that Calvinism was the moving force in those events. If, on the other hand, the preachers who did the violence called themselves Reformers, but acted as individuals, on personal initiative, then who can say that they were not acting in opposition to or at least disregarding the ideals and policies of the Calvinists, or that they were not motivated by any number of other things – e.g., being an alienated intellectual, being Flemish rather than French, etc.?

If we accept, for the moment, the hypothesis that Calvinists had either planned the iconoclasm or taken advantage of a spontaneous movement and shaped it to their own ends, we are then faced with the problem of explaining why the Reformers seemed to have no coherent policy toward the local authorities. At times during the autumn of 1566 they were provocative in their behavior; in December the minister Cornille de Lesenne executed a man without trial because he had been called a Catholic spy.[123] At other times they went to great lengths to avoid violence; on December 12 the minister Etienne Marmier exhorted a mob to allow the execution of a Reformer to take place, although the executioner himself was ready to withdraw for fear of violence.[124] Moreover, if the ministers did plan the iconoclasm in order to take over the cities, they were patently acting against their own interests, since the Reformers had been negotiating for months with the Germans on the basis of a compromise with the Lutherans; the events of the summer and autumn antagonized a good many Reformed nobles and effectively extinguished any possibility of tolerance by the Regent. If the Reformers had decided that they were strong enough to act without foreign alliances, why did the ministers not behave as they did in the 1570s, killing priests and forcing their way into the offices of local government?[125] If, on the other hand, the ministers'

---

[122] *Mémoires de Soldoyer*, p. 256.   [123] Pasquier de la Barre, *Mémoires*, II, pp. 215–16.

[124] *Ibid.*, p. 250. At Ghent the ministers quarreled over whether or not to ignore the magistrate and preach in the city, and ended by complying with the magistrate (van Vaernewijck, I, p. 176). At Armentières the minister was aggressive: he ignored the magistrates' order to leave the city and proceeded to hold a service inside a church (*Ibid.*, I, pp. 82–3).

[125] W. Brulez contends that the Netherlands revolt began in 1566, but admits that the leaders of the siege at Valenciennes – the ministers themselves – were moderate and insisted on legal behavior; they refused to collect money for the revolt and

original motive was simply to preach and to seek toleration, why did they try to raise an army in September, before there was any real repression?

In short, whether we describe the iconoclasm as an act of magic, a gesture of religious outrage or a symptom of social revolution, the behavior of most people during the Troubles – workers, magistrates, even ministers – remains unexplained. I think that this negative aspect of the Troubles requires our attention at least as much as the positive and more easily discernible feature of violence, and this remains true even though it is far more difficult to explain why people did not do things than why they did. For the fact is that in the Netherlands, violence was not a *mass* exercise; there was no aggressive *mass* attack against priests, magistrates – or images, for that matter. Certainly the Reformers were capable of violence, as they demonstrated in the murders in Flanders two years later. And certainly there were differences in the patterns of violence between one area and another.[126] But violence done to persons was not an element of the appeal of Calvinism as a mass movement. Priests were not mutilated or murdered, nor was a significant portion of church property stolen, by men who had been incited to act by the ministers at the hedgepreaching; the violence began only after the mass movement had been totally suppressed and punished.[127]

But if the thousands who attended the hedgepreaching were not incited to commit violence by the ministers, why did they go to the meetings? If the iconoclasm which seemed to climax the hedgepreaching was not a mass movement, perhaps the significance of the *prêche* itself was not to arouse the anger of the populace against the clergy or to inspire the audience to heights of religious frenzy. In any case, our concern with the sources of popular religious sentiment during the Troubles should lead us to focus less on the iconoclasm and military campaigns, which were the actions of a minority, and more on the phenomenon of the hedgepreaching, which was a genuine mass movement. And here the unquestioned leaders *were* the Calvinist ministers who presided over the meetings.

declined help from the French ('De opstand van het industrie-gebied in 1566,' *Standen en landen*, IV (1954), pp. 81–101). Kuttner dismissed this behavior as 'impractical' (*Ibid.*, p. 86).

126 The use of violence varied in different localities. Sometimes the minister prevented a popular uprising; at Bruges a *prêche* was interrupted by the bells from a church – the minister yielded and the crowd went elsewhere, where they were attacked by troops and dispersed (Janssen, *Bruges*, p. 18). Elsewhere the crowd was the passive element; at Antwerp there was a rumor that troops were coming – everyone at the *prêche* fled, leaving hats, coats, etc. (Bertrijn, p. 115). At other times the magistrates prevented violence; at Antwerp the officials prevented a crowd from breaking down the doors of the cathedral (Rijksarchief Antwerpen, PK 272, no folio numbers).

127 Van Vaernewijck, *Troubles*; in volume II the author cites no instances of public preaching (1567); but he does cite several instances of violence done to persons.

2

THE MINISTERS

In a village near Limbourg lived an old woman who was tormented by the belief that she and her children were damned. Having been exorcised in vain by the priests, she wandered alone in the forest, behaving 'like a demon.' One night she was persuaded to visit the Calvinist minister Junius, to whom she confessed that the cause of her despair was the reproaches of her neighbors, who told her she was damned because – a widow with nine young children – she had no time to attend Mass. She believed that her children were also damned, 'seeing that a serpent can only give birth to serpents.' Junius assured her that by being a good mother she was also a good Christian. The woman regained her sanity, and Junius was honored as a miracle-worker; despite his protestations, his followers brought many sick people before him to be cured.[1] In Tournai, the rumor spread that Etienne Marmier, another Calvinist pastor, had been attacked at a *prêche* outside the city. A group of Reformers immediately left on horseback to get news of his condition. 'And it seems to me,' wrote a contemporary, 'that if the matter had been true, that there would have been a great disorder and pity in Tournai, for the rumor had already spread among many that they were going to kill and plunder all of the priests or men of the church to avenge the death of their minister.'[2] In Ghent, thousands ignored the magistrates' warnings to stay away from the hedgepreaching: 'One sermon from the ministers,' they said, 'is worth a hundred others.'

While the ministers impressed their followers as heroic, almost super-human, their enemies viewed them as illiterate vagrants. 'To make few wordes,' wrote a Catholic professor at Louvain, 'the abjectes and outcastes, the most wicked and base of all sortes of men are gon to this gospellyth con-gregation like the chaf winowed out of God's flocke...'[3] In Bruges, the friar Cornelis tried to dispute with the minister at a *prêche*, but he found that the man knew no Latin: 'He was ignorant of dogma and church history.

[1] D. Lenoir, *Histoire de la réformation dans l'ancien pays de Liège* (Brussels, 1861), pp. pp. 95–7. The incident occurred in November, 1566.
[2] Pasquier de la Barre, *Mémoires*, I, 187–8.
[3] Peter Frarin, *Oration Against the Protestantes* (Antwerp, 1566), n.p.

He could only give the text in Flemish.'⁴ The ministers at another *prêche* looked to him like beggars:⁵

The first had a shabby pair of breeches which were full of holes. . .a second-hand jacket without sleeves. . .and no shirt; the second had an old shirt. . .and a wretched, dirty hat with a feather; the third had hose of dirty linen and a thin coat full of holes.

In the territory of Liège, a man approached the pastor Junius and stared fixedly at his feet. Finally the man said, 'Ah! Now I see that what people have told me is not true.' 'And what is that?' asked the minister. 'I was told that you have cloven feet.'⁶

Who were these men, whom the Catholics saw as devilish impostors and the Calvinists as messengers of God? François du Jon (Junius) and Peregrine de la Grange were French noblemen in their early twenties, who left Geneva together in 1565 to preach in the Netherlands – their first assignment as pastors. Junius was active at Antwerp with Herman Moded, a Fleming from the northern town of Zwolle. Moded was some ten years older than Junius, and had been both a monk and a professor at the University of Cologne. As a Calvinist, he preached at the Danish court, was briefly imprisoned at Utrecht in 1559, and spent the next six years as an itinerant minister in the Netherlands. Also at Antwerp in 1566 were Gaspar van der Heyden, member of a respected burgher family of Mechelen, who had run away from home at the age of sixteen to become a Calvinist, and Jean Taffin, a former humanist scholar who had served as librarian to Granvelle, the Regent's chief adviser, before joining the movement in 1558. Peregrine de la Grange preached at Valenciennes with Guy de Brès, a former glass painter from Mons. De Brès was twice the age of de la Grange, and had converted to the Reformed movement some twenty years earlier. Before coming to Valenciennes, de Brès had been a refugee in England, Switzerland and France; he had spent six months in a French prison, three years as the chaplain of the Duke of Sedan, and several more years as an itinerant preacher in the region of Tournai and Valenciennes.

Nicaise van der Schuere was a young, bourgeois Fleming from the city of Ghent, with no great reputation for learning or maturity; one witness called him an idiot.⁷ In 1566 he preached in his native city with Jean Micheus and

---

⁴ Broer Cornelis, *Historie*, quoted in M. Leblanc, *Les prédicants Calvinistes et leur rôle dans les Pays-Bas, de 1559 à 1567*, Diss. University of Brussels, 1949–51, p. 27.
⁵ *Ibid.*, Leblanc, p. 46.
⁶ F. W. Cuno, *Franciscus Junius der Altere* (Amsterdam, 1891), p. 39.
⁷ J. W. Te Water, *Historie der hervormde kerke te Gent* (Utrecht, 1756), p. 180. The insult probably meant that van der Schuere knew no Latin, or was immature in his behavior. Van Vaernewijck thought that he had studied medicine at Louvain (*Troubles*, I, p. 25).

Pieter Dathenus. Micheus was a bourgeois from Utrecht, in the North; three years before he had been a professor of languages at the University of Lausanne. Dathenus was a former Carmelite friar from Ypres who had been in the Reformed movement for over a decade, most of the time as a refugee in the Flemish churches of England and Germany, part of the time as chaplain to Frederick III of the Palatinate. Sebastien Matte, a former hatmaker who had been a member of the Flemish refugee church at London, preached in Flanders with Jacques de Buzère and Cornille de Lesenne. De Buzère was an apostate monk from the renowned Augustinian cloister at Ypres who had become a trained Calvinist theologian and pastor of the refugee church at Sandwich. De Lesenne, a blacksmith from French Flanders, was a self-taught minister who had cared for the children of executed Reformers while studying Scripture.[8]

In short, the ministers who preached during the Troubles were a highly disparate group of men, both in terms of their original background and in terms of their experience and relative eminence in the Reformed movement. Some, like Pieter Dathenus, were theologians and writers of international repute; others, like Sebastien Matte, returned to the Netherlands in 1566 as obscure members of refugee communities who had probably never even been consecrated as ministers. Still others were students, or artisans, or academics with no formal experience as pastors. In fact, the only experience which the ministers seem to have had in common was that of flight; almost every minister had spent some time as a religious refugee – in England, Germany, France, Switzerland or the northern provinces – in the years before the Troubles.

What does all of this tell us about the kinds of men who chose to join the Reformed movement? Peter Frarin thought that the ministers were recruited from ambitious members of the lower classes, 'like the chaf winowed out of God's flocke.' Jean Cateu, a former monk, was certainly not unusual in having been accused of joining the Reformers for money.[9] However, as the preceding description should already have suggested, many of the men who became ministers had very little to gain, either in terms of status or wealth, and sometimes a good deal to lose, by their new religious commitment. The ministers had not been an especially deprived group in Netherlands society, in terms of original background and education. They did come from every social and economic class, but they did not represent the lowest elements of those groups, while of those who had belonged to the Catholic clergy, the great majority came from large monasteries in the cities – they were not

8 Meyhoffer notes.
9 Desilve, *St Amand*, p. 73.

benighted parish priests.[10] At least one minister experienced a loss of status before his conversion, and certainly the Catholic clergy as a whole had suffered a loss of popular respect, both because of the Church's inability to perform its pastoral functions and because of the hatred of the Inquisition and the ecclesiastical courts.[11] But there were still avenues of advancement within the Church for those with talent; in fact the king had recently introduced a number of administrative reforms (the new bishoprics) which were partially intended to open important ecclesiastical offices to those with high intellectual qualifications. Yet many of these theologians and university students were the very people who chose to enter the Reformed clergy; those whom the bishoprics hurt – the younger sons of the nobility and the parish priests – did not.[12] For these educated men, admission to the Reformed ministry involved a sacrifice of opportunities to achieve greater status within the established clerical and professional hierarchies.

It also involved a sacrifice of physical and financial security. For the most part the Reformed ministers subsisted on salaries provided by the consistories or on charity which was collected by the deacons at the *prêches*; none had permanent lodgings.[13] And in the years before the hedgepreaching, many

[10] Seven were workers; of these, 5 were skilled artisans (1 glasspainter, 2 shoemakers, 2 hatmakers) 1 a weaver, 1 unskilled. 16 belonged to the Catholic clergy; on the academic training of the clergy from urban monasteries, see E. de Moreau, 'Le clergé des Pays-Bas méridionaux à l'époque des troubles,' BCRH, 5 ser. xxxiii (1947), pp. 195–214. 12 were bourgeois, 4 were nobles, the rest unknown (of these unknowns, 4 had studied at universities and probably belonged to the clergy or bourgeoisie). Of the educated men, 6 studied law, 5 theology (assuming the clergy who studied at universities did this) 2 languages, 1 pedagogy. Taffin was a librarian, Flaming ran a Latin school, Cubus started a school for Latin and French in London in 1569, Baerdeloos was a 'student.' The group was also divided in terms of age, place of origin, and language: 15 were young (under 35), 11 older. 24 came from Flanders, 1 from Liège, 2 from Brabant, 1 from Artois, 4 from Hainaut, 7 from the N. Netherlands including Emden, 10 from France, 1 from Spain, 1 from Germany. 31 spoke Flemish, 18 French.

[11] Herman Moded had been dismissed from the faculty of the University of Cologne by the Jesuits, at the time when he called himself a 'half-heretic.' (Brutel de la Rivière, *Het Leven*, p. 13).

[12] Only the Netherlands noble, Jehan Gillain, from the North, became a minister; the rest were Frenchmen.

[13] Contemporary accounts say that the ministers lodged with prominent Reformers where they preached. Marmier's in-laws had property, as did the families of the bourgeois ministers, but in general the ministers were too mobile to enjoy this wealth; in fact the *Comptes des confiscations*, which are so useful in determining property values for other groups, are of virtually no use in analyzing the ministers' holdings, since many arrived only in 1566 and preached in several locations. On salaries: Pasquier de la Barre wrote that at Tournai the only salary for the ministers was charity. At Deinze the deacons at the *prêche* circulated twice – once for the ministers' salary, and once for the poor. (J. van Vloten, 'Losse aanteekeningen betrekkelijk

had survived only by resorting to manual labor. Van der Heyden, a well-to-do bourgeois, went to work in Antwerp as a shoemaker. Cornille de Lesenne worked as a lace-maker, Dathenus as a printer. Junius, the son of a nobleman, subsisted in Geneva on two eggs and a glass of wine a day.[14] Taffin, a member of the Regent's entourage and the son of a wealthy bourgeois family of Tournai, became a refugee minister who was forced to beg for shelter.

Clearly, the ministers' recruitment to the Reformed movement cannot be explained as a function of their socio-economic origins. But can we discern some connection between the ministers' early background and their public behavior during the Troubles? Not all of the hedgepreachers committed iconoclasm or supported a policy of violence against the magistrate in 1566. If we find that the 'radical' ministers were also foreigners, or Genevan radicals, or members of the Flemish proletariat, in contrast to those who were merely active as preachers, then we might be able to explain the violence as the action of a fragmented, alien minority.[15] But were the Geneva-trained Calvinists more radical, more eager to break images and lead sieges, than their colleagues who were trained in Germany or Emden? Did the younger pastors behave differently from those who had several years of experience at accommodating themselves to foreign governments? Did the facts of being poor or rich, Flemish or French, German-trained or Geneva-trained, involved in secular politics or involved in theological disputes, make any difference in the way the pastors responded to the crises of 1566–7? Or were there any other patterns of background or behavior which might help to clarify their role in the Troubles and, by implication, the effect of different religious and political attitudes on patterns of social upheaval?

II

It is probably impossible to determine whether or not violence, in the form of iconoclasm, prison breaks, or the revolt of cities, was an element of the Reformers' original policy in 1566. Consistory records from the London Dutch church, where many ministers had taken refuge before the Troubles, have been lost for the period 1564–8, and there are no records of the

---

den vrijheidsoorlog: Deinze, Eekloo, Petegem,' *Bijdragen tot de oudheidkunde en geschiedenis inzonderheid van zeeuwsch-Vlaanderen*, Vol. II, p. 144.)

[14] Cuno, *Franciscus Junius*, p. 13.

[15] This is the thesis of several economic historians. Clark, for example, maintains that the iconoclasm in Flanders was not really Calvinist; it was a spontaneous uprising by radical lay preachers and vagabonds – he asserts that there were no trained ministers or organized consistories in areas where it started ('An Urban Study,' pp. 327–8, 337).

ministers' deliberations at Antwerp during the iconoclasm itself.[16] But, while we cannot say whether or not the consistories planned the violence of 1566, we do know that many pastors supported both the general principle of violence against the magistrate (particularly in the form of prison breaks), and the specific act of iconoclasm.

In the early 1560s a number of successful prison-breaks occurred in W. Flanders. At the same time a series of public letters and pamphlets were circulated in the area, defending the innocent blood that was shed by foreign tyrants and asserting that if certain Calvinist prisoners were not released, an army of footsoldiers and horsemen would rise and destroy the towns of Flanders. This agitation was the result of several discussions on violence which took place in England and the Netherlands in 1561–2.[17] The first meetings were held at Nieuwkerke in Flanders, and at the Dutch refugee church in Sandwich. At a synod held in Antwerp in 1562 the pastors again discussed the legality of using violence against the magistrate in order to free prisoners. Two members of the pro-violence faction, Herman Moded and Pieter Hazard, proceeded to a meeting in London to discuss the matter further. London finally forbade the use of violence, and Moded stopped corresponding with the London church.

This argument was renewed immediately after the Troubles, when the pastor Godfried Wingius preached vehemently against the iconoclasm, causing an uproar in the London community.[18] A party of radicals, including several ministers who were in the Netherlands in 1566, opposed him, and the issue soon polarized the consistory – the elders and Wingius versus the younger deacons. Wingius was temporarily suspended from preaching and a body of deacons withdrew to the more radical church of Norwich, from which another minister, Jan Michiels, returned to Flanders and committed three murders at Reninghelst. One John Engelram, a follower of Wingius, published an attack on iconoclasm and was forced to make a public confession of heresy. The minister who corresponded with other churches about the orthodoxy of Engelram's book, Antoine Escaille, preached immediately after the icono-

---

[16] For consistory meetings before 1564, see A. A. van Schelven, ed., *Kerkeraads-protocollen der Nederduitsche vluchtelingen-kerk te Londen 1560–1563* (Amsterdam, 1921). For the later period, see A. Kuyper, ed. 'Kerkeraads-protocollen der Hollandsche gemeente te Londen 1569–1571,' WMV ser. 1, Vol. 1. The archivist at the Guildhall in London, where the records of the refugee churches are stored, has informed me that the records for years 1564–8 have been lost.

[17] See the account in van Schelven, 'Het begin van het gewapend verzet tegen Spanje in de 16e eeuwsche Nederlanden,' *Handelingen en mededeelingen van de maatschappij der Nederlandsche letterkunde te Leiden over het jaar 1914–1915* (Leiden, 1915), pp. 126–56.

[8] See the account in J. Lindeboom, *Austin Friars. History of the Dutch Church in London 1550–1950* (The Hague, 1950), pp. 48–50.

clasm at La Gorgue and was cited by witnesses as one who had called the people to arms before the battle of Wattrelos–Lannoy.[19] Wingius' defenders finally addressed a letter to the Bishop of London, complaining about the dissensions within the consistory and against 'the corruption of our nation above all others, which is proven by the synod at Antwerp in 1562 (mentioned above), by the iconoclasm itself, and by the disturbances created by the pastor Isbrand Balck in his sermons and pamphlets.'[20]

That our church is not unanimous in doctrine, and that some of its members are more rational than others is proved by the...dissension between Georgius Vibotius [a Flemish minister] and Godfried Wingius on the breaking open of prisons...by the continual disputes...as to the ejection of idols from churches by private persons and the reformation of religion...by the public condemnation, by some members...of the orthodox doctrine of God as regards the duty of subjects toward a magistrate,...[and] by the repeated visions and asseverations of Georgius Vibotius as to the impending destruction of the Belgian–Dutch church.

On the issue of violence, the ministers were divided not only in theory but in practice. Nearly half the group committed some hostile act against the government during the Troubles; twelve were iconoclasts, and ten others preached directly before or immediately after the iconoclasm; two led prison breaks, fourteen participated in military campaigns, and one committed murder.[21]

Who were these ministers? All of the iconoclasts were Netherlanders, and all but two were Flemish-speaking.[22] Pieter Bert was a Flemish hatmaker who began preaching in 1565 – a man of virtually no importance in the Reformed movement. Pieter Hazard, who was variously described as a hatmaker and as an apostate priest, had been preaching secretly in the Netherlands for over twenty years. Gaspar van der Heyden had been the pastor of a refugee church in Germany and a correspondent of Calvin. He was also intransigent in matters of dogma. In Germany he had refused to compromise with the Lutherans on the definition of the sacraments, and during the Troubles he traveled to Amsterdam to admonish the local Reformers, who were leaning dangerously close to the Lutheran heresy. Herman Moded had also preached

---

19 De Coussemaker, *Troubles*, II, p. 212.
20 J. H. Hessels, *Ecclesiae Londino-Batavae Archivum*, II (Cambridge, 1889), No. 104, letter to Edwin Sandys, November 17, 1570.
21 See Appendix B. Also, a relative of Andreas Baerdeloos was arrested with 40 letters for English Reformers, part of a conspiracy to commit seditious acts (A. L. E. Verheyden, 'Le protestantisme à Nieuwport au XVIᵉ siècle,' BCRH, CXVI (1951), pp. 6–7). Bécourt lodged with a local Calvinist who committed the iconoclasm (de Coussemaker, *Troubles*, II, p. 245). Rudsemelis' father and brother committed iconoclasm (Delmotte, p. 160).
22 Moded came from the N. Netherlands; all the rest were from the southern provinces.

to communities in Germany and corresponded with Calvin, and he was also intransigent – but in matters of violence. It was he who refused to correspond with the London church after the consistory forbade the use of violence in 1562; in fact, he had already assisted in the planned escape of two Calvinist prisoners at Antwerp.

Iconoclasm was clearly an illegal act of violence. Public preaching, either directly before or immediately following the iconoclasm, was a more ambiguous action. Monsieur Aert, for example, was sentenced by the Council of Troubles for inciting the iconoclasm at Eindhoven.[23] This may have been true, or he may have been preaching on an unrelated subject; he may even have exhorted the people *not* to commit violence. In the case of Jean Taffin, who preached in the cathedral at Antwerp on the day after the iconoclasm, this was almost certainly what happened; according to Pensionary Wesembeke, the magistrates' envoy to the Calvinists, Taffin's sincere purpose was to mitigate, not to incite violence.[24] But for almost all of the ministers who preached at the time of the iconoclasm, this act of preaching was probably conceived as an act of aggression against the Catholics.[25]

The ministers who preached either to incite violence or to capitalize on a fait accompli were noticeably different in background from those who had actually directed the iconoclasm. The majority were French-speaking, middle-class and highly educated, and half the group had spent time at Geneva.[26] Jacobus van Culembourg studied at the University of Cologne and preached as a Lutheran in N. Germany until 1566, when he appeared as a Calvinist preacher in Bois-le-Duc; Jacobus had already directed the image-breaking in a Germany town nine years earlier. Charles de Nielles was a Geneva-trained pastor who had worked for several years in the clandestine churches of Ant-

---

[23] O. J. de Jong, *De reformatie in Culembourg* (n.p., n.d.), p. 118.

[24] Wesembeke, *Mémoires*, p. 297. Taffin committed no other acts of violence during the Troubles. His only aggressive act was to endorse the 3-million guilder request which may have been intended merely to placate Philip. William of Orange thought that he was reasonable in political matters (Boer, *Hofpredikers*, p. 30).

[25] De Nielles, Marmier and Wille appeared before the magistrate after the iconoclasm, declaring that they were holding the treasure of the church (Hocquet, *Tournai*, p. 334). The ministers at Valenciennes, de Brès and de la Grange, wrote to Wille at Tournai asking his advice on how to deal with the magistrates – they had meanwhile appropriated two churches. De Lesenne preached before the iconoclasm at Lille; later the image-breakers justified the image-breaking in his name. Jacobus van Culembourg, who preached at Bois-le-Duc, had directed the iconoclasm in a German town five years earlier. Joris Wybo, who preached in Lierre after the iconoclasm, had advocated violence against the magistrate since 1562, when the matter was discussed at Antwerp.

[26] De la Grange was a noble, de Nielles a bourgeois, Marmier a lawyer, Jacobus a priest, Pieters a monk, Wybo in one of the liberal professions, de Brès and de Lesenne were artisans, Crapandiau unknown.

werp and Tournai. Like Jacobus, de Nielles was willing to compromise with the Lutherans on dogmatic questions; in 1564 he and Guy de Brès were summoned to a meeting with William of Orange, where they agreed to compromise on doctrine for the sake of an alliance with the Lutherans. Etienne Marmier, on the other hand, was a rigid defender of Calvinist orthodoxy; three years after the iconoclasm, Marmier participated in a vendetta against another Calvinist pastor, Antonio Corro, who was accused of denying the doctrine of the Elect.

While a majority of the iconoclasts supported a general policy of violence against the magistrates, only two of the ministers in this second group, Wybo and Jacobus, ever endorsed any such policy; all of the others who had any experience in the pastorate before 1566 were moderates, de Nielles and de Brès, explicitly, and de Lesenne – because he did nothing to antagonize the authorities during his years in Antwerp – implicitly.[27] Perhaps these moderates conceived of the preaching as a pragmatic act, a response to the emergency created by the iconoclasm. If so, it was only the first of many such acts, for almost all of the ministers participated in military campaigns during the autumn of 1566.[28] Cornille de Lesenne committed personal violence as well; it was he who executed a supposed Catholic spy without trial in December of 1566.

What can we learn from this brief survey about the real causes of the violence in 1566? The ministers came from Reformed communities in England, the N. Netherlands and Emden, Germany, France and Switzerland, but the radical pastors came largely from England and Geneva. While Geneva was indisputably the chief stronghold of orthodox Calvinism, the situation in England was more complex. There, the Reformed communities consisted both of pastors and of families of artisans who had escaped from the Netherlands, particularly from Flanders. The churches of London and Antwerp were in continual communication and individual pastors, like Pieter Hazard, often traveled back and forth between England and Flanders in the years before 1566. Thus the 'English' pastors were well-informed about the upheavals in the Netherlands, and were doubtless affected as much by this atmosphere of social unrest as they were by the very rigorous training and discipline to which they were subjected in church. Moreover, it was the Flemish ministers, most of whom had spent time in English churches, who

27 De Lesenne worked as a lace-maker in Antwerp to conceal his identity as a preacher while Wille was organizing public demonstrations in Tournai. A story was told of de Nielles that in Antwerp, while the flames of a martyr's pyre illumined the room, he told his followers to pray quietly for the dying.
28 De Lesenne was a captain at Wattrelos–Lannoy. De Brès and de la Grange defended Valenciennes during the siege. Dathenus directed the recruitment of troops. Marmier was present during the siege of Tournai.

committed the iconoclasm, which, in turn, triggered the invasion of churches and the barricading of cities. The ministers who tried to capitalize on this initial act of violence – to rationalize it, as it were – were also the French-speaking pastors from Geneva. Thus the iconoclasm might be interpreted as a product of social unrest as well as the outcome of discussions on the legitimacy of violence which were held in the Calvinist consistories.

The only thing wrong with this theory of the Troubles is that, while it purports to be merely descriptive – a breakdown of the mentality of the radical ministers – it also implies that the two elements of this mentality, social discontent (England) and Calvinist ideology (Geneva) *caused* the particular type of behavior which these ministers exhibited during the Troubles. If this is true, then the biographies of the other thirty-one ministers who were not radical should be very different from those I have summarized already.[29]

Who exactly were these moderates? Jan Lamoot and Erasmus Top were Flemish cloth-weavers who fled to England and joined the London Dutch church. Junius, Micheus and Jean Rudsemelis (two bourgeois, one noble) all arrived in 1566 from Geneva. Godfried Wingius was active in Emden, Flanders and England in the years before the Troubles. At Emden he collaborated in a translation of the Bible; in Flanders he edited the national Confession of Faith; in England, as pastor of the London Dutch church, he initiated a controversy on baptism, insisting on a strictly Calvinist interpretation of the sacrament. In 1569 he initiated a second controversy in the London church by preaching against the iconoclasm. Jean Taffin was a refugee pastor in Germany, a visitor to Geneva, and then a pastor in the French city of Metz, where he established contacts with the local nobility and published Calvinist literature; he was also an advocate of the proposed Lutheran Accord which had been negotiated with William of Orange in 1554.

[29] By 'moderate' I mean that they were either explicitly opposed to violence or were simply passive during the Troubles. De Brès was a moderate during most of his career; he opposed all violence before 1566, and during the siege of Valenciennes he wanted to surrender immediately and in good grace, while de la Grange insisted on dictating terms to the Regent's army (E. Braekman, *Guy de Brès: sa vie (premier partie)* (Brussels, 1960), p. 251). Taffin, de Nielles and Carpentier were moderates. De Nielles only negotiated with the magistrates; he did not participate in military campaigns. Carpentier's only act of aggression was to advise the military captain Jean Denys to burn his list of recruits after the Reformers' defeat. Wingius preached against the iconoclasm; Jan Lamoot defended him. Junius tried to prevent the image-breaking in Ghent and took no part in military campaigns. The remaining ministers who were active in the Troubles simply did nothing. Robert Flameng was accused of 'scandalous acts' at Ypres; this could mean he simply preached. The magistrates said they preferred him to Pieter Hazard; when they dismissed him in October, after he had held baptism in a house, he left the city (Diegerick, *Documents*, I, p. 130). Three other ministers are not discussed here: Valencijn came for only a short while in May, 1566; Louis Cappel arrived from France in 1569; Jean Capito arrived in 1568.

TABLE I: *Training and experience*

	Geneva	England	Germany, Emden, N. Netherlands	Several countries	France	No travel
Radicals	Wille	Bécourt	Balck	Dathenus	van der	Cubus
	de la Grange	Bert	van Culembourg	Hazard	Schuere	
	Leseur	de Buzère	de Lesenne	v. d. Heyden		
	Marmier	Garcia	Ryckwaert	Le Bron		
		Matte		Moded		
		Michiels				
		de Quekère				
		Wybo				
Moderates	de Nielles	Baerdeloos	Lantsochtius	Bacquereel	Cateu	Lippens
	Junius	de Brune	Mostaert	Boquinus		Missuens
	Micheus	Carpentier	Pontfort	de Brès		van Vyve
	Rudsemelis	Flameng	Rhetius	Taffin		Pieters
		Lamoot	Sterkenbrugge	Wingius		
		May	de Voghele	Corro		
		Platevoet	Gillain			
		de Schildere				
		Strobbe				
		Top				

TABLE II: *General background*

	Radicals	Moderates
Under 35 yrs old in 1566	9	8
Over 35	4	7
French-speaking (11 Walloon, 5 French)	7	7
Flemish-speaking	16	25
Experienced minister	11	13
Inexperienced	12	19
Eminent in Reformed movement	7	10
Unimportant	16	22
Artisan or unknown	6	9
Catholic clergy	9	9
Middle class or noble	8	14

Clearly, there is almost no discernible difference between the radical pastors and the moderates in terms of training or experience. The fact of being a Geneva-trained Calvinist or a Flemish refugee in England was simply no guarantee of a particular type of outlook or behavior. Nor were other personal factors, such as age or degree of eminence in the Reformed church, important in this sense. The one factor which might have played a role in determining the pastors' behavior during the Troubles was socio-economic class; of thirty-one moderates, sixteen were artisans or priests and fifteen were bourgeois or noble; of the twenty-two radicals, seventeen were artisans or priests and fourteen were bourgeois or noble. But these numbers are clearly so small that the differences between them reveal very little. True, the first acts of iconoclasm in W. Flanders were instigated by Sebastien Matte, a Flemish artisan of no distinction in the Reformed movement before the Troubles; but they were also committed by Jacques de Buzère, a pastor of considerable eminence. Likewise, of the five young, Geneva-trained ministers only two, de la Grange and Marmier, were radicals. Both Gaspar van der Heyden and Godfried Wingius were absolutely intransigent in defending Calvinist orthodoxy; Wingius was accused by consistory members of being a power-hungry fanatic. But during the Troubles each interpreted his theology differently; while van der Heyden led a group of iconoclasts into the church at Hulst, Wingius preached vehemently against the legality of breaking images. This is not to deny that Calvinist ideology and economic grievances encouraged certain types of behavior by the ministers and their audiences; but the same number of ministers, with exposure to these same influences, reacted in a very different manner to the crisis of 1566 – and this was also true of their audiences. More important, there were many ministers who simply did not fit into the mould of the fanatic Calvinist radical or of the liberal compromiser. On the contrary, when confronted with violence many ministers simply vacillated. Guy de Brès opposed the radical, de la Grange, during the siege of Valenciennes; yet he himself had brought on the siege by holding public communion after it had been expressly forbidden. Taffin, de Brès, Dathenus and de Nielles were all involved in negotiations with the German nobility in which their priorities were clearly for political survival rather than integrity in matters of dogma; yet all four took very different actions both in the iconoclasm and the subsequent military campaigns.[30]

What this suggests, and what I have already suggested in the last chapter, is that the synthesis of Calvinist ideology and economic unrest simply does not work as a complete explanation of the Troubles, either from the viewpoint of popular participation or from that of the Calvinist leaders. In order to understand the ministers' ideology more fully, and by implication, their effect on their audience, we must look more closely at their early experience in the Reformed movement, both at home and in exile.

---

[30] Taffin did nothing, either during the iconoclasm or the sieges; de Brès led the siege and preached after the iconoclasm, but advocated surrender before the other ministers; Dathenus was the chief military organizer in the S. Netherlands; de Nielles preached after the iconoclasm but took no active part in the siege of Tournai.

3

THE REFORMED MOVEMENT
1544–1565

...and as for those who are of the (true) Church, one can recognize them by the mark of Christians, which is faith...loving the true God and their fellow man, without turning to the right or to the left, they crucify their flesh... not, however, because there is a great infirmity in them; but they battle against it by the spirit all the days of their lives, having continual recourse to blood, to death, and passion, and obedience to the Lord Jesus...

Confession of Faith, 1561.

I implore you, my friends, to feel yourselves in the place where I am, so that by this means you will understand what great need I have of you, so that you will pray to God for me, so that I will not incline either to the right or to the left, so that I will remain firm until the end.

Letter from Michael Robillart,
in prison, 1562.

In 1543, Calvin sent to the Netherlands over two hundred copies of a pamphlet, 'A Short Treatise Showing what the Faithful Man, Knowing the Truth of the Evangile, Must Do when he is among the Papists.'[1] The message of this short polemic was that God requires us to serve Him in body as well as spirit. The true believer must either retire to a place where it is lawful to worship publicly, or he must abstain from all idolatry and instruct the ignorant without fear of death, 'for the glory of God...must be more precious to us than this frail and transitory life which is only a shadow'.

The reaction of the Netherlanders was immediate and hostile; several even wrote letters of complaint to Valerand Poullain, a local Reformer then living at Strasbourg, who had originally requested that the pamphlets be sent.[2] In the first place, the Erasmian traditions of the Netherlands went totally counter to the intransigence of Calvin. The tendency of most people was to applaud the anti-clericalism and sacramentarian ideals of the religious re-

---

[1] Quoted in G. Moreau, *Histoire du protestantisme à Tournai jusqu' à la veille de la révolution des Pays-Bas* (Paris, 1962), p. 90.

[2] In response they got an even sterner tract, 'Excuse à Messieurs les Nicodémites sur la complainte qu'ils font de sa trop grande rigeur,' 1544. (E. Léonard, *A History of Protestantism*, tr. R. M. Bethell, II (London, 1967), p. 81.)

formers, without feeling the need to take a stand on either the Catholic or the Protestant side.[3] Second, the Netherlands Protestants had no real need of another, Genevan Confession of Faith, because the country had been inundated by evangelical doctrines emanating from Germany and France for over twenty years. Luther's works were read and discussed in Antwerp and Tournai almost as soon as they were published, and when his rebellion against the Emperor in 1520–1 made religious issues a popular topic of conversation, the writings of other reformers, Erasmus in particular, were re-issued. While Lutheran churches were established only at Antwerp, the indirect influence of Luther's writings was far more widespread. In Tournai, Lille and Valenciennes, clandestine religious conventicles were held to discuss the Scriptures, the nature of the sacraments, and the duties of a Christian; a common fund was also maintained to aid the poor and finance religious propaganda. These conventicles, which soon spread to the smaller villages of French Flanders and Artois, were often conducted by former priests, who had responded most intensely to Protestant propaganda, and who provided the movement with its first martyrs.[4]

At most, religious writings and conventicles might serve to occupy a literate and at least partially committed elite.[5] That Protestant ideas actually penetrated a much broader spectrum of society than this was due to the popularity of the plays produced by the Chambers of Rhetoric. These Chambers, or local dramatic guilds, existed throughout the Netherlands and especially in Flanders.[6] Their source was the religious processions which were organized by the church, and the tableaux and plays produced by local associations, called 'Confrères de l'Eglise' or 'Confrères de Jeu.' The Chambers produced not only plays, but held poetry contests and pageants; their spectacles, first organized in the fourteenth century, eventually became annual events, with prizes for the finest plays. During the early sixteenth century the Chambers played the role of a critical press, attacking clerical abuses in particular: '. . .some monk or nun always has a part in the comedy,' wrote a contemporary historian. 'People can not seem to enjoy themselves without making fun of God or the Church.'[7]

The religious sentiments expressed in the plays of the Rhetoricians were overwhelmingly those of Erasmus. Christ and the apostles were portrayed

[3] *Ibid.*, p. 79 and Moreau *Histoire*, p. 73, 81–2.

[4] Moreau, *Histoire*, p. 63.

[5] G. Moreau, 'La correlation entre le milieu social et professionel et le choix de religion à Tournai,' SHRB pp. 286–301. During the period 1520–44, the Reformers who were prosecuted, with few exceptions, belonged to the clergy and the ruling class.

[6] H. Liebrecht, *Les chambres de rhétorique* (Brussels, 1948).

[7] Ch. Piot, *Histoire des troubles des Pays-Bas par Renon de France*, I (Brussels, 1886), p. 46.

not as miracle-workers, but as preachers and ethical teachers. At Ghent, where a national competition was held in 1539, the playwrights had to answer the question, 'What is the most comfort to a dying man?' The answers – the word of God, the hope of Grace, faith in Christ – reflected Erasmian ideals; no one thought it necessary to receive the last rites of the Church. Despite the efforts of the authorities to prevent the spread of the published plays, the collection of 1539 went through several editions; thereafter, all works by Rhetoricians had to be approved by officers of the law before they could be produced on the stage.[8]

So there seemed to be no reason why the Netherlands Protestants should be amenable to the dictates of Calvin's pamphlet. Even the most radical plays of the Rhetoricians, which were denounced as Lutheran by the authorities, reflected the sentiments of Erasmus and Zwingli rather than the more uncompromising doctrines of Luther or Calvin. Yet in 1544, the year after the pamphlet appeared, a delegation from Tournai arrived in Geneva to request that a Calvinist minister be sent to the Netherlands. The delegates went to Geneva because they felt that the new religion was being increasingly threatened by two great evils, paganism and the millennarian heresy, and that ministers from Geneva were the only men capable of defending it.

The pagan element of popular Catholicism had been criticized as much by educated Catholics as by Protestant polemicists. For the vast majority of believers in the Netherlands and elsewhere, prayers, pilgrimages and the celebration of the sacraments were conceived not as modes of worship but as varieties of incantation, as magic formulas which guaranteed good fortune. Images of saints and other cult objects were sanctified not as symbols of a higher spiritual reality, but as tokens of the Church's magical power, which might be turned to one's own use if certain rituals were followed to the letter. Relics were invoked against rain and storms, ill health and the French; they also served as talismans to ensure the protection of the prince, a good harvest, or the salvation of souls. The veneration of Mary and the saints as demigods who might be more directly and easily propitiated than Christ Himself, became so highly specialized that arguments were conducted as to which Mary was more powerful, that of Aardenburg or Rosebeke.[9] As for the seven holy sacraments, baptism and the last rites were celebrated almost universally, while those of confession, confirmation and matrimony were

[8] H. A. Enno van Gelder, 'Erasmus, schilders en rederijkers,' TvG LXXI (1958), pp. 1–16, 206–41, 289–331. The author analyzes 25 plays, all of which were Erasmian; neither the sacraments nor the need for penance are ever mentioned. He also discusses contemporary painting, where saints are portrayed as preachers, not as miracle-workers.

[9] J. Toussaert, *Sentiment religieux, vie et pratique religieux des fidèles en Flandre Maritime* (Paris, 1968), pp. 287, 292.

observed sporadically, if at all; Communion was effectively limited to once a year, on Good Friday.[10] This suggests that the overriding religious sentiment among the masses was the fear of Hell, and that this fear might be assuaged not by spiritual striving during one's lifetime, but by the correct pronunciation of certain words in an unknown language.

These various elements of primitive religion – polytheism, the use of supernaturally-endowed cult objects, the magical powers of the priest, who alone understood the ritual which he intoned – were condemned with some bitterness in the plays of the Chambers of Rhetoric. In 1539 an actor at the festival in Ghent delivered the following diatribe:[11]

> Our mouths are at church but our hearts are at home,
> We drink ourselves drunk, we observe the holidays,
> We hear masses, we swear, we make fun,
> We dedicate churches with other men's goods,
> We set up candles, we silence the spirit
> In order to see another's confusion;
> We visit the smith's puppets, we leave the smith,
> We serve the saints and place God aside.

But even though the substance of the plays was anti-clerical and Erasmian, the spectacle itself, reflecting the contemporary penchant for allegorical figures and mechanical wonders, was bound to impress many people as a reinforcement of the magical powers of the Catholic church. In 1547 the Chamber of Valenciennes presented the Life and Passion of Jesus Christ:[12]

> ...strange and admirable things were made to appear, the secrets of Paradise and of Hell were prodigious, and capable of being taken by the populace for enchantments. For one saw Truth, angels, and diverse other personnages descend from above, sometimes visibly, sometimes invisibly...from Hell Lucifer was raised up, carried by a Dragon, without our being able to see how...the souls of Herod and Judas were carried through the air by devils...One saw water changed into wine, but so mysteriously, that one couldn't really see it...

Clearly, the mystical piety which has often been attributed to the Netherlands at the close of the Middle Ages was actually confined to a very small elite, and this was in large part due to the virtual absence of religious education. There was no such thing as methodical catechism. Popular works, such as the

---

10 *Ibid.* pp. 89, 223. Clark ('An Urban Study') notes the carnival-like atmosphere at Mass, the local myth that merely to see the Host was to be preserved from evil, so the flock left after the elevation of the Host (p. 134). An official of Granvelle's reported that engaged couples seldom confessed before receiving the sacrament of marriage. (Ch. Rahlenbeck, 'Les chanteries de Valenciennes,' BCHEW III (1888), p. 129).

11 Moxey, *The Image Debate*, p. 153. This was delivered by the Bruges Chamber.

12 Quoted from Fr. Oultreman, *Histoire de la ville et comté de Valenciennes* (Douai, 1639), pp. 396–7; printed in *Bibliotheca Belgica*, I, p. 526.

'Mirror of a Christian' (1550) consisted of ethical homilies, not explanations of dogma, while the use of the Bible was confined to monastic schools and universities; many Books of Hours contained no Scriptural texts whatsoever.[13] The local vicar, if he was not absent from the parish, might also be a notary, gendarme or farmer. He might have been ordained simply because he was literate and had received some rudimentary instruction from the former vicar, or had served as a choir boy. In any case, his office was not really a spiritual one; the vicar conducted the rites according to form and acted as a kind of policeman in the community. He was rarely called by families to instruct their children, and his sermons were devoted to moralizing and to topics of secular interest; in times of political crisis he might be given to patriotic harangues, often delivered in the open air. Even if the vicar *were* highly educated, he did not thereby fulfil the role of pastor and educator in the community.[14] More likely he held his office as a minor benefice and followed his own interests. The humanist Martin de Smet, vicar of the village of Sleydinghe, seems to have spent most of his time before becoming a Reformed minister in editing his private collection of Latin inscriptions.[15]

But the profane character of religious life in the Netherlands, as elsewhere, was less a product of ignorance than of the socializing function of Catholic ritual. Religious ritual was a means of affirming not only the order of the universe, but that of the community as well. Baptism, for example, was necessary not only to save the infant from limbo, but to mark its formal entry into the community, which was synonomous with the parish. Thus religion permeated every aspect of life, but not in the same way that it does for the orthodox Jew, who sanctifies the mundane activities of cooking and bathing by uttering a particular prayer. Rather than elevating everyday life to the level of spirituality, the rituals of late medieval Catholicism seem to have taken on the character of the mundane, even festive life functions which they were intended to sanctify. Pilgrimages, for instance, were not religious activities in the sense that they were somehow different from or opposed to secular activities. The most common sentence against blasphemy, sorcery, prostitution, or bathing in the municipal ponds, was to make a pilgrimage. The pilgrimage also functioned as an ideal rendezvous and as a purely festive outing; at Aelter, a large group paid tribute to the Virgin, circled the church three times, dined at an inn, and spent the rest of the day dancing and

---

[13] Toussaert, *Sentiment*, pp. 68–71. Also see Coulton, *Art and the Reformation*, p. 296, on the absence of biblical subjects in pre-Reformation art.

[14] Toussaert, *Sentiment*, pp. 75, 559, 574. One of the first policies of the Trent decretals was to suggest readings and titles of books useful in sermons. Priests were also instructed to get rid of animals, quarreling, etc. (Clark, 'An Urban Study,' p. 137).

[15] BN, v, p. 764.

walking in the woods.[16] The church itself was at once an asylum for criminals (and, in times of communal disaster, for the entire populace), a center for local festivals, and a setting for both personal violence and outrages against the church building itself. At Tournai, a procession was held to venerate Mary in September; a few months later, a gathering was held to burn down the bishop's house.[17]

Popular superstition and indifference to spiritual values were chronic evils with which the Netherlanders had long been familiar. Indeed, Calvin had accused the Protestants themselves of sharing in the prevailing spiritual apathy, since so many of them were willing to maintain their outward allegiance to the Roman Church. A more easily perceived and immediate threat to the movement was the success of competing Protestant sects, particularly that of the Spiritual Libertines. Calvin reserved his most virulent attacks for the Libertines, whom he distinguished from those Anabaptist sects which accepted the validity of the Scriptures. The Libertines denied not only the holiness of Scripture but also the dichotomy between man and God; they were pantheists who believed that each soul was a particle of God, and that to sin was therefore inconceivable.[18]

The Libertines in the Netherlands were led by one Eloi Pruystinck, a native of Antwerp who conceived the desire to unite his own movement with that of Luther's. In 1525 he traveled to Wittenberg and disputed with Melanchthon in the presence of Luther, who immediately fired off a letter of denunciation to the Protestants at Antwerp. Pruystinck was arrested and abjured his heresy, but twenty years later he emerged as the leader of an even larger sect; dressed in rags sewn together with jewels, he ordered his followers to embrace each other in public. Pruystinck was captured and executed in 1544 and his sect, called the Loïstes, was forgotten, but the Libertines continued to flourish under the leadership of Quintin Thierry, an illiterate tailor who propagated the new faith in the neighborhood of Lille and Tournai and then moved to France, where he enjoyed the patronage of Marguerite de Navarre. His successor was Antoine Pocquet ('ce reveur et Phantastique' wrote Calvin), who developed the quietist and mystical side of the Libertine movement. After preaching in Strasbourg and at the court of Navarre, Pocquet settled in the Netherlands in about 1540 and introduced

---

[16] Toussaert, pp. 234, 276, 734. Clark describes saints' days and processions at Valenciennes, which were like public entertainments. Crowds were admitted into the city to buy from local markets, there was dancing and drinking, etc. (pp. 145–6).

[17] Toussaert, p. 266.

[18] Calvin's pamphlet is quoted in Moreau, *Histoire*, p. 83. On the theology of the Loïstes, see J. Frederichs, 'Un Lutherien français devenu libertin spirituel: Christophe Herault et les loïstes d'Anvers 1490–1544,' BSHPF xli (1892), pp. 250–69.

himself into the Protestant communities of Tournai, Lille and Valenciennes, preaching in secret and distributing Libertine writings. In the absence of any local leadership adequate to challenge him, Pocquet almost succeeded in taking over the movement in these cities. Calvin spoke of 'the ruin caused in the country of Artois and Hainaut...by Messire Antoine Pocquet'; elsewhere he accused him of causing the perdition of ten thousand souls, 'besides the scandal and setback to the Evangile.'[19]

Calvin's pamphlet arrived at the very moment when the Libertines were seriously competing with the orthodox Protestant movement in Antwerp, Tournai and Valenciennes. In the resulting confusion within the local communities, it was decided that a delegation should travel to Strasbourg, where a number of Walloon refugees had settled, to request that a consecrated pastor be sent to the Netherlands. But Martin Bucer, to whom the delegates addressed their petition, was already sheltering Libertines in his own house. For fear of antagonizing them (as well as their patrons at the court of Marguerite de Navarre) he refused to write anything against the Libertine sect, and contented himself with merely consoling the envoys. With nowhere else to turn, the Netherlanders wrote to Calvin, who disdained to answer their letters. They then traveled to Geneva. Calvin responded by writing a pamphlet against the Libertines, and a Calvinist pastor, Pierre Brully, was sent to the Walloon provinces to assure 'the stable preaching of the Word of God...the administration of the sacraments and to give form and impetus to the Church for the future.'[20]

Calvinism was reluctantly embraced by the Netherlands Protestants not for the greater purity of its doctrine or because the style of life at Geneva seemed especially congenial to them; for this the reformers would surely have preferred the more tolerant, evangelical Protestantism of Strasbourg.[21] Ministers from Geneva were invited to the Netherlands because they were the only group which was thought to be sufficiently organized and intransigent to ensure the safety and legitimacy of the orthodox Reformed church. But this intransigence was needed not only to achieve greater coherence within the movement;

[19] Letter to Marguerite de Navarre, April 28, 1545, quoted in Moreau, *Histoire*, pp. 87–8. On the Libertines, see N. Cohn, *Pursuit of the Millennium* (New York, 1961), pp. 177–9. Another sectarian group was the Family of Love (Familists), which was founded in Emden in the 1540s. The Familists were dedicated to living in communal holiness in obedience to a 'begodded' hierarchy of elders.

[20] Jean Crespin, *Histoire des martyrs*, I, p. 427. On the Reformers' trip to Strasbourg and Geneva, see Moreau, *Histoire*, pp. 91–4.

[21] Actually Calvinism as a particular doctrine was not recognized by contemporaries. Godfried de Hamal, who succeeded Brully, called himself a Lutheran. The brother of Guy de Brès was incarcerated in 1562, 'que aucuns du village l'appelaient allesfois hughenois ou luther, à raison qu'il ne allait à la messe,' Braekman, *Guy de Brès*, p. 23.

in order to attract new converts, the ministers would have to somehow overwhelm both the magical aura of the Catholic priest and the bizarre and cathartic magnetism of the Libertine preachers. They would have to generate a sense of their own miraculous powers, and here the ministers' fanaticism, which was originally so repellent to the Netherlanders, would be their most valuable quality. The new pastors were to act as educators, administrators and organizers; but most of all they were to be witnesses to the purity of Reformed worship in the face of Catholic paganism and sectarian Protestantism. Their mission was an apostolic one. Just as in contemporary painting, the depiction of Christ and the apostles in the act of preaching had superseded the depiction of miracle-working saints, so the Calvinist ministers were expected to authenticate the new faith not by miracles or by performing the rites of the new Church, but by preaching and by the perfection of their exemplary morality. They would thus establish the authenticity of the orthodox Reformed Church by the superior, indeed miraculous purity of their own lives.[22]

II

As it turned out, these expectations fell not only upon the shoulders of highly-trained and ardent ministers dispatched by Calvin, but upon a much larger group of lay preachers and pastors who had never even been close to Geneva.[23] In the first place, persecution nearly decimated the Reformed movement in the late 1540s. Pierre Brully was executed in 1545; the leaders of the Libertine sect, with whom he had disputed during his short pastorate, in 1547.[24] The next two pastors sent from Geneva, Evrard Erail and Arnold Banc, were apparently unwilling to play the heroic role which Calvin had dictated in his pamphlet. Erail arrived in Antwerp in May, 1557, at the beginning of a new wave of persecution, and departed for London a year later without the authorization of either the Antwerp or the Genevan consistories.[25] His successor, Arnold Banc, arrived in June, 1559, but re-

[22] Williams asserts that the Calvinists adopted the ideals of apostolic life from the Anabaptists, and that such ideals were characteristic of the radical sects, not the 'magisterial' Reformation (*The Radical Reformation*, p. xxviii). But it is also true that the Calvinists adopted these modes of behavior as a means of establishing the spiritual validity of their own church and that, if they were to succeed, the behavior of the new apostles would have to be uncommonly pure, indeed superhuman.

[23] Of eighty-four Reformed ministers active during the period 1544–65, only 12 had been in Switzerland, and this included 2 foreigners (Cassiodoro de Reyna and William Cole) who remained in the Netherlands for only a short time. Three lay preachers spent time there: Alexander Dayke, François Varlut and Michel Robillart.

[24] Moreau, *Histoire*, pp. 98, 116.

[25] F. de Schickler, *Les églises du refuge en Angleterre*, i (Paris, 1892), p. 90.

turned to Geneva six months later and was reassigned to a church in France. Thus, while Calvin's pamphlet provided an ideal of intransigent leadership for the Netherlands Reformed movement, the leadership itself, with a few notable exceptions, came from elsewhere.

Not only were the sources of pastoral training more diversified in the Netherlands than in other countries; by far the largest number of Reformed ministers had almost no pastoral training whatsoever. The practical demands of the expanding local communities and the losses suffered in periods of persecution meant that lay Reformers were forced to become lay preachers as well. Gaspar van der Heyden was one such case: Van der Heyden fled to Antwerp at the age of about sixteen and joined the local Reformed community. Soon after (1551) the minister, Jan van Ostende, was executed, and van der Heyden assumed his ministerial duties, meanwhile supporting himself as a shoemaker. Not until 1555, when the community offered to support him as a full-time minister, did he travel to Emden to be ordained.[26] Jean de Lannoy, a former upholsterer, became an elder at Tournai by 'his good conversation.' He soon acted as the first assistant of the pastor Guy de Brès, holding secret conventicles and catechizing in the area of Tournai and Valenciennes, until he was arrested in the autumn of 1562.[27] De Lannoy's experience was typical; consecrated pastors frequently accepted men of very inferior background and training as colleagues, although they repeatedly attempted to limit the activities in which lay preachers might legitimately participate and to maintain their personal basis of authority in the consistories.[28]

But these attempts to limit the authority of the lay preachers were inevitably superficial, because the ministers had not yet come to grips with the more fundamental problem of defining the actual significance of ordination. Not

[26] van Lennep, *Maximiliaan Frederick. Gaspar van der Heyden 1530–1586* (Amsterdam 1884), pp. 2–16. Jean Taffin converted at Antwerp shortly before Erail left and inherited responsibility for the Walloon church before he became a pastor (Ch. Rahlenbeck, 'Jean Taffin,' BCHEW II (1887), p. 123).

[27] De Brès had several other disciples who served as lay preachers: Guillaume Cornu, Alexander Dayke, Robert Dufour, Philippe Mallard and Simon Faveau. Of these only Dayke, who visited Geneva, had any considerable education in Reformed doctrine. Mallard studied in Geneva, but after his activities in the Netherlands (P.-F. Geisendorf, ed. *Le livre du recteur de l'académie de Genève 1559–1878* (Geneva, 1959) p. 94).

[28] At the synod of Teurs (April 26, 1563) Article 14 ruled that in the absence of the pastor, the elder or deacon can recite prayers, but he may not preach or administer the sacraments ('De synoden der Nederlandsche hervormde kerken onder het kruis, 1563–1577,' NAvKG, IX (1849), p. 128). Clearly this ruling indicates the existence of a problem, not its solution. Guillaume Damman, a lay preacher, administered communion in Flanders in 1562; so did Jehan Bonniel in Quesnoy.

until 1563 did the pastor Herman Moded travel to Emden to discuss this question with the church council. Their conclusion was hardly calculated to simplify the problem of pastoral authority; an inward call from God, they said, was of greater validity than the mere act of consecration, or laying-on of hands.[29] It was actually more common to recognize a minister by his eloquence than by any formality of office; when François Varlut was interrogated in prison he maintained, 'I am an artisan, and not a minister.' The officer replied, 'You are eloquent enough to be one.'[30] And in fact, Varlut was a lay preacher in Valenciennes.

There was therefore nothing to prevent a man who believed himself to be consecrated by God from preaching on his own authority; and as consecrated pastors became more successful in disseminating Reformed doctrines, the number of laymen who felt inspired to preach also increased. Thomas Watelet, a coal miner in the territory of Liège, was so impressed by Reformed doctrine that a few days after his conversion he learned to read and began evangelizing in the countryside; 'he instructed according to his capabilities those of his village who worked with him.'[31] Loys Brochart, an elderly woolcomber, moved to Valenciennes after the death of his wife, found a room in which to hold meetings, and installed himself as a preacher; at his first conventicle he spoke to a group of about ten people on the letters of St James.[32] Brochart was allied to the Reformed community at Valenciennes and his son became a deacon of the consistory; but Kackhoes, formerly a priest in Germany, preached for five years in the neighborhood of Maastricht without making contact with any organized Reformed church.[33]

There was also nothing to prevent a man who *was* a formally ordained pastor from doubting his own spiritual calling. Paul Chevalier was trained and consecrated as a pastor in Rouen, where he had fled as a refugee from Tournai. He returned to the Netherlands, was examined by the consistory of Valenciennes, and formerly charged with the leadership of the local Calvinist community. After some hesitation, Chevalier refused to be confirmed in his post, insisting that he felt unprepared for his new responsibilities.

[29] A. A. van Schelven, *De Nederduitsche vluchtelingen kerken der zestiende eeuw in Engeland en Duitschland in hunne beteekenis voor de Reformatie in de Nederlanden* (The Hague, 1908), p. 119. They also had the example of the English churches, where the right of a layman to expound publicly on doctrine was institutionalized in the prophecy (P. Collinson, *The Elizabethan Puritans and the Foreign Reformed Churches in London* (London, n.d.), pp. 51, 169).

[30] Ph. Muret, 'François Varlut et Alexandre Dayke, martyrs Calvinistes à Tournai en 1562, cx (1964), p. 26.

[31] Crespin, *Histoire des martyrs*, iii (Toulouse, 1889), pp. 261.

[32] Ch. Paillard, *Histoire des troubles religieux de Valenciennes*, 1560–1565, iii (Brussels, 1876) p. 141.

[33] Bax, *Het protestantisme*, p. 127.

The consistory had no choice but to send him back to France for further study.[34]

Given this diversity of training and experience, how could the Netherlands ministers possibly convey a sense of their united apostolic mission strong enough to counteract both the magical attractions of the Catholic priest and the charisma of the sectarian preachers? They attempted to do this chiefly through the ritual of the conventicle, which was clearly intended to approximate those of the early Christians. At Tournai, meetings were generally held in the evenings, at the home of a Reformer or in a deserted house; a deacon or elder read from the Bible and then directed psalm-singing, catechism and the recitation of prayers. These conventicles, as well as the prayer meetings held out of doors, catered to the community at large; their purpose was chiefly to attract new converts.[35] The secret conventicles, presided over by a consecrated pastor, were attended only by Reformers who were well-instructed and had sworn an oath to defend the movement; usually they numbered from six to ten people, including members of the consistory and a selected number of the faithful. At Tournai, the pastor Guy de Brès held these nocturnal meetings in private homes. The company listened to a sermon and then dined together, after which the pastor lectured on a biblical text; he might also celebrate Communion on these occasions.[36]

The function of the secret conventicle, where the atmosphere was one of community and friendship and Communion was associated with the literal breaking of bread, was clearly to reenact the relationship between Christ and his apostles. The ministers' intention was to raise the mundane activities of eating, drinking, reading, and singing to the level of spirituality, whose attainment by the community as a whole was symbolized by the ceremony of Communion. But the focus of the Reformed conventicle was not Communion,

[34] L.-E. Halkin and G. Moreau, 'Le procès de Paul Chevalier à Lille et Tournai en 1564,' BCRH, cxxxi (1965), pp. 8–9.
[35] Jean de Lannoy regularly catechized the youth of Tournai on Sundays. Michel Robillart was captured after a group of soldiers, whom he had arranged to instruct, denounced him (Moreau, *Histoire*, p. 233). De Brès preached in the woods near Lille (Braekman, *Guy de Brès*, pp. 82–3); Hansken van Brugghe in the woods near Ypres in 1562–3 (Diegerick, ii, p. 179); Nicolas Cuvelier near Douai in 1560 (P. Beuzart, *Les hérésies pendant le Moyen Age et la Réforme jusqu'à la mort de Philippe II, 1598. Dans la région de Douai, d'Arras et au pays de l'Alleu* (Paris, 1912), p. 166); Claude Duflos in the woods near Valenciennes in 1564 (Paillard, *Histoire*, iv, p. 97); Pieter Hazard outside Ypres in 1559–60 (BWK Prot., iii, p. 594); Guillaume Damman near Hondschoote – Damman wrote his own music for the *prêches* (de Coussemaker, iv, p. 234). With the exception of Guy de Brès, all of these men were lay preachers, working out of doors.
[36] Van Langeraad, *Guido de Bray*, pp. 37, 49–50. The pattern was the same at Antwerp; Christophe de Smet preached to groups of less than twenty in abandoned houses or inns (AA Vol. ix, pp. 172–5; inquest of July, 1564).

but preaching; whereas in the Roman Church, the worshipper confessed in order to purify his soul to receive the Host, the participants in a conventicle at Lille publicly confessed their sins in preparation to receive the Word of God:[37]

> When we were assembled in the name of our Lord to hear His holy Word, we prostrated ourselves all together on our knees, and in humility of heart we confessed our sins before the majesty of God; afterward we all prayed that the Word of God be correctly announced and purely preached.

It is difficult to evaluate the actual impact of these secret conventicles. The meetings, as they are described above, were necessarily infrequent, due to the lack of pastors qualified to celebrate Communion. In the area of Tournai–Lille–Valenciennes, for example, Guy de Brès was virtually the only consecrated pastor active before 1563. With the exception of Antwerp, where services were conducted several times weekly by ordained ministers, the burden of catechism and preaching fell to the lay preachers, who functioned either as adjuncts to the pastor or as independent agents. In these cases, it can only be conjectured whether the conventicles raised mundane activities to a spiritual plane, or whether spiritual discussion was actually degraded to the level of everyday conversation.[38]

Consider, for example, the case of Wilhem Heckelers, a lay preacher in Hasselt. By allying himself with a local nobleman, Heckelers obtained entry into various houses where he held informal prayer meetings.[39] At one such conventicle, ten or twelve men sat around a table set with candles and books and discussed the Scriptures, while Heckelers uttered such biblical phrases as 'Man must believe in one God and hold no other gods before Him.' A tavern keeper testified that Heckelers and a group of friends came in at nine o'clock in the morning, ordered beer, and stayed until evening, talking about the Bible with various people who came in during the day. At another meeting in a private house, Heckelers stated that Moses and Jesus both fasted, and so 'must we be always sober and fast for our sins and punish our flesh.' After this exhortation the group went to another house for dinner and Heckelers sang a German religious song. The Bible and various heretical writings and

---

[37] Braekman, *Guy de Brès*, p. 82.

[38] On Antwerp, see W. G. Goeters, 'Dokumenten van Adrien van Haemstede,' NAvKG, v (1907), p. 4. The synod of Teurs, April 26, 1563, Art. 24 ruled that ministers must visit neighboring communities where there are no pastors, or to establish a new community. Art. 12 of the synod at Armentières (1563) ruled that Communion must be administered at least four times a year. Thus de Smet traveled from Antwerp to Bruges, Chevalier toured all of French Flanders, although he was based at Valenciennes, and de Brès preached in the area of Tournai–Lille–Valenciennes.

[39] Bax, *Het protestantisme*, pp. 34–5. Heckelers preached in 1562. He spoke against the saints and maintained that Mass and confession are human inventions.

songs were thus brought to the attention of the local citizenry; one witness confessed to actually borrowing a work of Calvin's and reading it at home. But whether Heckelers or his congregation can be considered part of the Calvinist movement is clearly another question.

The pastor also gave the greatest personal attention to instruction and conversion, as exemplified in the case of Christophe de Smet, who was betrayed by a woman named Grande Marguerite, a hat-seller.[40] Marguerite gave out that she wished to talk to a wise man in order to understand the difference between true and false doctrine, promising to abandon the Catholic church if she could be convinced of the rightness of the other side. After her first meeting with de Smet, pastor of the Flemish church of Antwerp, she was taken to a secret conventicle, after which she demanded further personal instruction. When, after several private meetings, Marguerite expressed the desire to hear the opinions of another learned man, de Smet introduced her to Olivier de Bock, a professor at the University of Heidelberg. Marguerite then arranged a debate between de Smet and a Catholic priest, assuaging his fears of capture by promising that if she could be won over, several hundred others would join the movement with her. Finally, having gained ample evidence of de Smet's heretical opinions, the authorities arrested and executed him in 1564.

In other instances the pastors were more successful in effecting valuable and lasting conversions. Paul Chevalier, a Catholic priest in Tournai, ceased to believe in the Real Presence and found that he could no longer bear to perform the Mass. A colleague put him in touch with Jean Cornu, brother of one of Guy de Brès' assistants. In July, 1561, both monks fled the cloister and were sheltered by the Reformed community and instructed by Jean de Lannoy; Chevalier later became a consecrated pastor in Valenciennes.[41] Adrien Saravia, a Cordelier, was aided in escaping his cloister, given money and lodged by Jacques Taffin, brother of the pastor Jean Taffin and an important lay Reformer; Saravia later became a pastor and established the first Calvinist church in Brussels.[42]

The Reformers also attempted to propagate their doctrines by exploiting the existing institutions of the Chambers of Rhetoric which, as we have seen, were already well-disposed toward the Reformed movement. In a period when public preaching was not feasible, the Reformers were thus able to reach an audience of thousands, as they often did in Tournai. In the 'Histoire d'Hélie et Jesabel,' performed in 1559, the prophet spoke: 'You have

---

[40] Crespin, *Histoire des martyrs*, Bk. VII.
[41] Moreau and Halkin, 'Paul Chevalier,' pp. 5–6.
[42] Letter of Jacques Taffin to the council of Flanders, February, 1562 (quoted in van Langeraad, *Guido de Bray*, p. 99).

abandoned the living God to adore Baal and your idols...You make gods of wood, of stone, of plaster.'[43] Prominent Calvinists were also Rhetoricians and the consistories went so far as to adopt secret code-names which had belonged to the various chambers; Tournai was 'La Palme,' Armentières was 'La Bouton,' Antwerp, 'La Vigne.'[44]

The Calvinist ministers attempted to formalize these activities of preaching, catechizing and assisting converts by means of provincial synods, which met frequently during the period, 1563–5.[45] A good portion of the resolutions deal with the duties of pastors, the importance of missionary activities, the privileges of deacons and elders, etc. But beyond this concern to legitimize the activities which were already being carried on in individual Reformed congregations, the ministers clearly hoped to extend their moral control over the private lives of the entire Reformed community. The consistory was voted the right to decide whether the parents' refusal to consent to a marriage was justified; public crimes had to be atoned for by public penance; it was forbidden for the individual to assist the poor without acting through a deacon; a man who had been seen drunk three times was suspended from Communion; the life and morals of the minister could be censured by the consistory.[46] The sacraments were discussed not as spiritual precepts, but as signs of the adherent's membership in the community; parents submitting their children for baptism by the Catholic church were suspended, and no one might receive Communion who had not first been catechized and found sufficient in morality and doctrine.[47] Finally, the ministers were anxious to remain untainted by either Roman superstition or Anabaptist preaching; illicit assemblies were forbidden as schismatic, specifically those held by Anabaptists; no prayers could be recited at funerals, to avoid any hint of superstition in the Reformed cult; printers, writers, painters, etc. could produce nothing which might favor Roman superstition.[48] Finally, every newly-chosen elder or deacon was ordered to sign the Belgian Confession of Faith.[49]

The Confession of Faith, composed by the pastor Guy de Brès, was originally presented to the magistrates of Tournai and the Regent in 1561, as proof

[43] Moreau, *Histoire*, p. 139.
[44] In Ypres, plays were used as school texts (J. Decavele, *De dageraad van de reformatie in Vlaanderen (1520–1565)* (Brussels, 1975), p. 217). On the importance of the Chambers, both as sources of written propaganda and as centers of Reformers who were later active in the iconoclasm, see Moxey, *The Debate on Images*, pp. 25f.
[45] Eight synods were held during the period; five at Antwerp, two at Armentières and Tournai, one at 'Teurs.'
[46] Teurs, 1563, art. 2, 16, 27. Antwerp, 1564, art. 37. Tournai, 1563 art. 16.
[47] Teurs 1563, art. 5, 9.
[48] Tournai, 1563, art. 9. Antwerp, 1564. art. 40–1.
[49] Armentières, 1563, art. 1.

of the legitimacy of the Reformed cult.[50] 'By this confession,' wrote de Brès, 'the king will see that the Reformers are neither schismatics, nor rebels, nor heretics, but believers in Jesus Christ and in his Church, as it was before it was corrupted by human inventions, and in Holy Scripture.' In 1563, it became a provincial confession, accepted by the synod at Armentières; two years later it was decided to read the confession at the beginning of each synod, when it would be open to revision by the delegates.

Both the provincial synods and the publication of a national confession of faith undoubtedly gave the Netherlands Reformers a measure of formal unity and a sense of their legitimacy as members of the international Calvinist movement, but there is no indication that the actual practices of Reformers in different cities were successfully standardized as a result of these efforts. In Antwerp, for example, the local consistories appear to have been quite powerful; the Flemish church was influential enough to initiate proceedings against the pastor Adrien van Haemstede when he began holding private conventicles without their permission. In Tournai and Valenciennes, the prestige and authority of the pastors was considerably greater than that of the consistories; even in 1566, when the pastor of Tournai, Ambroise Wille, wrote to Guy de Brès at Valenciennes, he cautioned him to keep the Reformers' plans a secret from members of the consistory. Moreover, the Flemish pastors in Flanders and Antwerp, who maintained active relations with Netherlands refugees in Emden and London, were more closely supervised by these foreign churches than the Walloon ministers who corresponded with the consistory at Geneva.[51] These differences in the ministers' authority should not be exaggerated; all of the established churches in the Netherlands corresponded with each other and with churches abroad. But the fact remains that the Reformed churches in the Netherlands turned to different foreign churches for advice, and that the degree of control exerted by these foreign church councils varied greatly.

The Reformed ministers thus attempted to propagate the word of God by two very orthodox methods. They imitated the behavior of the apostles by preaching and catechizing in intimate groups, often during a shared meal, and they legitimized these activities by holding synods and by maintaining communication with each other and with churches abroad. By doing so they were not only provided with a higher authority on questions of theology and

[50] E. Braekman, the biographer of de Brès, asserts that de Brès was the sole composer, and that the Confession is not derivative of the Confession of the French Calvinist churches. Moreau maintains that it was the joint venture of the Antwerp consistory (*Histoire*, p. 156).

[51] See, for example, the relations of the English preacher William Cole with the bishop of London (Collinson, *The Elizabethan Puritans*, p. 67).

discipline; they were also able to supervise the activities of religious refugees, who would strengthen the Netherlands churches abroad until the Kingdom of God should be established at home.[52]

There was a third method which the ministers might have adopted to strengthen the Reformed movement – that of public demonstrations; under a repressive government, this inevitably involved the danger of violence. I have already described the discussions on violence which took place in England and the Netherlands in 1561 and 1563, when a party of Flemish pastors advocated a policy of delivering prisoners by force. These pastors supported clandestine violence to counteract religious persecution, but none of them ventured, during this early period, to advocate public celebrations of the Reformed cult. The great majority of ministers and leading Reformers were opposed to such public demonstrations as dangerously imprudent, but given the primitive character of church organization at the time and the undefined relationship between the minister and the community, they found themselves without the formal means to prevent it.

The first incident of aggressive behavior by a Reformer occurred in 1557, when Adrien van Haemstede preached and disputed publicly in Audenarde and Antwerp. Van Haemstede was an ordained pastor, sent from Emden in 1555 to preach to the Flemish community at Antwerp.[53] The new minister immediately bridled against the extreme caution exercised by the Reformers in their efforts to escape persecution. He particularly resented the necessity of changing his residence every month to avoid detection by the authorities, because it involved moving his extensive library. He also resented the limits which the consistory attempted to impose on his pastoral activities; in turn, the church council accused him of neglecting the majority of the faithful by creating a special community of wealthy Reformers and holding what amounted to religious salons in private houses.

In the summer of 1557, van Haemstede staged a public disputation in Audenarde with Jan Daelman, a 'Libertin Nicodémite' who advocated formal submission to the Catholic church. He also preached publicly outside Antwerp and then left for Emden, refusing to return until he was expressly requested by the Antwerp consistory. Van Haemstede did return, having agreed to submit future quarrels with the consistory to the council at Emden

---

[52] e.g., the letters of recommendation by the minister Cornille de Lesenne for Walloon refugees settling in London in 1561. E. Johnston, *Actes du consistoire de l'église Française de Threadneedle Street, Londres*. Vol. 1, *Publications of the Huguenot Society of London*, Vol. 38, pp. 39, 46, 90.

[53] See J.-F. Gilmont, 'La genèse du martyrologue d'Adrien van Haemstede, 1559,' RHE LXIII (1968), for biographical notes. Gilmont asserts that van Haemstede was not a nobleman but a *roturier* who studied at Louvain and was ordained at Emden. He was about thirty years old in 1555.

for arbitration, but the following year, despite the consistory's opposition, he resumed public preaching. One demonstration was held in the center of the city, directly in front of a Catholic procession of the holy sacrament. The result, as the Reformers had feared, was a new wave of persecution. The other Flemish pastor, Gaspar van der Heyden, fled to Germany when his house was invaded by the authorities, and several lay Reformers were imprisoned, whose relatives all blamed van Haemstede for the disaster. In October, 1558, van Haemstede and another pastor, Gilles Verdickt, traveled to Brussels to arbitrate a local dispute; three days later Verdickt was arrested. Van Haemstede continued to preach in Antwerp until 1559, when he too fled the Netherlands.

Van Haemstede was thus the first minister in the Netherlands to preach publicly; but this innovation was clearly a personal one, not the result of any Reformed policy. The next public *prêche*, held in the village of Boeschepe, in West Flanders, was also the project of an individual minister, Ghislain Damman.[54] Damman was a lay preacher who had recently returned from exile in England and begun holding conventicles in Flanders, financed by local Reformers. A few days before the *prêche* at Boeschepe, which occurred on July 12, 1562, Damman distributed leaflets with the names of Reformers who were to be informed that, on the following Sunday, a learned doctor from England would preach the Evangile and expose the false prophets. On Sunday, at nine o'clock in the morning, the service commenced in the church cemetery, despite the entreaties of the priest who was conducting Mass inside the church. Damman, holding a book, stood on a bench surrounded by the crowd, who were armed with knives and sticks. The *prêche*, which included psalm-singing and collective prayers, lasted for two hours. Damman then rested at an inn, where he disputed on points of Scripture with one Robert de Crook, a laborer, the discussion being interspersed with songs. A few days later Damman fled to England; there is no record of his ever having preached again. This second *prêche*, which was more highly organized than van Haemstede's, had a very great negative effect; ninety-three people were

[54] Damman was the brother of the lay preacher, Guillaume Damman. Leblanc thinks that he was insane, referring to a statement by Pieter Heuzeeck that the brothers in London had to restrain him by force from coming back to preach in Flanders (de Coussemaker, *Troubles*, 1, p. 346). Guillaume's participation in an organized prison break may mean that his brother also had connections with radicals in England, but this is conjecture. On the *prêche* at Boeschepe, see A. Cordeweiner, 'Prêche Calviniste à Boeschepe, 12 juillet 1562,' BSHPF, cxii (1966), pp. 105–20. Cordeweiner assumes that this *prêche* was typical of meetings which were regularly held; but this is hardly likely, in view of the scandal that the incident caused. There is a record of another public *prêche* by Loys de Voghele, who held a service in the chapel of Casuele, in E. Flanders, during Easter, 1562, at the invitation of the local chaplain (Decavele, *Dageraad*, p. 368).

prosecuted for their attendance and at least nine were executed. The armed demonstration also convinced a larger public of the strength and connections of the Reformed movement. 'That these new preachers were supported by powerful men is obvious,' said one near-contemporary, 'since the preacher was protected from justice by many armed men.'[55]

On the night of September 27–8, 1561, a group of Reformers in Valenciennes walked through the streets, singing psalms in French to the melodies of popular songs.[56] The following night Robert Dufour, a deacon of the consistory, led more than three hundred Reformers through the streets of Tournai; the leader sang the first line of each verse and the crowd completed the psalm. The next day the group had grown to more than eight hundred, and the crowd sang and shouted insults at the windows of the deputy bishop's house for over two hours. The singing finished, one of the leaders began speaking to the crowd:

Messieurs, now that we have praised the Lord each must return to his own lodging to thank Him that He has given us the grace to announce His truth and His word, praying also that He allows us to persevere and grants us victory.[57]

The leaders of the *chanteries* were the young deacons of the churches of Tournai and Valenciennes.[58] They had met ten days before, under cover of an annual Catholic procession held in Tournai, and decided to organize public demonstrations similar to those in France. The pastor Guy de Brès and his assistant, Jean de Lannoy, attempted to dampen the Reformers' enthusiasm by displaying copies of the Confession of Faith about the city, in which it was declared that they opposed any disturbance of the public peace. After the fact, de Brès continued to disavow the demonstrations, for which he was criticized by the deacons. The *chanteries* thus endangered the Reformers not only by inciting persecution; they seriously threatened the local movement with a schism. De Brès, faced with the impending execution of several leading Reformers, was finally pressured to write to the commissioners, requesting that they be set free. He addressed them, 'in the name of the bourgeois, workers and inhabitants of Tournai.' Although he could not approve the *chanteries*, he deplored the ensuing persecution even more.

What have you gained when by your threats and terrors, you constrain God's poor people to idolatry?. . .If the people are not treated more gently. . .we fear

---

55 Heinderycx, *Jaerboeken*, p. 7.
56 For an account of the chanteries, see Rahlenbeck, 'Les chanteries.'
57 Report of the magistrates on October 12, 1561. Quoted in Moreau, *Histoire*, p. 170.
58 The deacons included Mallard and Faveau from Valenciennes, and Varlut and Cornu from Tournai. A 'Lannoy' was accused; this might have been the minister Mathieu de Lannoy (Moreau, pp. 162–3).

that a horrible confusion will descend on all the cities of the realm, for we can no longer contain the people with discipline and patience...For God is our witness how greatly we fear the tumults of the people.[59]

The letter was thrown, along with a copy of the Confession of Faith, inside the castle gate, and then sent to Margaret (November 2), but with no result. In the ensuing persecution, de Brès fled to France and the Calvinist church was effectively dismantled.

Two months later occurred the affair of the 'maubrulés' in Valenciennes.[60] Two deacons, Philippe Mallard and Simon Faveau, were arrested for holding false opinions on the Mass and for possessing forbidden books. Their prison became almost a place of pilgrimage, where Reformers gathered at night to pray and sing psalms; on the night of March 23, 1562, the group included over two hundred armed men, wearing hoods and false beards, who stood in the rain and sang until four o'clock in the morning. Leaflets were issued which threatened tumult, and the populace committed intermittent acts of iconoclasm. On the day of execution, Faveau appeared and called out, 'O Eternel...', at which point a riot, which had clearly been organized in advance, broke out, and the prisoners were liberated and taken to a private house where they received their friends, while a crowd gathered nearby to celebrate a public service of thanksgiving.

The 'maubrulés' escaped in April; by August, 1561, secret conventicles were resumed in Tournai with the addition of public preaching outside the city walls. The mood of the Reformers was now more aggressive than before; ecclesiastics were reluctant to imprison Reformers for fear of attack, and it was said that a Jesuit could not cross the road without risk of insults or flying rocks. By the spring of 1563, public preaching had become a regular institution in both Tournai and Valenciennes and the *chanteries* were resumed.[61] The impetus for this revival of the Reformed movement came from a newly ordained pastor, Ambroise Wille, who dominated activities in both cities after de Brès had fled to France. Wille had just spent four years in Geneva, and was authorized to preach in the Netherlands in 1562. With the assistance of several other preachers who appeared for the first time in 1563, he proceeded to organize a consistory in Valenciennes and to reactivate the community in Tournai.[62] Altogether, nine public *prêches* were held in Tournai under Wille's leadership. At one meeting, one thousand Reformers appeared,

[59] *Ibid.*, p. 183.

[60] See the account in Clark, 'An Urban Study,' pp. 274–5.

[61] And perhaps also at Antwerp. On October 21, 1563 the Margrave received a letter from Margaret, discussing the rumor of a *prêche* of 400 people, held in the streets (AGR, E & A, 1739/1; no folio numbers).

[62] The preachers were Gerard de Bailleul, a native; Martin Desbuyssons and Mathieu de Lannoy, from France. Only the latter was a pastor.

armed with sticks; when the magistrates attempted to disperse them, the people rioted.

But before the end of the year all public demonstrations had been effectively smothered in another wave of repression. The only significant public action taken by Reformers before the Troubles occurred in 1564, during the execution of a minister, Christophe de Smet, at Antwerp.[63] When de Smet was placed on the funeral pyre, some of the witnesses began to throw stones; they succeeded in wounding several officers, including the executioner, but they failed to free the prisoner. After this final outbreak, the Reformed movement remained clandestine until the public preaching of 1566. In Tournai and Valenciennes, one of the measures imposed by the government was a compulsory oath of loyalty to the Catholic church, an oath which was taken by the majority of the Reformers. Guy de Brès, who had always believed that the demonstrations were premature, now lamented the weakness of the brothers under the cross:[64]

. . .for what is it to avow by oath the infernal doctrine of the Roman church. . .if not to separate from your son Jesus and leave the heavenly doctrine? Alas, it is now our lot to suffer the knowledge that in this time of shadows we have blasphemed too much, and not only served you in vain, but have wickedly disavowed you. . .

For more than a year, the ministers made no collective statement on this issue; not until the synod of November 21, 1564 did they declare, 'that it is not licit and still less expedient to take an oath which contravenes the glory of God and the edification of our neighbors.'[65] Thus they belatedly and, it seems, reluctantly vindicated the ideal of intransigent loyalty to the true faith which had been espoused by Calvin in his pamphlet twenty years before.

That the Netherlands Reformers found it difficult to emulate the standard of religious fanaticism set by Calvin is not surprising. They lacked the advantage possessed by the Geneva Company of Pastors in France, a network of revolutionary Calvinist pastors, all trained in one church and all reporting back to one church council. Partly because of this diversity of background, partly because of the uncertainties of life in a Catholic country, they were unable to formulate standards of church organization which would define the relationship between the pastor and the consistory, and among the pastors themselves. Both the van Haemstede affair and the *chanteries* of Valenciennes and Tournai were the result (and the cause) of conflicts within the Netherlands church, not the symbolic demonstration of a united movement. And even if the movement *had* been united, it had not yet established

[63] AA, IX, p. 188f.　　　　[64] Quoted in Moreau, *Histoire*, p. 240.
[65] Synod of Antwerp, November, 1564; article 7.

sufficient contacts with the nobility to make a public demonstration anything other than suicidal; the Reformers imitated the Calvinists in France, but as yet they had no Coligny to protect them from the royal commissioners.

The depth of the Reformers' confusion on the question of authority within the church is pathetically obvious in the exchange of letters between the churches of Antwerp and Emden on the activities of Adrien van Haemstede. The Antwerp church wrote of van Haemstede: 'He has said that he wishes to be free and not held in check, as if he were in a cloister. . .that he may not come and go as he pleases; but. . .whoever wants to be free, cannot be a minister [*dienaer* = servant].'[66] Van Haemstede also complained that he wished to preach outside the community, that one must neglect the ninety-nine lambs in the fold and search out the hundredth. 'But how,' the Reformers wondered, 'shall we then care for our ninety-nine sheep?'[67] During his sojourn at Emden, van Haemstede maintained that he would never act against the word of God and would rather serve God than man. He also defended the right to preach 'hier ende daer,' citing the example of the apostles; the church of Emden maintained that van Haemstede was not an apostle, and thus entitled to move from place to place, but a shepherd over the Antwerp flock, and should therefore remain in his own church.[68] The importance of defining the role of the pastor as somewhere between a free apostle of Christ and a member of an organized ecclesiastical hierarchy was recognized at the provincial synods held in 1564 and 1565. Several articles were directed toward limiting the status of the minister: He could not usurp primacy over other ministers; he could not leave his flock without obtaining leave from the consistory; if he taught 'mauvaise doctrine' or lived scandalously, he was subject to excommunication.[69]

This confusion over the status and authority of the minister applied even more to lay preachers than to pastors. The activities of an untrained preacher such as Wilhem Heckelers, who did little more than discuss the Bible and sing Lutheran songs, might have resembled those of a consecrated pastor, but Heckeler's relationship to the organized Calvinist movement was certainly tenuous, and may even have been non-existent. Heckelers himself was said to have followed the Lutherans; he may have had closer connections with the Lutheran Reformers in Germany (Hasselt was relatively close to the German border) than to the Calvinists from Emden or Geneva – if indeed he had any formal religious connections at all. Even in cases where the lay preachers were allied with the Calvinist movement, they did not necessarily confine

[66] *Brieven uit onderscheidene kerkelijke archieven*, ed. H. Q. Janssen and J. J. van Toorenenbergen, WMV, ser. 3, Vol. 3, pp. 50–88.
[67] *Ibid.*, p. 54.   [68] *Ibid.*, p. 55.
[69] Synod Antwerp, May, 1564, articles 2, 6–9.

their activities within the limits imposed on them by the synods. The magistrates of Tournai and Valenciennes each reported at least one case of attempted exorcism by a Calvinist deacon. In Tournai, Alexander Dayke, who had attended sermons at Geneva, appeared at the house of a man possessed by the devil and attempted to exorcise the evil spirit by instructing the victim not to trust in the saints but in God alone.[70] In Valenciennes, a worker from Cambrai approached the deacon Simon Faveau and told him that a man possessed by the devil had requested his assistance. Whatever the result of the exorcism which then took place, it could hardly have contented Faveau's superior, the pastor Guy de Brès.[71]

Not only did the Reformers fail to eradicate Catholic superstition; they also failed to eradicate the Anabaptists. The disappearance of the Libertine sect had been as much the work of the Catholic prosecutors as the Calvinist ministers. The Anabaptists, whose adherents in the southern provinces followed the pacifist doctrines of Menno Simons, survived the rigors of the Inquisition; by 1550 the Mennonites had established communities throughout the Netherlands, despite the Reformers' attempts to discredit them, and they continued to flourish until they were finally overshadowed by the Calvinists in the 1560s. In Antwerp a placard against religious conventicles mentioned a list of pastors who had been exceptionally notorious; the list included van Haemstede and five other ministers, all Anabaptists.[72] At Armentières, Mass had to be held three times because of the size of the Anabaptist congregation. 'And as for Hondschoote,' the Inquisitor Titleman wrote in 1561, 'there is not a number to be given; it is a bottomless abyss.'[73]

But despite the difficulties which confronted the Calvinist ministers in their attempt to establish the authenticity of their particular church, they did succeed in dominating the Netherlands Reformed movement by 1566. They could only have done so by providing some sense of their genuine superiority – their own miraculous powers – in contrast to those of either the Catholics or the Anabaptists. Enough has already been said to demonstrate that the ministers could not have achieved this merely by their exemplary life-style, by the uniqueness of their doctrine, or by their public intimidation of the

---

[70] Halkin and Moreau, 'Le procès,' p. 24.
[71] Clark, 'An Urban Study,' pp. 152f.
[72] AA, ix, p. 130 (March 7, 1562). A letter to Margaret lists churches in Ypres, Poperingue, Menin, Armentières, Hondschoote, Tournai and Antwerp (V. Gaillard, ed., *Archives du conseil de Flandres* (Ghent, 1856), p. 230. Williams accepts the inquisitors' estimates of 700 in Bruges in 1568 and 2,000 in Antwerp in 1566 (p. 765). Verheyden mentions churches in Bruges, Ghent, Douai, Tournai, Roeselaere, Menin, Ostend, Hondschoote, and Gistel (*Anabaptism in Flanders* (Scottsdale, Pa., 1961)).
[73] Verheyden, *Anabaptism*, p. 55. Decavele mentions Anabaptists in Antwerp, Ghent, Courtrai, Bruges, Hondschoote, Ypres, Diksmude (*Dageraad*, p. 515).

established church. The necessary miracle by which they impressed many of their adherents was rather contained in the way that they chose to die.

III

Calvinist Reformers actually comprised only a minority of the total number of martyrs in the Netherlands, but it was the Calvinists who exploited the heroic suffering of their adherents most successfully.[74] They did this by comparing Calvinist martyrs to the Jews of the Old Testament – the Chosen People, who knew that God loved them most because they suffered most. 'For we know for certain, if we are punished for a short time, that we are children of God,' wrote Guy de Brès.[75] 'See how the ministers of the Word of God are persecuted,' wrote Adrien van Haemstede; 'that was why the books of the prophet Jeremiah were burnt...that is why Daniel was thrown into the lion's den; that was why the prophet Amos [was]...accused of being a rioter before King Jeroboam, and forbidden to preach...'[76]

It should not seem strange to you, that for the Evangile, and for confessing Jesus Christ, I am imprisoned, oppressed and in hell, and that I will finally be put to death as if I were a murderer and malefactor. For by this seal the truth has been defended and sustained through all time, and will be until the end of the world.[77]

The Calvinists also drew an obvious parallel between their Catholic persecutors and the evil kings of the Bible, who were scourged by God for their rejection of Jewish prophecy. All of this was clearly similar to the Calvinist doctrine of Election as it was taught by the ministers. Indeed, the martyrs openly called themselves God's Elect:[78]

It has therefore pleased my good God and Father, who has elected me before the foundation of the world, to carry and manifest his name to men, and for

[74] The *Bibliotheca Belgica*, IV, p. 231, states that of 877 martyrs listed in the three major martyrologies, only 260 were Lutherans or Calvinists. But the writings of the Anabaptist martyrs, who expected the millennium to arrive at any moment, were more passive in tone than those of the Calvinists, who were still interested in establishing a godly society in this world. One example: 'Hence it is better to weep now, than afterwards since the time is coming which will endure forever; and the things which now are must soon perish (T. J. van Braght, *The Bloody Theater or Martyrs Mirror of the Defenseless Christians*, trans. J. Sohm (Scottsdale, Pa., 1951). Also see W. Keeney, *The Development of Dutch Anabaptist Thought and Practice from 1539–1564* (Nieuwkoop, 1968); 'The characteristic Anabaptist emphasis on surrender or yieldedness...required the acceptance of suffering without resistance.'
[75] Guy de Brès, *Histoire notable* (Antwerp, 1565), Preface, n.p.
[76] A. van Haemstede, *Historien der vromer martelaren* (Dordrecht, n.d.), Preface, n.p.
[77] Crespin, *Histoire des martyrs*, III, p. 447; testimony of Christophe de Smet in 1564.
[78] *Ibid.*, p. 473.

this to abandon my life. This thing must be accomplished in me, so that the secret ordinance of God be manifest.

Van Haemstede was even more explicit: 'Think, whenever you see God's ministers before you, that Christ himself stands before you...and that he speaks to you.'[79]

By identifying the heroism of biblical figures with that of their contemporaries, the martyrologists were contributing to a new historiography of Protestantism. The continuity which they saw between their own sect and the originators of their religion was an excellent means of buttressing their claims of authenticity as opposed to the innovations of the Roman Catholics.[80] The Calvinists were also able to transmit their theology in a highly effective polemical fashion, and to a wider audience than they had ever reached during the period of the hedgepreaching.[81] Calvin himself went to considerable lengths to publicize the heroic suffering of the Reformed martyrs, in contrast to the cowardly behavior of the Anabaptists. The execution of the pastor Pierre Brully in 1545 prompted him to issue a new pamphlet against the Libertines, in which he ridiculed the martyrdom of the preacher Quintin Thierry.[82] Four years later, when a lay preacher who had studied in Geneva was burned alive in Tournai, Calvin wrote a sermon on the event.[83]

A young man, who has lived here with us...was condemned to be decapitated if he abjured, and to be burned alive if he persisted in his beliefs. When he was asked what he intended to do, he answered simply: He who gives me the grace to die...will certainly give me the grace to endure the fire.

It was at least partially due to these efforts of Calvin that by 1547 the Libertine sect had perished entirely, while the Calvinists in Tournai were stronger than ever.

The ability to withstand torture was thus given a special resonance by the Calvinists. Readers were constantly reminded that heroic suffering was a miraculous sign of grace or election, and that the sufferer, far from being a heretic, was heir to an authentic Christian tradition; 'we abandon our bodies to the fire, to the cross, to death...for then we know that we are children and heirs of God, true servants and disciples of Christ.'[84] By depicting the serenity of the Reformed martyrs in this fashion, the Calvinists were fully aware that they were in danger of breeding a new kind of saint. The Genevan Council

[79] Van Haemstede, Preface, n.p.
[80] J.-F. Gilmont, 'Les martyrologes protestantes du XVIe siècle,' thesis, University of Louvain, 1966.
[81] *Ibid.*, p. 375. Crespin had twelve editions in the period of 1554–70.
[82] Moreau, *Histoire*, p. 115.
[83] *Ibid.*, p. 117. The martyr was Michael Destoubequin.
[84] Guy de Brès, *Histoire Notable*, Preface, n.p.

originally gave Crespin permission to publish his martyrology without using the words 'saint' or 'martyr,' but the word 'martyr' was included after all, with the injunction that the author's object was not to write 'golden legends' but to render homage to God and to console others in the same position as his subjects.[85] Nevertheless, since the virtues of the martyrs were described in the same awed tones as those of the saints in Catholic hagiographies, it does not seem far fetched to suggest that the public responded to both kinds of literature in the same way.

The immense popularity of the Calvinist martyrologies began in 1554, with the publication of Jean Crespin's *Histoire des Martyrs*. Crespin had been implicated in the trial of the first Calvinist pastor in the Netherlands, Pierre Brully. He was also acquainted with the pastor Guy de Brès, who supplied him with documents concerning new martyrs. When de Brès' lodgings were invaded by the magistrates of Tournai in 1562, the officers found a letter to de Brès from Crespin asking for a list of true martyrs, 'which he knew to be deserving of this title and rank.'[86] The second great Calvinist martyrology was written in 1559 by the pastor Adrien van Haemstede while he was still preaching in Antwerp and in personal danger of martyrdom himself. Both works were therefore enhanced by the author's personal involvement in the sufferings of the victims; van Haemstede was often writing about his own friends, while Crespin's accounts consisted largely of testaments and letters written by the martyrs themselves while awaiting execution.[87] The two works were also characterized by a strict definition of martyrdom. While Crespin acknowledged the virtues of pagan heroes, and van Haemstede devoted one sixth of his work to pre-Reformation martyrs, both refused to publish confessions of any martyr whose theology was not strictly Calvinist.[88] They were thus able to exert greater control over the statements of lay preachers than they could ever have done in real life. Thomas Watelet, the lay preacher who supposedly learned to read after his conversion to the Reform, was undoubtedly heard by a very few people; but his confession, written in prison and published by Crespin, was read by thousands. Had Watelet's doctrines not conformed to those of orthodox Calvinism, however crudely conceived, his writings would not have been published.[89]

[85] L.-E. Halkin, 'Hagiographie Protestante,' *Mélanges Paul Pieters II, Analecta Bollandiana,* LXVIII (1950), pp. 458–9, 461.

[86] Van Langeraad, *Guido de Bray,* p. 46.

[87] They were also enhanced by greater accuracy; see Muret, 'François Varlut,' p. 41, and Halkin and Moreau, 'Le procès,' p. 2.

[88] Gilmont thesis, p. 281 and Gilmont, 'La genèse du martyrologe,' p. 399.

[89] Crespin, *Histoire,* III, p. 262. Jan Hendrix, an adjunct of Pieter Hazard, was known for his dissolute life. He was executed in 1564, having been denied aid from Hazard; he is not mentioned in any martyrology, and was probably ostracized from the Re-

The impact of these martyrologies on the public, and of the actual sight of the martyrs at the scene of execution, is indisputable. In 1555, Charles de Croy wrote to the Emperor Charles V:[90]

the basis of these heretics' strength,...[is] merely that simple people, seeing the public execution of such heretics with firm constancy and hearing their resolutions and the prayers which they address to God before dying, fall into vacillation and doubt of their faith...

Two years later, when the young pastor Ange Merula, endured execution by fire at Mons, many in the crowd thought that a miracle had occurred.[91] When the preachers François Varlut and Alexander Dayke remained firm during their execution, several other prisoners who had abjured the Reformed faith returned to their original opinions; one of them later avowed that the cause of his sudden change 'was having seen and heard the constancy of the preachers.'[92] Varlut and Dayke were executed in the castle of Tournai, despite Margaret's order that it be done at the scene of the last public *prêche*, because the magistrates feared the tumult which would ensue if the martyrs' constancy were witnessed by the crowd. After the bodies were buried in a ditch outside the city, a laborer was asked what he thought of the two martyrs; he answered, 'They spoke so well that they seemed to be angels...'[93] While still in prison, Varlut had written, 'The monks...have all but said that it was for our own glory that we spoke, that we wanted to maintain our opinions so that they would be included in the beautiful book of martyrs from Geneva...'[94] Margaret herself wrote to the judges, 'they take pleasure and seek a perverse glory in dying in the cities before the people...'[95]

When the pastor Gilles Verdickt was interrogated in prison, the news spread through Brussels that a young man of twenty-four had confounded his inquisitors. As he was being led to his execution, Verdickt spoke to the crowd: 'Do you think, Messieurs, that you can expel and extirpate these poor Christians by killing and burning them?...you delude yourselves greatly; the ashes of my body will make the Christians multiply.'[96] The people of Brussels 'were amazed to see the constancy of this young man, who did

formed community. (J. Decavele, 'Jan Hendrix en het Calvinisme in Vlaanderen (1560–1564),' *Handelingen van het genootschap te Brugge*, xvi (1969), pp. 17–32).

[90] Moreau, 'Correlation,' p. 293.

[91] E. Mahieu, *La réforme à Mons des origines à 1575*, Diss., University of Liège, 1961–2, p. 167.

[92] Moreau, *Histoire*, p. 214.

[93] Muret, 'François Varlut,' pp. 31–2.

[94] *Ibid.*, p. 27.

[95] Moreau, *Histoire*, p. 212. Letter of September 19, 1562.

[96] Crespin, *Histoire des martyrs*, Book vi.

not seem troubled or changed.'[97] When a rumor was circulated that the pastor Christophe de Smet intended to abjure in prison, the scandal threatened to seriously damage the Reformed movement until de Smet issued his Calvinist confession of faith. Even after his execution the Catholics tried to capitalize on the rumor by publishing a libel, 'proving' that de Smet had temporarily abjured.[98]

De Smet's letters from prison, which often took the form of sermons to his wife or to the congregation as a whole, achieve the quintessential ideal of the Calvinist saint. He orders his congregation to march courageously in the path of the Lord:[99]

Take His yoke on your shoulders, and you will find peace fully armed. Abandon the world with its affections; for it will pass and perish. . .even he who would be a friend, in case he is an enemy of God. Crucify the flesh with its concupiscence; for it is necessary that the spirit live and the flesh die. . .

The other ministers are likewise exhorted to be firm, and to be assured of the worth of their labors:[100]

March constantly and virtuously, let nothing deter you: preach, indoctrinate, admonish, console, reinstate, have no regard for the appearance of anyone, whether he be rich or poor, young or old, man or woman. Let your voice be raised like a trumpet.

By his suffering, the Christian becomes exalted and purified, as iron is purified by fire. De Smet asks his congregation not to betray this suffering, but to become saints themselves: 'Do not be merely contemplators, but be imitators of the salutary admonitions which God has addressed to you through his ministers.'[101] These exhortations were rendered all the more convincing by the inclusion of the martyr's accounts of his own physical discomfort. De Smet describes his illness in prison, the pains which torment him whether standing or at rest: 'There is no one here to be near me, who would render me assistance, who would give me aid.'[102]

De Smet's execution in 1564 occasioned a popular riot which was quickly put down by the authorities. But the authorities were not able to muzzle the Calvinist polemicists, who issued pamphlets and songs to commemorate his death. A history of de Smet's life and imprisonment was published in Flemish by a Calvinist pastor, Joris Wybo, which went into several editions, and a French translation was offered in 1565 by the pastor Guy de Brès.[103]

The constancy of the Reformed martyrs not only convinced many people

---

[97] *Ibid.*, Book VI. Of 15 martyrs among the clergy, we know the ages of 9; seven of these were young men.

[98] Gilmont thesis, pp. 111-13. [99] Crespin, *Histoire des martyrs*, III, 449.

[100] *Ibid.*, p. 460. [101] *Ibid.*, p. 450. [102] *Ibid.*, p. 457.

[103] *Histoire notable*, trans. Guy de Brès, 1565.

that the Calvinists were the Elect; it also convinced the martyrs themselves. Having rejected the marks of spiritual status enjoyed by the Catholic priests, the ministers had no means of verifying the sanctity of their vocation other than by their own faith. A minister who had endured torture and the expectation of death without losing this faith must have been doubly convinced that his vocation was God given.

> ...this is how I console myself...I diligently consider not only what is going to happen to me, but how the name of the Lord will be magnified, exalted and praised by my constancy and by my death...I am not certain of myself...but I am fully certain of the promises of Christ.[104]

Indeed, the conditions of life in prison, of constant sleeplessness and hunger, must have created in some martyrs a hyper-conscious sense of spiritual alertness. Michael Robillart, a lay preacher, wrote in prison: 'It is true that at the beginning the flesh was in torment, but now I have accustomed myself to it; so much so that the spirit is more prompt and vigilant in the vocation to which the Lord has called me.'[105] One might conjecture that the highly formalized poem or canticle composed in prison by Varlut and Dayke symbolized the clarity of vision which they hoped, by the act of writing, to achieve in their own minds:[106]

> Reconnoissant aussi la petitesse
> Qui est en nous, recourons pour adresse
> A nostre Dieu, l'invoquant au besoin,
> Disant: c'est toi qui promets d'avoir soin
> De l'affligé qui après toy s'écrie:
> Assiste-nous donc et nous fortifie.

Varlut and Dayke worried that since they were to be executed by the sword and not by fire (in order to avoid a public demonstration), they would be thought inconstant; they would have preferred burning.

Other martyrs found this constancy much more difficult to achieve. Paul Chevalier and Jean Castel both abjured during their imprisonment, hoping to avoid execution by burning, but both eventually reaffirmed their faith and demanded the ultimate punishment.[107] Even Christophe de Smet, whose letters were so strident in their affirmation of purpose, wrote to another pastor, 'I beg you... that wherever you go you will recommend me...to the brothers, so that I will be able to remain firm and stable in the faith, and be sustained in combat.' And again, 'Pray to the Lord for me with a pure heart and a good conscience, so that...my faith will remain firm and immut-

[104] Crespin, *Histoire des martyrs*, III, p. 459.   [105] *Ibid.*, p. 428.
[106] Printed in Ch. Frossard, *L'Eglise sous la croix, pendant la domination Espagnole. Chronique de l'église reformée de Lille* (Lille, 1867), pp. 301–2.
[107] Halkin and Moreau, 'Le procès,' p. 20.

able, that by this means I may obtain the reward of pure grace...'[108] The most poignant example of this self-doubt was Michel Robillart, who endured the imprecations of his entire family, all good Catholics, and the jesuitical manipulation of his inquisitors:[109]

And when I think that I have answered one of them the other suddenly begins another question, such as, 'And who has ordained your Calvin? Why are you causing yourself to be burned? I have read the books of Calvin. . .he has made four sermons expressly to incite his followers to have themselves burned. . .and when Calvin is dead, another will arise. . .

Just before his execution Robillart pleaded, 'My brothers, this is written with sweat and tears. I beg you to pray to our good Father, that He may give me the grace to persevere until the end.' The next day Robillart was burned alive, and in a state of grace.

IV

A common explanation for the ministers' apparent control of their mass audience during the hedgepreaching is the success of Calvinist methods of organization. Indeed, simply to say that the ministers were Calvinist is sufficient to conjure up an image of a fanatically dedicated party member, an obedient official in the Calvinist system, a participant in consistories, colloquies, synods and international debates – a servant of Geneva. The mystique of the Calvinist genius for organization extends to every level of religious activity. One historian remarks that whereas Anabaptist conventicles were small meetings for sympathetic listeners, the Calvinist conventicles were formal religious services. The life of a believing Calvinist, he writes, was comparable to that of a cloistered monk: 'His rule of life in the cloister had the same charismatic quality as discipline in the Calvinist community.'[110]

The ministers who preached in the years before the Troubles would probably not have recognized themselves in this description. The Calvinists did have more sophisticated methods of ecclesiastical organization and a larger and more disciplined pastorate than the Lutherans, and they certainly enjoyed greater prestige among Reformers than the Mennonites. This capacity for discipline and dedication was probably the chief reason for the Reformers' success in the years before 1563, and for their ability to sustain a clandestine movement in the period just before the Troubles. But it could not have been the only reason, simply because there were too few ordained pastors, who were trained in too many different Reformed centers, to make an overall

108 Crespin, *Histoire*, III, p. 447.
109 *Ibid.*, p. 427.
110 Enno van Gelder, 'Erasmus,' p. 290.

network of consistories, with a shared system of ecclesiastical government, feasible at this time. Of course the cities of Antwerp, Tournai and Valenciennes had had consistories since the 1540s; in these centers of the Reformed movement, consecrated pastors were almost continuously active in the years before the hedgepreaching. But in the smaller cities and in communities where the Inquisition was powerful, the Reformers' activities were superficial and intermittent.[111] Breda, for example, was served primarily by Lodewijck de Voghele, who had failed the examination for ordination at Emden. The only other ministers who visited Breda before the hedgepreaching were Jan Lippens, a lay preacher, and François Junius, a pastor from Antwerp; both appeared – and departed – in 1565.[112] The smaller towns of E. Flanders were sometimes visited by ministers from Ghent and Antwerp; the villages of Axel and Hulst once welcomed Pieter Hazard, who conducted a Communion service and discussed the Netherlands Confession of Faith. But the main source of spiritual enlightenment for these communities was a merchant named Jan Claeyssone, who had established relations with the mother church at Antwerp and who continued to practice his trade while serving as an itinerant preacher in the area. There is no evidence of a local consistory, and the majority of believers remained Catholic in name.[113] As for Calvinist discipline – it simply did not exist before 1566.[114]

One reason it did not exist was the intensity of persecution after the public demonstrations of 1561–3; in fact there were, to my knowledge, only nine consecrated pastors continuously active in the southern provinces in the three years before the Troubles.[115] Undoubtedly these pastors were successful

[111] Decavele describes the contacts among various churches in Flanders in the early 1560s, and notes that the mobile labor force in the area of Brussels–Tournai–Audenarde enabled Reformers to move about a great deal. He mentions churches in Ghent, Bruges, Audenarde, Renaix, Axel, Hulst, Eekloo and Ostend, but says that several were disbanded in the period before 1566 (pp. 359–64, 384–5, 433).

[112] A. J. M. Beenakker, *Breda in de eerste storm van de opstand 1545–1569* (Tilburg, 1971), pp. 42–3, 122, 167.

[113] Decavele, 'Axel,' pp. 2–4. The author doesn't know if Claeyssone was a pastor or not. He describes a corps of local Reformers, naming five men from both towns.

[114] This was also true in towns like Mons, where there was no consistory, but where there were said to be 2,000 Reformers in 1566 (Mahieu thesis). In the Lille-Douai region there were two itinerant preachers around 1564 (R. du Plessis, *Urban Stability in the Netherlands Revolution. A Comparative Study of Lille and Douai*, Diss. Columbia University, 1974, p. 590).

[115] Five ministers came in 1565 (Marmier, Junius, de la Grange, Carpentier, Moded). De Brès visited during this period, but was in exile most of the time. Those active in 1563–6: Pieter Hazard at Antwerp and E. Flanders; de Lesenne in Antwerp and French Flanders; Jan Missuens at Antwerp, Brussels and Flanders; Wille at Tournai and Valenciennes; de Nielles at Antwerp, the area of Tournai; Gabriel, based at Antwerp, traveled to Bruges; Mostaert at Bois-le-Duc; Wybo at Antwerp and Mechelen; Balck at Antwerp. Cole preached in 1564, but as pastor to the foreign

in introducing Calvinist doctrines into communities whose inclination had been simply to reject Catholic rituals and to attend occasional meetings for the discussion of Scripture. But it is hard to believe that this network of Reformed communities and the secret conventicles which sustained them in the years before the Troubles can really be called a Calvinist underground. This underground may have existed in the minds of the ministers in exile who corresponded with consistories at home, but it did not exist on the popular level outside the major Reformed centers. The acts of aggression which occurred before 1566 – prison breaks, *chanteries* and public *prêches* – were committed for the most part by lay preachers, not pastors; more important, they were never the result of a united Reformed policy, but the acts of a radical minority which was condemned by the churches in Antwerp, England and Geneva. In view of the government's persecution and the Reformers' lack of connections among the Netherlands nobility, it would have been impossible for the ministers to organize and sustain a vast popular movement, as they did so effectively in 1566.

There was therefore little to convince a sceptical or indifferent Catholic that the Calvinists had any claim to God's special favor or, failing that, at least the favor of the high nobility. One contemporary, speaking against the Reformers at the University of Louvain in 1565, put it most succinctly:[116]

If a man might be so bold as to aske you nowe, right Honorable Gospellinge Captaines. . .where hence came you? Who sent you? By what authoritie doe ye all these thinges?. . .[You should] be driven plainlye to confesse and graunte, that ye. . .have no authoritye at all, neither ordinarie power in earth, nor extraordinarie communion from heaven. For ye shal never be able to prove either this by Miracles, or that by letters patentes.

Nothing was left, it seems, but for the Reformers to exploit the serene deaths of their adherents as miraculous proof of their claim to be God's chosen sect. Through the martyrologies, which included the letters and Confessions of their ministers, they could also disseminate their theology to a very wide audience at a time when, for safety's sake, it was impossible to deliver sermons to congregations of more than twenty people. Van Haemstede wrote that his conscience commanded him to preach to the uninitiated in public, but the results of his attempts to do this were catastrophic for the Antwerp community.[117] Van Haemstede's martyrology, written during the same period in Antwerp, undoubtedly quieted his conscience.

___

church of Englishmen. All of the provincial synods (four, in 1564–5) were held at Antwerp.

[116] Peter Frarin, *Oration Against the Protestantes* (Antwerp, 1566), n.p.

[117] Letter to Emden, quoted in E. Meiners, *Oostvrieschlandts kerkelyke geschiedenisse*, I (Groningen, 1738), pp. 371–5.

All of this possibly tells us something about the ministers' effectiveness, but it tells us little about their ideology or character. The Reformed ministers were not a group of suicidal fanatics, eager to prove their election by their death; the group of eighty-four included only eighteen martyrs. Nor was the fanaticism of these few necessarily a product of Calvin's personal influence; of the eighteen, only four had even been to Geneva.[118] Moreover, the fact that martyrdom was the ministers' most effective means of propaganda does not mean that the radical preachers conceived of their spiritual destiny in terms of martyrdom, or that they accepted a passive martyrdom because they had already failed to achieve a godly society on earth. In fact, the martyrs and the social radicals formed two distinct groups; of the eighteen martyrs, only three committed acts of violence.[119]

It is therefore pointless to speak of the ministers' collective mentality, or of a 'typical' Reformed pastor. The single trait which did characterize them as a group must be stated in negative terms; the ministers did not succeed in defining either the status or the function of their own office. Training and ordination were clearly necessary to enable them to organize consistories, dispense the sacraments, or write letters to Calvin; but there was no training or ritual which would automatically set the minister apart from the ordinary layman, either in his own eyes or in the eyes of the community. Paul Chevalier possessed citations from the churches of Rouen and Valenciennes, but, as he maintained to the pastors at Valenciennes, he did not *feel* qualified to preach. The pastors had no answer for this. Adrien van Haemstede was apparently quite certain of his own spiritual vocation, but incapable of reconciling his personal conception of the ministry with that envisioned by the consistory. Guy de Brès was also certain of his own pastoral function, and of the best course for the Reformed community, which was secrecy and moderation; but despite de Brès' personal status, he lacked the formal authority to impose his views on even his own deacons.

Of the eighty-four ministers whose activities have been discussed in this chapter, twenty-two were still preaching during the Troubles.[120] For these men, and for the future ministers who were first exposed to the Reformed movement during this early period, their most important legacy was this problem of authority – the problem of confirming one's status as an apostle of God, both to oneself and to the Reformed community.

---

118 Of these, only one studied for the pastorate, Gilles Verdickt (who lived in Zurich). The others were Varlut, Dayke and Robillart.

119 Varlut, Dayke, Cornu.

120 Martin Desbuyssons was active in the Antwerp consistory in 1566 under the name of M. Dulac (Clark, 'An Urban Study,' p. 180); Claeyssone was also active in Eekloo (Decavele, 'Axel,' p. 6).

4

EXILE

Gentle reader...with the manners and behavioure thou seest in our Ministers at home compare and laye together these straunge doinges of their Fellowes and companions abrode in other countries. So shalt thou perceive, they are of one spirite and stampe, and...know them by their workes...and by that meanes learne to avoid them, and beware of them.

Peter Frarin, *Oration Against the Protestants*, 1565.

It is desired to bring us into accord with the Germans in one Confession... so as to break the power of the pope utterly...It would also serve to shut the mouths of those who say we are not united. And our own country too would be greatly relieved by such a step; when they inquire to which rule or to which reformation of doctrine it is proposed to lead them, it would then be easier to answer.

Guy de Brès to the Antwerp consistory, 1565.

John Calvin had given all true believers a choice between martyrdom or exile in his pamphlet of 1543. And in fact, for almost every Reformed minister who was active during the early years of the movement, the only alternative to martyrdom – whether by choice or by coercion – was the experience of exile.[1] In the trials and executions which began in 1558 and culminated in 1563, many Reformers were either liquidated or banished, the survivors dispersing to refugee communities in England, the North Netherlands or Germany, and to hospitable churches in Switzerland and France. Some endured exile for a decade, until the Moderation of April, 1566 brought hundreds of religious refugees back to the Netherlands to celebrate the triumph of the Reformed cult.

The motivation for flight varied with individuals. Many who returned to the Netherlands as pastors in 1566 had fled as simple laymen with vague Reformed sympathies. In England, Elizabeth had granted several charters which allowed a fixed number of skilled workers and their families to settle in various cities and to practice the new religion. Several Netherlands

[1] Fifty-one ministers spent some time abroad before 1566.

Reformers sought the shelter of these refugee communities, where they participated in the life and government of the church and emerged, in 1566, as Calvinist ministers. For others, the motivation to travel abroad was less a matter of physical insecurity at home than an explicit desire to pursue formal study for the pastorate. These Reformers often traveled to Geneva, where the Academy had been established since 1559, and where they lived in what was perhaps a more refined and academic milieu than their future colleagues who had fled to England.

What did the experience of exile mean to these ministers? Was there some process of selection which determined where they fled? Was the refugee experience fundamentally different – ideologically, politically, psychologically – in different churches? How was the popular image of the Calvinist clergy as an all-powerful, international corps of pastors furthered during this period? And did this image have any basis in reality? Were the Reformers in exile actually members of an international organization, or did the refugee experience tend to isolate them from each other and from Reformers at home? What was, in short, the real significance of exile and of the type of experience and training which the pastors received in exile, in the formation of the Netherlands Reformed clergy?

GENEVA

The original impulse for the formation of a Calvinist movement in the Netherlands came, as we have already seen, from Geneva. Aside from publishing several short polemics addressed specifically to the Netherlands Reformers, Calvin wrote to the Antwerp church in 1556 and 1558 in order to stimulate their activities and to answer questions on the proper procedure for baptism and marriage.[2] But this original impulse from Geneva never evolved into a formalized and continuous relationship between the two countries; Geneva did not become the 'mother church' of the Netherlands.[3] The Netherlands Reformers imitated Genevan models of church organization in their synods, but they also turned for advice to the churches of Emden and England. Moreover, in the decade before 1570, Geneva dispatched no formal missionaries to the Netherlands who were bound to maintain regular contact with the Geneva Company of Pastors.[4] Ministers from Geneva who

---

[2] On the pamphlets, see R. L. Rutgers, *Calvijns invloed op de reformatie in de Nederlanden* (Leiden, 1901), pp. 18–23, 29–30, 222–6.

[3] R. Kingdon, *Geneva and the Consolidation of the French Protestant Movement 1564–1572* (Geneva, 1967), p. 14.

[4] On the missionaries dispatched from Geneva, see 'Liste de 121 pasteurs envoyés par l'église de Genève aux églises de France de 1555 à 1566,' BSHPF, VIII (1859). Kingdon lists only one missionary for the Netherlands, who arrived in 1572 (p. 205).

served in Netherlands churches were often requested directly by the local consistories; they were not dispatched by the Genevan council, nor were they subject to its authority.[5] The main focus of proselytizing activity throughout this period continued to be France, particularly the southwest provinces where aristocratic support was concentrated. Few pastors were sent to the northern provinces of France, from which they might have penetrated into Hainaut or French Flanders.

But despite the absence of strong formal ties between the churches of Geneva and the Netherlands, no less than fourteen ministers visited Geneva before 1566.[6] The atmosphere and training which they found there was of the strictest sort. The Genevan Academy, founded in 1559, was a school specifically for the training of pastors, emphasizing the study of theology and languages in the form of public lectures.[7] Candidates for membership in the Calvinist clergy were then subjected to rigorous examination of their character and scholarship by the church council, and to periods of practical apprenticeship, during which they traveled to outlying towns and villages in Switzerland to preach. Under Beza's leadership (from 1564), this strictness increased. Beza was a far more fanatic ideologue than Calvin, and felt threatened by the existence of other, potentially divisive Protestant sects; the pastors whom Beza dispatched from Geneva were, according to one historian, 'even more clearly than before Geneva's product, accustomed to Geneva's rigid discipline.'[8]

Which of the Netherlands ministers who traveled to Switzerland were really 'Geneva's product?' Eleven ministers studied in Geneva, but few of them underwent the rigorous pastoral training which Kingdon describes. François Junius arrived in Geneva in 1562, intending to study languages. Until 1565, when he was summoned by the Walloon church of Antwerp, he worked as a private tutor, attended public lectures, and spent the bulk of his time in private study from his personal library of four volumes; at one point he refused the offer of a post as preacher to the inmates of a local hospital.

---

[5] e.g., Antonio Corro received a letter directly from the Antwerp consistory, requesting his services (P. Hauben, *Three Spanish Heretics* (Geneva, 1967), p. 22). Jehan Leseur was summoned to Valenciennes in the summer of 1566 by Guy de Brès (Desilve, *St. Amand*, p. 48). Ambroise Wille received permission to accept a call to the ministry in his home country of Flanders (Kingdon, *Geneva and the Coming of the Wars of Religion in France* (Geneva, 1956), p. 44).

[6] The eleven who studied there were Marmier, Junius, Leseur, Cappel, de la Grange, Wille, Corro, de Nielles, Micheus, Rudsemelis, and Taffin. Three others who visited Geneva did not study there: Moded, Dathenus, Lebron.

[7] H. Meylan, 'Le récrutement et la formation des pasteurs dans les églises réformées du XVI⁰ siècle,' *Colloque de Cambridge*, 1968, pp. 130–2. Also see Kingdon, *Geneva and the Coming*, pp. 14–24.

[8] Kingdon, *Geneva and the Consolidation*, pp. 18, 36.

When Junius agreed to become a pastor in Antwerp, he was examined by the Genevan church council and deemed worthy of the pastorate; clearly he had established a considerable personal reputation, since he was advised in this decision by the famous martyrologist Jean Crespin, also a resident of Geneva.[9]

It is also clear that the council's authorization to preach in the Netherlands was no proof that the minister had completed a program of formal training for the pastorate. Jehan Micheus taught languages for several years at the University of Lausanne until 1566, when he conceived the desire to preach in the Netherlands. He received leave to do this, along with the promise of his old job if he should ever return to Switzerland, but he was certainly not 'Geneva's product' in Kingdon's sense of the word.[10] Nor was the Walloon pastor, Jean Taffin, who settled in Strasbourg with a community of refugees from Antwerp, and visited Geneva only long enough to be examined for his doctorate in theology – about six months – before returning to Strasbourg.[11] Of the remaining ten ministers who spent time in Geneva, only four were registered at the Academy.[12]

But it would be foolish to belittle the influence of the Genevan Church on the Netherlands pastors who resided there simply because they were not members of the formal Company of Pastors. Formal connections might have been lacking, but Marmier and Junius established sufficiently close ties to the Genevan pastoral elite to receive personal greetings from Beza in 1566, while Jean Taffin corresponded with Beza for several years.[13] Ambroise Wille lived in Geneva for four years, Guy de Brès for three. All were to some degree affected by the rarified atmosphere of the Genevan community of Reformers. Geneva's relative freedom from outside political influence combined with an atmosphere of militant piety within the city to permit, indeed to enforce, a spiritual integrity and orthodoxy which their co-religionists in other countries could not imitate. By no means all of those who spent time in Geneva were radicals; but to those who were, the Genevan environment posed the fewest limitations to an uncompromising stand in matters of doctrine.

The 'Genevan' ministers were also unique in sociological terms; they did not have the status of refugees who lived in a virtual ghetto and followed a trade in order to survive, but the status of academics. Requirements for

---

[9] Cuno, *Franciscus Junius*, pp. 11–16.
[10] H. Meylan, 'L'Eglise d'Anvers sous la terreur. Lettres inédites de Johannes Helmichius (1567), '*Mélanges historiques offerts à Monsieur Jean Meyhoffer, docteur en théologie* (Lausanne, 1952), pp. 73–4.
[11] Rahlenbeck, 'Jean Taffin,' p. 127.
[12] Corro, Leseur, Rudsemelis and Cappel.
[13] H. de Vries de Heekelingen, ed., *Genève pépinière du Calvinisme Hollandais*, II (The Hague, 1924), p. 165.

admission to both the Academy and the city itself were stringent, and the expense of traveling to Switzerland was considerable. This was not a community for refugees, but for students, and if these students did not always have ample means of support, they did have relatively high social and intellectual stature. Of the twelve ministers who studied at Geneva (ten of whom spoke French, four of whom *were* French), eight came from bourgeois or noble families and eight had received a humanist education; only two, Guy de Brès and Ambroise Wille, had been artisans.[14] They were also an extremely young group; ten were described as youthful, and seven were definitely in their twenties. In view of their extreme youth, it is surprising that six had had practical experience as pastors (two in the Netherlands) before 1566. The ministers who studied in Geneva were not a formally organized corps of pastors, sharing a common training and subject to a common discipline, but they did constitute a social and intellectual elite within the Reformed clergy.

FRANCE

Margaret of Parma was convinced that the Reformed ministers were Frenchmen, that the French Huguenot noblemen, Condé and Coligny, were agitating among the Netherlands nobility, and that her own subjects would view the peace of Amboise as a pretext for demanding religious toleration. Her suspicions were at least partially correct. Marnix of Thoulouse asserted that Philip should grant freedom of worship, 'which experience has shown the king of France to be the sole remedy for such a great shedding of blood.'[15] Condé's agents did visit border towns in French Flanders and Artois, which were refugee centers for Huguenots, and heretical works printed in France were smuggled into the Netherlands by Protestant merchants. Reformers living near the French border went to Picardy to attend religious services and to celebrate weddings and baptisms.[16] And ministers from France did cross over the borders to preach in the Walloon provinces.

But the actual, direct influence of French Protestantism on the development of the Netherlands Reformed movement was considerably less than Margaret supposed.[17] Many Confederates, as Burgundian noblemen, were

---

[14] Wille had the advantage of traveling to Rome before he visited Geneva, while de Brès was already a pastor at the time of his arrival. This conforms to the pattern described by Kingdon; the French pastors included very few artisans or peasants.

[15] G. Hoffman, 'French Calvinism. A "Subversive" Movement in the Spanish Netherlands,' *The Dawn of Modern Civilization* (Ann Arbor, Mich., 1964), p. 208.

[16] *Ibid.*, pp. 204, 209, 215.

[17] Only one minister crossed over the border from France during the Troubles: Jean Cateu, a native of Picardy, arrived at St Amand in the autumn of 1566, having

politically hostile to France, and therefore averse to forming an alliance with the Huguenots. At least one Reformed pastor shared these sentiments; during the siege of Valenciennes, the pastor Guy de Brès rejected offers of aid from Condé, preferring to wait for help from the Germans, which never came.[18] Several ministers whom the inquisitors assumed to be French, because they spoke 'good' French and not a Walloon dialect, were actually natives who had studied or preached for a time abroad. The fact was that France, although for different reasons, was no more a suitable haven for religious refugees than Geneva. The political situation was too unstable to admit of the intrusion of a group of foreigners whose religion differed from that of the Crown. Thus, with very few exceptions, there were no refugee communities in France, and certainly no facilities to shelter Flemish-speaking Reformers; only one Flemish minister, Pieter Hazard, was rumored to have fled there in order to escape persecution.[19]

The Netherlands pastors who did visit France were sent there to preach after their ordination in Geneva, or, like de Brès, they were welcomed informally because of the reputation they had already established. Jehan Leseur, a native of Arras, matriculated at the Genevan Academy in 1563 and was then assigned to the French churches of Montcornet and Tupigny. He also functioned as an itinerant pastor in the area of Cateau and Prémont, which bordered on the S. Netherlands, and in July, 1566 he became a pastor at Valenciennes.[20] Louis Cappel and Pierre Boquin (Boquinus), both native Frenchmen, were active for several years in France before coming to preach in the Netherlands in 1566 – Cappel as pastor of the church at Meaux and delegate to the national synod at Paris in 1565, Boquin as a professor of Reformed theology at Bourges.[21] Antonio Corro, a Spaniard, spent several years in France after completing his studies at Geneva, in order to establish a

preached for three years in France (Haag, *La France Protestante*, 2nd ed., III, p. 854). The Netherlands Reformers did make direct requests for ministers to be sent from the Academy at Orléans to the churches of Lille and Hainaut (*Correspondance de Théodore de Bèze, 1566*, ed. Aubert and Meylan. Letter 488: Des Gallars to Beza, 12 August 1566 (Geneva, 1960–), VII, p. 196). Of course, many of the lay preachers discussed in Chapter 6, whose backgrounds are unknown, could have come from France. Jean Grincourt, who preached at La Gorgue in 1566, came from Picardy; Crapandiau was recruited from France by Calvinists from Armentières. Decavele sees the violence of the early 1560s as imitative of France; Hazard in particular was in France during the massacre of Vassy in 1562, (*Dageraad*, p. 426). But Hazard was already a radical; de Brès, who was also in France at the time, was anti-violence.

18 Braekman, *Guy de Brès*, p. 141.
19 Hessels, *Ecclesiae*, II, letter of Buzère, April 27, 1562 (No. 64).
20 Desilve, *St Amand*, p. 59.
21 On Cappel, see Haag, *France Protestante*, 2nd ed., III, pp. 736–9; on Boquin II, p. 400.

Calvinist church for Spanish refugees.[22] Guy de Brès, having fled Tournai after the *chanteries* of 1561, preached for four years in various churches in France and served as chaplain to the Duke of Sedan.[23]

By far the most important Reformed church in France, in terms of its effect on the Netherlands Reformed movement, was that of Metz. The community was first organized in 1525 by Guillaume Farel, and received official status, with permission to conduct public religious services, in 1560.[24] Jean Taffin was called there in 1561 to serve the rapidly growing refugee community. Taffin organized a consistory, ministered to the needs of the neighboring churches of Montigny, Montoy and St Privat, and supervised the construction of a Calvinist temple; on September 21, 1561, the ministers celebrated Communion in the presence of ten thousand worshippers. The church at Metz also maintained close ties with Geneva; Taffin wrote to Beza for advice in handling a controversy concerning baptism, and on the problem of dealing with the local Catholic clergy.[25]

Thus the church at Metz, as well as that of Sedan, where Guy de Brès preached from 1563 until 1566, seemed to offer an ideal refuge to the Netherlands Reformers. One elderly Calvinist, complaining of the dissension within his own refugee church at Frankfurt, wrote to a colleague in 1562:[26]

As my old age makes me unfit for such troubles, I have looked out for a place where I might find a little rest. The church at Metz seems the most blessed of all recently established communities. It is served by two excellent young men: Petrus Colonius. . .and Jean Taffin, with so much success that the congregation consists of between fifteen and eighteen thousand members.

The French churches also enabled the ministers to establish personal contacts with the Huguenot nobility. On July 13, 1565, Taffin received a letter from Pierre de Salcède, governor of numerous chateaux in the neighborhood, inviting him to preach on his lands, 'where I am sure you will have a large audience, since all of the Netherlands Reformers will be invited.' Salcède also invited Taffin to bring along 'some good gentlemen.'[27] The year before, Taffin had received François de Coligny, who had recently been married by another Reformed pastor near Metz. Guy de Brès also enjoyed the patronage of the Huguenot nobility, as chaplain to the Duke of Sedan, while Antonio Corro preached at the courts of Jeanne d'Albret and duchess Renée of Fer-

[22] Hauben, *Three Spanish Heretics*, p. 10.
[23] Braekman, *Guy de Brès*, p. 192.
[24] Accounts of the Metz church are in Boer, *Hofpredikers*, pp. 7–20, and Rahlenbeck, 'Taffin,' pp. 127–33.
[25] Boer, *Hofpredikers*, pp. 17, 19.
[26] Hessels, *Ecclesiae*, II, letter of Aegidius Becius to Utenhove, April 5, 1562 (No. 63).
[27] Rahlenbeck, 'Taffin,' pp. 130–1.

rara.[28] Louis Cappel, François Junius and Peregrine de la Grange, all of whom studied in Geneva, were themselves members of the French nobility.

But for the most part, the benefits which the ministers enjoyed as a result of their association with the French churches were illusory. The same elderly Reformer from Frankfurt who sought a quiet haven in Metz was nonetheless moved to remark, 'I should wish to go to Metz, if rumors of war did not deter me, which are all the more to be feared in a town, which is always occupied by a strong garrison on account of the vicinity of the enemy.'[29] Pierre de Salcède, the French nobleman who assured Taffin of complete safety on his lands, was routed soon afterward in a campaign against him by the bishop of Metz. Nor were the ministers' other noble connections more durable than this. De Brès' patronage by the Duke of Sedan would be of little help to him during the Troubles, since de Brès refused to become involved in the French uprising by accepting aid from the Huguenots. Corro was forced to leave the court of Renée when her husband, a Catholic, returned home. Louis Cappel, a French nobleman himself, was more interested in the affairs of France than in those of the Netherlands, and remained in Antwerp for only a few weeks in 1566. Junius' Huguenot connections were broken when his father was killed by Catholic soldiers; in fact, his main purpose in coming to preach in the Netherlands was to avoid all further contact with France.[30]

Whatever Margaret may have thought about the Reformed ministers and their relations with the French Huguenot movement, the facts were quite different. But these illusions, which Margaret shared with other important officials, conferred very real advantages on the ministers when they returned to the Netherlands in 1566. And because many in the population shared Margaret's estimation of the support enjoyed by the ministers, they were able to attract a huge popular following during the summer of the hedge-preaching.

GERMANY

The Lutherans of Saxony, to witt the zelous Lutherans agree with the Calvinists denying free will, and braule with the Melanchthonistes for allowing free will against the doctrine of their Father Luther...Yet againe these zelous Lutherans in the article of originall sinne, agree with the civill Lutherans, and defie the Calvinistes. But in the articles of Justification, of good workes, of the supper of Lorde...in these the zelous Lutherans dissent bothe from the Civill Lutherans and from the Calvinistes.[31]

[28] Hauben, *Three Spanish Heretics*, pp. 9f.
[29] Hessels, *Ecclesiae*, ii, No. 63. [30] Cuno, *Junius*, p. 14.
[31] Thomas Stapleton, *A Returne of Untruthes Upon M. Jewelle's Replie* (Antwerp, 1566), n.p.

The most important decision which confronted both the Reformed refugees and the German Lutherans was whether or not they might safely consider each other as true Christians. Largely because of their recent troubles with the Anabaptist sects, the Lutherans were militantly hostile to any religious group whose tenets did not conform quite literally to their own; to them, every Netherlander was a potential anarchist. The Reformers, for their part, were concerned to maintain their religious integrity against Lutheran pressure to compromise on dogmatic questions. After prolonged quarrels with the Lutheran preachers, Pieter Dathenus, pastor of the Dutch church of Frankfurt, declared himself prepared to adopt Lutheran practice in the celebration of baptism and other church ceremonies, in order to ensure the survival of the refugee church; his colleague, Gaspar van der Heyden, insisted that any compromise in matters of doctrine was tantamount to heresy. This conflict between the ideal of religious integrity and the necessity of religious compromise for the sake of survival agitated almost every Reformed community in Germany in the years before the Troubles.[32]

Ten Netherlands pastors visited communities in Germany, where the most important refugee churches were in the Palatinate under the auspices of Frederick III, and on the lower Rhine.[33] At Frankfurt, two small communities, French and Flemish, existed from 1555 until 1562, when the Reformers were ordered to accept Lutheran practice.[34] The Lutherans originally welcomed the Reformed refugees, most of whom had fled to Germany from England after the accession of Mary Tudor; in 1555 the new church, consisting of about two hundred members, received the Fleming, Pieter Dathenus, as its first minister. For the next seven years, Reformers from the Netherlands, France and England shared the use of a single church building, in which they engaged in almost uninterrupted quarrels on matters of theology and ecclesiastical authority:[35]

Ministers, who could not get along with the church council or with each other; elders who, when things did not go their way, left before their time, or those... who insisted on remaining after their time; and members of the community who wanted to govern the church themselves.

The minister Pieter Dathenus wrote to a colleague in 1561: 'In truth you are the overseer of a people signing under the Egyptian load, [while] I

[32] A. A. van Schelven, *De Nederduitsche*, p. 315.
[33] Dathenus and van der Heyden preached at Frankfurt and Frankenthal; Boquinus at Heidelberg; Taffin at Aachen; Bacquereel at Frankfurt and Aachen; Jacobus van Culembourg in Cleves, de Lesenne at Wesel; Wingius at Frankfurt; Ryckwaert visited Frankenthal; Moded studied at the University of Cologne. A lay preacher, Nicholas Panquert, studied at the University of Heidelberg.
[34] van Schelven, *De Nederduitsche*, pp. 214–34.
[35] Rutgers, *Calvijns invloed*, pp. 26–7.

preside over a people in the wildnerness, free from the yoke of tyrants, but querulous, inflexible, arrogant and murmuring.'[36]

The lack of discipline within the Reformed churches made it all the more difficult to reply to the charges of the Lutheran pastors, who maintained that the Reformers had entered the city under false pretences, as co-religionists (i.e. as Lutherans), only later revealing themselves as Calvinists. The Lutherans objected above all to the Reformers' 'dishonest' practice of Communion, baptism and various church ceremonies, and repeatedly demanded that the local magistrates take measures against the refugee community.[37] In 1557 Dathenus wrote to the church council at Emden, requesting that Marten Micronius, their most eminent pastor, come to Frankfurt to settle quarrels within the church and to participate in a debate with the Lutherans – but to no effect.[38] Four years later, Dathenus wrote to a colleague in England:[39]

We have been expecting the end of our tragedy, but nothing has as yet been decided, wherefore we are in great straits. The ministers of this town are furious against us, and the greater...part of the Senate is on their side; hence we have little hope, unless the Lord aid His Church.

The conflict between the Reformed refugees and the Lutheran preachers eventually attracted the attention of Reformers in other countries. Calvin and Dathenus exchanged a series of letters on the subject, a minister from England, Godfried Wingius, arrived in 1561 to conciliate the two parties, and letters to the local senate, pleading for toleration of the Reformed cult, arrived from the Elector Frederick III, the Landgrave of Hesse and the theology faculties of the University of Heidelberg and Marburg.[40] Meanwhile the refugee church itself was divided between the partisans of Dathenus, who wished to accept the Lutheran form of baptism, and another Flemish pastor, Gaspar van der Heyden, who insisted that the Lutherans were not members of the church of Christ and that no basis for compromise existed.[41] In 1562 the Lutheran preachers finally convinced the Senate to forbid religious worship to all non-Lutherans, and the refugee community, after repeated and futile attempts to petition the Senate, was forced to leave the city.

The Reformers also had a difficult time of it at Aachen, where a tiny group

---

[36] Hessels, *Ecclesiae*, II, letter to Wingius, April 22, 1561 (No. 50).
[37] van Schelven, *De Nederduitsche*, p. 219.
[38] *Ibid.*, p. 216. Emden sent Delenus and John Dirkens. In 1561 Dathenus again discussed the possibility of a debate with the Lutherans in a letter to Utenhove (Hessels, *Ecclesiae*, letter of April 28, 1561, No. 51).
[39] Hessels, *Ecclesiae*, II, letter of July 7, 1561, No. 55.
[40] van Schelven, *De Nederduitsche*, p. 228.
[41] Dathenus wrote to Calvin for advice on April 28, 1562 '*Calvini Opera*, XIX, No. 3777).

of Walloon weavers had emigrated in 1544.[42] Reformed worship became public after a Lutheran burgomaster was chosen in 1552 (Aachen, being a free Imperial city, was not subject to territorial jurisdiction); but in the next few years, local pressure by Catholics against the Reformers increased so much that the Walloon pastor Jean Taffin was refused admission to the city in 1558.[43] Wesel, unlike Aachen, was subject to the outside jurisdiction of the Duke of Cleves, who vacillated between Catholic and Protestant.[44] During the 1540s, a number of local magistrates became Lutheran, and Reformed preaching was tolerated as long as the sacraments were held only in the Lutheran church; Reformed refugees also had to sign the Augsburg Confession.

The only refugee church in Germany to enjoy a degree of security was that of Frankenthal, in the Palatinate. Following the Reformers' expulsion from Frankfurt, Frederick III, a Calvinist sympathizer, admitted Dathenus and sixty families, on condition that the minister sign a capitulation submitting all future quarrels to the arbitration of the Heidelberg church council. For the next three years (1553–6), the Netherlands refugees enjoyed a period of relative quiet. Another debate between Lutherans and Calvinists took place in April, 1564 at Maulbronn, at which the issues which had been discussed at Frankfurt were re-opened; but Dathenus, who participated on the Calvinist side, was now secure in the patronage of Frederick. Dathenus also acted as a diplomat during this period, making at least one trip to Zurich on behalf of the community.

Given the extreme insecurity of the Reformers in Germany, it is not surprising that only two refugees, Corneille de Lesenne and Nicolas Panquert, lived and studied there before preaching in the Netherlands. Nor is it surprising that only four ministers were active in Germany for more than a few weeks, and that three of them, Dathenus, van der Heyden and Boquinus, were sheltered by Frederick.[45] The activity of the other ministers in Germany consisted of the presentation of requests to local magistrates, asking them to accept a group of refugees within the walls of their city – usually in vain. Thus Jean Taffin and Hermes Bacquereel traveled to Germany in 1558 to find a haven for a group of Walloon refugees from Antwerp. After they were refused admittance by the magistrates of Aachen and Worms, Frederick III intervened and convinced Duke Christophe of Wurttemberg to take the group – until his spiritual superintendent advised him that Taffin was too

[42] van Schelven, *De Nederduitsche*, pp. 273–81.
[43] During this period Corneille de Lesenne also fled to Aachen, where he remained for five years as elder of the Walloon church.
[44] van Schelven, *De Nederduitsche*, pp. 281–97. Karel le Bron visited Wesel during the Troubles. Jacobus van Culembourg preached on the land of the Duke of Cleves.
[45] The fourth was Jacobus van Culembourg.

unorthodox. The community finally settled at Strasbourg. With the exception of van der Heyden, who insisted that observance of the Reformed cult be conducted in the orthodox manner or not at all, each of these ministers agreed to compromise on issues of dogma and church ceremony in order to win admittance by local communities. Jacobus van Culembourg preached according to the Augsburg Confession for several years before coming to the Netherlands in 1566 as a Calvinist minister. Taffin and Bacquereel submitted a pro-Lutheran Confession at Worms, while Dathenus, as we have seen, encouraged his congregation to submit to Lutheran baptism at Frankfurt, with the full approval of Calvin.

Paradoxically, the Reformed ministers in Germany, who were so consistently maligned by the Lutheran ministers and city magistrates, were highly successful in establishing contacts with the German nobility – contacts which they could later exploit in their relations with the confederate nobles and with William of Orange. The Reformed church of Frankenthal became an important link between those German nobles who were sympathetic to Calvinism and the Calvinist nobility in the Netherlands. When Dathenus, who became Frederick's personal chaplain, arrived in the Netherlands in the autumn of 1566, he was able to appear before the local magistrates with letters of recommendation from his patron.

EMDEN

In Germany, the lines of demarcation between the Lutheran and the Calvinist camps were absolutely rigid; despite the Reformers' willingness to make substantial concessions to the local ministers, they had great difficulties in receiving even temporary physical shelter from the Lutherans. The churches of the N. Netherlands and Emden were quite different in this respect; here the lines of demarcation between Protestant sects were so blurred that scholars have argued at length over the exact point at which they should be drawn.

Historians formerly asserted that the North was moderate and tended toward Lutheranism, while the southern provinces were more strictly Calvinist.[46] Against this view, both Rutgers and van Schelven have argued that the Lutherans were actually a very small minority, consisting chiefly of German soldiers and merchants who penetrated only a few areas. Both writers point out, and rightly, that the terms 'moderate' and 'strict' are more appropriately applied to individuals than to groups. Certainly the Emden church was a strictly Calvinist church; when the English refugees at Wesel were ordered to participate in Lutheran ceremonies, Geneva and Lausanne

[46] Rutgers, *Calvijns invloed*, p. 126 and van Schelven, *De Nederduitsche*, pp. 213, 222.

advised compliance, while Emden's first reaction was to advise the Reformers to stand firm against Lutheran pressure. Still, Lutheran communities did co-exist with Calvinist communities in the northern provinces; Gaspar van der Heyden made a special trip to Amsterdam in 1566 to remonstrate with the local Reformers against compromise with the Lutherans there. One reason for the decision of the Frankfurt community to settle at Frankenthal rather than in the North was that the Emden church was enduring pressure from the magistrates to adhere to Lutheran ceremonies, while the church at Norden had its own troubles with the Lutherans in that city.[47]

But these internal conflicts did not prevent the Emden church from functioning as a 'mother church' to the most important community in the southern provinces, that of Antwerp. Seventeen Netherlands ministers visited churches in the North before 1566, seeking physical shelter, advice and education.[48] Pastors studied at the Latin schools of Emden and Norden and were examined by the Emden church council before consecration. When Gaspar van der Heyden was ready to be ordained as pastor of the Antwerp church, he insisted on traveling to Emden for the ceremony. 'I will accept such [an office] not of my own choosing,' he wrote in 1556, 'nor by their choice [i.e., the Antwerp church], but by your command, so that we [have] no false prophets...'[49] Ministers also consulted the Emden church council on matters of theology and discipline; in 1555 van der Heyden wrote to Emden about his struggles against the many Protestant sects in Antwerp, asking in particular for arguments to be used against the Lutherans.[50] Emden was also forced to intervene in the dispute between the Antwerp consistory and Adrien van Haemstede. Two ministers who were active during the Troubles, Jean Taffin and Hermes Bacquereel, acted as mediators during this particular quarrel, and when van Haemstede's public preaching led to intensified persecution of the Reformers, they assumed the responsibility of conducting the local community to Germany. In 1563, Herman Moded appeared before the Emden consistory on behalf of the Antwerp church to discuss standards for the ordination of ministers and to be advised whether or not the minister may preach without being assigned to a specific church. Emden's response, which was reminiscent of her criticism of van Haemstede six years earlier, was that the privilege of preaching without a church affiliation belonged only to the apostles of Christ.[51]

[47] van Schelven, p. 235.
[48] The following ministers lived in or visited Emden and the northern provinces: Moded, van der Heyden, Bacquereel, Wingius, Balck, van Culembourg, Top, Sterkenbrugge, Rhetius, van Vyve, Lantsochtius, de Voghele, Mostaert, Pontfort, Gillain, Valencijn, Mostaert.
[49] van Lennep, *Gaspar*, p. 18.   [50] *Ibid.*, p. 33. Letter of December 17, 1555.
[51] van Schelven, *De Nederduitsche*, p. 119.

Calvinist preaching and Iconoclasm in the Netherlands

The role which Emden played in relation to the churches of the southern provinces was similar to that played by Geneva in relation to the churches of France, in a very limited sense; limited, because the ministers who corresponded with the Emden church – Dathenus, Taffin, Moded – also considered the churches of Geneva and London as higher authorities. Moreover, the practical jurisdiction of the Emden church extended to only a portion of the Netherlands churches. With the exception of Taffin all of the ministers who dealt with Emden were Flemish; the Walloon ministers of Tournai and Valenciennes turned for training and advice to churches in Switzerland and France. Emden also differed from Geneva in its function as a church to which people fled, with or without the desire or the money for formal study, in times of persecution. This accounts for the lower social and intellectual origins of the ministers who belonged to the Emden community, or who preached in other churches in the North.[52]

ENGLAND

... profitable and gentle strangers ought
to be welcomed and not to be grudged at.

Archbishop Parker, referring to the
Flemish refugees at Sandwich, 1563.

England was the only country to welcome refugees from the Netherlands not merely from a sense of compassion toward co-religionists 'under the cross,' but because of the positive benefits which the Reformers could bring to England. In 1550, Edward VI established two refugee churches in London, one French and one Flemish-speaking. The members were forced to disperse during the Marian persecutions, but many returned in 1560, when the churches were reconstituted by Elizabeth; churches were also established at Canterbury, Norwich and Sandwich.[53] Edward and Elizabeth were both concerned to increase the number of skilled workers in these cities. At Norwich, when the local magistrates resolved to invite a group of skilled Flemish workers, hoping thereby to revive the local economy, Elizabeth issued letters patent admitting thirty master workmen in textiles and their families, to form a church of about three hundred members. The refugees were successful in finding both employment and a hospitable atmosphere in

[52] Six belonged to the Catholic clergy, 4 were artisans or unknowns, 6 middle class, 1 noble. The Emden community attracted many poor weavers from the area of French Flanders (R. van Roosbroeck, *Emigranten* (Louvain, 1968), p. 98).

[53] The church at Canterbury was formed before 1561, that of Norwich in 1564 (J. S. Burn, *The History of the... Protestant Refugees Settled in England* (London, 1846), p. 38). Sandwich was founded in 1561 (van Schelven, *De Nederduitsche*, p. 178).

England. 'Friesland,' wrote one exile of the Emden church, 'is much less congenial than Norwich...I earn so much that I can easily make ends meet with a family of three children.'[54] Not surprisingly, a high proportion of the Netherlands ministers trained in England belonged to artisan families, and the great majority came originally from the industrial area of West Flanders.[55]

King Edward's second reason for admitting the Netherlands refugees was to counteract the threat of Anabaptism by establishing a well-organized and stable religious community which might serve as a model to the English Reformers. Theology and discipline in the English churches was therefore strictly orthodox, and close ties were established between these communities and Calvinist churches on the continent. Nicolas des Gallars, minister of the French church of London, was sent from Geneva with Calvin's personal recommendation, while Beza utilized the consistory of the French church as mediators in his correspondence with English Reformers.[56] The Dutch Austin Friars church was influenced more directly by the Reformers at Emden; Micronius and John à Lasco, who wrote the catechism, liturgy and Confession used by the congregation, were also members of the Emden church. Both churches met regularly at a 'coetus' where the ministers, elders and deacons discussed matters of church government in concert. The consistories were particularly concerned to maintain a high standard of morality and education among the laity. Prospective members of the Walloon church had to prove their sincerity by answering questions on doctrine or by submitting letters of recommendation from a recognized church abroad; no member was admitted to Communion who was on bad terms with a brother of the church; finally, members were not permitted to take disputes before the civil courts until they had submitted to the arbitration of a committee chosen by the consistory.[57] While the London churches were formally subject to the jurisdiction of Bishop Grindall, in practice the Netherlands refugees enjoyed a greater degree of autonomy than the English Reformers who subscribed to Calvinist doctrine. The English Puritans apparently envied the foreigners this spiritual independence. In 1566 one English minister complained, 'This with them: they an eldership, we none; they freely elect

---

[54] van Schelven, p. 194.
[55] Eleven were artisans or unknowns, 6 middle class, 8 members of the Catholic clergy. (At least 3 of the 'middle class' ministers were schoolmasters; Wingius, Bacquereel and Bécourt worked as tutors in England; Baerdeloos was a student.) All but 3 came from Flanders.
[56] P. Collinson, *The Elizabethan Puritans*, p. 114. The strict Calvinism of the English churches is argued at some length by T. van Oppenraaij, *La Doctrine de la prédestination dans l'église réformée des Pays-Bas* (Louvain, 1906).
[57] Johnston, *Actes du consistoire*, I, pp. xviii, xvix, xxxvi.

the doctor and pastor, we may not; they their deacons and church servants with discipline, and we not.'[58]

In quantitative terms, the English refugee churches were of greater significance in the formation of the Netherlands clergy than those of any other country. Twenty-five ministers visited England: fourteen were affiliated with refugee churches for an extended period, three visited England to discuss issues pertaining to the Netherlands movement, and five more traveled to England during the Troubles, returning to preach in Flanders in 1567–8.[59] Almost all of the ministers who lived in England had fled there as newly-converted Reformers, having no apparent status within the organized Calvinist community in the Netherlands. The context in which their names appear in consistory minutes and personal correspondence occasionally offers hints as to their status in the refugee communities: Octavien Bécourt, a schoolmaster attached to the Walloon church of London, was summoned before the consistory with regard to a quarrel over the fees he had charged a customer.[60] Andreas Baerdeloos, a student and member of a wealthy merchant family in Hondschoote, married the sister of an important Reformer in Sandwich.[61] Sebastien Matte was received as a member of the London Dutch church in 1560; three years later he attended a conference to discuss the legality of prison breaks.[62] Jan Lamoot became an elder of the same church.[63] A few Reformers attained the status of ordained pastor during the period; Erasmus Top was assigned to the church of Middelburg in Zeeland, and Pieter Carpentier to that of Antwerp.[64] Jacques de Buzère earned his doctorate in theology in London and became the first pastor of the Flemish church of Sandwich in 1561.[65]

Unlike the churches in Germany, which were nearly decimated by theological controversies with other Protestant groups, the issue which preoccupied the 'English' ministers more than any other was that of violence. The reason for this was the unique situation of the English churches. The Netherlands

---

[58] Collinson, *The Elizabethan Puritans*, p. 114.
[59] Ministers who visited England: Bécourt, Bert, de Buzère, Garcia, Matte, Michiels, de Quekère, Wybo, Baerdeloos, de Brune, Carpentier, Flameng, Lamoot, May, Platevoet, de Schildere, Strobbe, Top, Dathenus, Hazard, Le Bron, Moded, Bacquereel, de Brès, Wingius.
[60] Johnston, *Actes*, vol. 1, pp. 56–9.
[61] Hessels, *Ecclesiae*, II, letter of Petrus Scagius to Wingius, No. 61.
[62] A. A. van Schelven, ed., *Kerkeraads-protocollen der Nederduitsche vluchtelingen-kerk te Londen* (Amsterdam, Johannes Muller, 1921), p. 35. Matte was admitted on August 27, 1560. He was also involved in the van Haemstede dispute.
[63] NNBW III, pp. 733–5, and KP, p. 4. Lamoot was also involved in the van Haemstede dispute.
[64] Leblanc, 'Les prédicants,' pp. 85–6. On Carpentier, see KP, p. 56.
[65] Hessels, *Ecclesiae*, II, No. 57.

Reformers in England enjoyed a degree of physical security and religious autonomy which they found in no other country, but they were rarely assimilated into the life of the local society.[66] On the contrary, the 'English' refugees maintained close and reciprocal contacts with their co-religionists at home, and they were particularly sensitive to the religious persecution there. The correspondence of Jacques de Buzère, pastor of the Flemish church at Sandwich, contains numerous references to the persecution in Flanders. 'Our church is prospering,' he wrote in 1562; 'Since the persecutions in Flanders have increased, very many pious and industrious people have sought refuge here.' Six months later Buzère wrote to a pastor in London, 'because of the persecution in Flanders so many come daily, that we can hardly hold them. Help us or we shall have to send you a number of brethren.' Buzère described the ordeal of an elder of the Sandwich church who had been captured in Flanders:[67]

His brother Francis landed here and brought us a letter by him in prison to our consistory indicating what Confession of faith he had made at Ypres. . .and how he had been taken to Ghent and kept in chains there. He wants the council or Bishop of London and other leading men to write on his behalf to the Chief Council of Flanders.

Communication between England and Flanders was so easy, in fact, that it was common for Reformers to travel back and forth between the two countries; the minister Pieter Hazard made several trips in the years before the Troubles.[68]

In short, the geographical proximity of England to Flanders, combined with the leniency of the English ecclesiastical authorities and the relatively insular character of the refugee communities there, made England an ideal center for revolutionary agitation. The conferences on the legality of prison

[66] Collinson mentions several instances of the English Reformers participating in ceremonies of the Netherlands churches. But it is difficult to believe that the average Reformer, knowing no Latin, could have communicated very well with those around him. In 1568 the bishop of Norwich reported that the Walloons and Flemings did not go to the parish churches because they did not understand English (W. J. C. Moens, *The Walloons and Their Church at Norwich 1565–1832* (Lymington, 1888), p. 26).

[67] Hessels, *Ecclesiae*, II, letters to Delenus, dated April 27, 1562 and October 23, 1562 (Nos. 64 and 68). Wingius wrote to London on behalf of three prisoners in Flanders, July 19, 1560 (KP, p. 22).

[68] In 1561 Hazard was at the meeting at Sandwich; in 1562 he was in W. Flanders; in 1563 he was at the London meeting; from 1563–6 at Antwerp (van Schelven, 'Het gewapend verzet,' p. 134; de Coussemaker, *Troubles*, I, p. 55; BWK Prot., III, pp. 593–6). Matte and Lamoot were also reported to have preached secretly in Flanders during their period of residence in England. David Cambier, a preacher in Nieuwkerke in 1560, had a helper whose special task it was to bring exiles from the Westkwartier to Nieuwport for the trip to England (Decavele, *Dageraad*, p. 407).

breaks which were held in Sandwich (1561) and London (1563), as well as the organized prison breaks which occurred in W. Flanders in the early 1560s, have already been described. I have also described the murders which were perpetrated in Flanders by Reformers coming from the churches of Norwich and Sandwich in 1567. Several Netherlands ministers were reported to have fled to England in 1566, returning to commit violence in Flanders with the assistance of consistories in both countries.[69]

II

Having described the varieties of experience which confronted the ministers during emigration, it would seem that nothing is left but to advance the rather modest conclusion that the ministers who preached during the Troubles had virtually nothing in common. We cannot even say that the experience of residing in different countries led to the formation of certain different types of ministers; if a Flemish weaver fled to England, he did not always come back a social revolutionary, nor were the 'German' pastors all 'survivors,' willing to make any compromise for safety's sake and unable to converse with the fiercely idealistic and intellectual pastors from Geneva. The evidence of the pastors' behavior during the Troubles has already shown us that a simple correlation between place of training and degree of radicalism or ideological rigor will not work. The biographies of the radical pastors, when compared with those of the moderates, demonstrated that training in Geneva or London or Emden was no guarantee of a particular type of outlook or behavior. The evidence of the pastors' experience in exile confirms this hypothesis; Reformed institutions were not *per se* either strict or moderate in terms of ideology. Willingness to tolerate doctrinal differences, even those of the Lutherans, depended more on personal preference than on the formal doctrines of the churches. For example, the image of the Genevan church as supremely fanatic in its efforts to maintain moral discipline and to safeguard the purity of Calvinist theology is, at least for the period of Calvin's leadership, quite simply false. Calvin himself was a moderate; when Dathenus and van der Heyden wrote to him for advice on the question of accepting baptism in the Lutheran manner, Calvin replied that Dathenus, who wished to compromise, was in the right. Beza, on the other hand, *was* a fanatic Calvinist, as were the pastors Gaspar van der Heyden and Godfried Wingius, both of whom were ordained at Emden – the only refugee center where Calvinists actually co-existed with Lutherans.

The ideological posture of the Reformers in different countries was also

---

[69] The preachers were Jan Michiels and Pieter Bert. Two lay preachers also fled to England during the Troubles: Adrien van Maeldegem and Pieter de Hase.

determined by the political environment. The independence of Geneva and its relative immunity from outside attack meant that its pastors did not have to compromise on points of theology, whereas the pastors in Germany did. This in spite of the fact that the Genevan church made a greater effort to nurture the Calvinist movement in Germany than in any other country except France.[70]

Given these obvious disparities in outlook and behavior, it is curious that so many people, including the ministers themselves, were convinced that they belonged to a vast international movement, a movement which had already penetrated into half the countries of Europe and was soon to engulf the Netherlands. Peter Frarin's *Oration Against the Protestants*, delivered at the University of Louvain in 1565, was published the following year and translated into English, French and Dutch, accompanied by a summary of the book in cartoon form for the benefit of the illiterate. After accusing the leading Reformers of deviant sexual behavior and general immorality, Frarin comes to his main point, which is that the ministers are not content to suffer calmly for their beliefs like the apostles, but seek to destroy society by force of arms. 'O master ministers, it is a very hard word that ye bring us, for ye speake gonnestones, your Gospel is too hot, ye preach fire and powder. . .and put on a corselet not of faith, but of iron and steele.' Frarin views the violence in Germany and France as part of a vast, anarchistic movement. 'Ye have heard,' he warns, 'what they have done otherwise; you understand thereby what you yourselves also ought to feare.'

These hyperboles were echoed, in less dramatic form, by the author of a pamphlet, *Brief Discours*, which appeared in Antwerp in the spring of 1566.[71] The polemic is addressed to Philip, and the author – actually the Calvinist pastor François Junius – assumes the position of Philip's advocate, seeking a means to prevent the spread of the Reformed faith:[72]

Inasmuch as in the Netherlands, as well as in France, England and Scotland, and even in Germany. . .a great part of the population has been overwhelmed by those who are called Evangelical. . .The question is how, following the will of the king, we can maintain the people in the old faith.

Since the new faith cannot be extirpated by physical punishment, the people must be persuaded by logical argument. Where the Anabaptists have been persecuted, they increase; where they have been invited to public debate,

---

[70] Kingdon, *Consolidation*, p. 14.

[71] François du Jon (Junius), *Brief discours envoyé au roy Philippe. . .pour le bien et profit de sa maieste. . .*, (n.p., 1565). Léonard thinks that Junius was assisted by Charles de Nielles, Louis of Nassau, Marnix of Thoulouse and de Hames (*A History*, II. p. 80).

[72] *Brief discours*, p. 4.

their strength evaporates. Moreover, freedom to celebrate the outward practices of the Reformed cult will maintain the people in a state of order, encourage fear of the magistrate, and thereby prevent another Münster. Junius' strategy is not merely to exploit the popular fears of the Anabaptists in the service of the Calvinists; his main point is that religious toleration is inevitable, since it has already been granted in France, Germany and England. In fact, there are probably three hundred thousand Reformers in Europe and the Netherlands – 'un nombre infini.'

...one can see at Utrecht, an episcopal city full of powerful canons of the church, a man of their party...who has preached this doctrine publicly in the pulpit for a year...and...who cannot be apprehended, since all the people together accompany him in and out of the church.[73]

The Reformed movement has become an international, evangelical crusade, and Philip would do well to accept the reality of their power before he is overwhelmed by it.

These exaggerated views of the ministers' unity and power are worth noting because they explain, at least in part, the Reformers' immediate successes during the summer of the hedgepreaching. But had these impressions any basis in fact? Did the ministers in exile form a community, in any sense of the word, by the time they returned to the Netherlands in 1566? Van Schelven has argued, quite plausibly, I think, that the ministers did constitute a spiritual community at the end of their period of exile.[74] He maintains that the diversity of the exiles' experience had the effect of making the Netherlands Reformers more uniformly Calvinist than they had been before. The early Reformed movement was nourished, as we have seen, by followers of Luther, as well as by those of Erasmus and the evangelical Catholics in France. Van Schelven argues that the ministers' experience in exile narrowed this focus: King Edward's desire to institute a model Reformed community in England encouraged the exiles there to develop a strict ideal of apostolic life. The contact which other Reformers had with the Lutherans in Germany had a similar effect; the Lutherans persecuted the Reformers because they associated them with the Münsterites, who had also come from the Netherlands, and the Reformers reacted by upholding the same ideals as their co-religionists in England. This impulse, added to the influence of à Lasco, Bullinger and Calvin on the refugee communities, resulted in the evolution of the Netherlands Reformed movement into a genuinely Calvinist movement.

Not only did the ministers in different countries share certain spiritual ideals; they extended their activities outside the bounds of their individual

[73] *Ibid.*, pp. 38–9.
[74] van Schelven, *De Nederduitsche*, pp. 312–28.

refugee churches by means of popular and liturgical writings. Guy de Brès published a tract against the Anabaptists and translated the *Histoire* of the martyrdom of Christophe de Smet during his residence at Sedan. Pieter Dathenus utilized his peaceful residence at Frankenthal to publish a Flemish translation of the psalms and a new Reformed liturgy, containing the forms for baptism, communion and marriage, which was adopted for use in the Netherlands. During his pastorate at Metz, Jean Taffin published works by various authors in collaboration with a former member of the Plantin publishing house in Antwerp. And in England, a Flemish Reformer named Jan Sheerlambrecht directed the publication of Calvinist propaganda to be sent to his home church at Bruges.[75] The Reformers also maintained contact among the refugee churches through personal correspondence. Crises in individual churches were discussed and arbitrated by Reformers in several countries; during the theological controversies at Frankfurt, Dathenus wrote to Calvin in Geneva, to Utenhove and the pastor Wingius in London and to the Emden church council for advice. Nor did their communication stop at the exchange of letters. At different stages of the crisis, Calvin traveled from Geneva, Bacquereel from Emden and Wingius from London to act as mediators. When the London Dutch church was disrupted by a controversy concerning baptism, ministers from Antwerp and Emden were sent as arbitrators. The ministers' correspondence also dealt with current Reformed literature: Antonio Corro and Cassiodoro de Reina, both Spaniards, corresponded between France and London about the proposed publication of a Spanish edition of the Bible.[76] Dathenus wrote to Jacques de Buzère in London, defending one of his recent works, and enclosing the opinions of Calvin, the minister of the French church at Strasbourg, and the Heidelberg theologians.[77]

The ministers in exile also maintained close contact with those who had remained in the Netherlands. In 1558, Dathenus consulted with Calvin on behalf of the Reformers in Antwerp, who requested advice on the correct practices of baptism and marriage.[78] Dathenus also corresponded with Guy de Brès when the latter was pastor of the Walloon church at Tournai.[79] De Brès returned from his refuge in Sedan to attend the Netherlands synod of 1563; his Confession of Faith, published in 1561, was sent to the Walloon church of London for further editing.[80] The clandestine preaching in W.

---

[75] Decavele, *Dageraad*, p. 336.
[76] Hauben, *Three Spanish Heretics*, p. 15.
[77] Hessels, *Ecclesiae*, ii, letter of Buzère to Delenus, October 23, 1562, (No. 68).
[78] Letter to Calvin, Sept. 20, 1558 (*Calvini Opera*, xvii, No. 2963), quoted in Rutgers, *Calvijns invloed*, pp. 28–9.
[79] Braekman, *Guy de Brès*, p. 80.
[80] Moreau, *Histoire*, p. 156.

Flanders was often conducted by ministers who traveled between England and the Netherlands. There was therefore no question of the Reformers in exile losing contact with their co-religionists at home.

These activities, which took place largely on paper, hardly added up to an organized, politically active movement, nor could they have resulted in the Reformers' acceptance by the Netherlands government. But they did have one important and tangible result; the project of unification with the Lutherans which was initiated by Louis of Nassau and William of Orange. In 1564, Orange summoned the pastors Guy de Brès and Charles de Nielles to Brussels to discuss the possibility of a religious Confession which would be palatable to both Lutherans and Calvinists. The effect was expected to break the power of the pope utterly for, as de Brès wrote to the Antwerp consistory, 'if we were unified in doctrine no one would be able to touch us without offending all of Germany, which would be of inestimable value for us.'[81] After the initial conference with Orange, de Brès received a copy of the Wittenberg Concord, which he was highly reluctant to accept. He then traveled to Metz in order to confer with Jean Taffin; both agreed that certain articles were 'hard' – those on communion, baptism, absolution and church ceremony – and proceeded to draft a new Confession, to be analyzed by Geneva and the Netherlands churches. De Brès urged the Antwerp consistory to accept the new Confession, which would give the Reformers freedom to preach the true Word of God, and asked that they arrange for the recall of Taffin and himself to the Netherlands, so that they might witness the beginning of the new era of toleration.[82] Beza objected to the project, predicting that people would turn away from the True Word if there were a 'false' religious peace, but the Calvinists pursued their alliance with the German nobility; by 1565, emissaries from the Antwerp consistory were negotiating with Louis of Nassau to prepare for the Confederates' request.[83]

Clearly, the Netherlands clergy was not merely an aggregate of tiny, discrete groups, each one the product of a unique and insular experience in exile. Admittedly, the ministers' period of exile was often of long duration, and emigration also accentuated the differences of language, class and education which had originally divided the ministers. The church of Geneva attracted French-speaking, well-bred intellectuals, while of those who visited the churches of England, Emden and Germany, the vast majority were Flemish-speaking, and only a few had studied at universities; the majority belonged either to the artisan class or to the Catholic clergy. These two groups, artisans

[81] van Langeraad, *Guido de Bray*, pp. iii–vii.
[82] Letter of August 24, 1565 to Taffin, cited in Braekman, *Guy de Brès*, pp. 198–9.
[83] See van Deventer, *Het jaar 1566*, pp. 16–17 on the relations between the Antwerp Calvinists and the Germans.

and priests, were the least represented among the Genevan pastors; artisans could not have afforded the trip or the preliminary education, and priests were not highly acceptable to the Genevan council as future pastors.[84] Not only did the ministers arrive at the refugee churches with different backgrounds; once there, their functions varied according to the church in which they had settled. In Geneva they were academics, in France and Germany they were active as ministers, and in England many worked as artisans.

But the actual effects of these sociological differences may not have been very great, at least in relation to the pastoral elite. Ministers in different countries did correspond in Latin, and at least nine pastors circulated among churches in several countries. Moreover, the Reformed elite which emerged in 1566 – those who corresponded with Calvin or Beza, headed important refugee churches, or had contacts with the nobility – was not formed exclusively of the former inhabitants of Geneva. On the contrary, we find that the group is equally split between French and Flemish-speaking pastors, and between pastors who had been socially prominent and those who came from obscure backgrounds. Moded, Dathenus, de Nielles and Corro were Catholic clergymen, de Brès an artisan, Taffin and van der Heyden bourgeois, Wingius a university student, Cappel a nobleman.

During the period of exile, then, there were obvious signs that the Reformed clergy might have been capable of building a unified movement, despite their obvious differences in background and experience. But rather than enhancing this possibility, the ministers' return to the Netherlands fundamentally undermined it. Indeed, the most serious obstacle to the formation of a cohesive movement in 1566 was rooted less in the sociological or spiritual differences which I have described than in the facts of contemporary politics. The Reformers who sought to form a movement of truly national proportions faced a difficult and paradoxical situation: in order to advance the cause of the Reform at home they would need the support of the Netherlands nobility. They stood a better chance of obtaining this support if they improved their relations with the Germans, not only because the Netherlands nobles had stronger personal and political affiliations with Germany than with France, but also because the Confederates had too little wealth or power to challenge Philip without assistance from abroad. But when it came to matters of theology, rapport between German Lutherans and Netherlands Calvinists was non-existent; one historian of the exiles in Germany asserts that the refugees there faced as much hostility from the Lutherans as the Reformers in Catholic countries.[85] Even if Beza had been less adamantly opposed to William of Orange's proposed compromise, the plan could hardly

[84] Kingdon, *Geneva and the Coming*, p. 10.
[85] van Schelven, *De Nederduitsche*, p. 312.

have succeeded, given these basic antagonisms. In short, there was very little practical basis for an alliance of the Netherlands ministers with either the Lutherans or the Huguenots.

This was a problem of politics, but its significance was not merely that the ministers lacked political connections; it meant that they lacked any possibility of establishing a sense of ideological unity among themselves, a unity which would have lent some credence to the vague and exaggerated claims of the author of the *Brief Discours*. The ministers had achieved a degree of unity in matters of theology, and they had circulated any number of tracts and letters among the churches of England and the continent, in which they expressed their common hopes for the future of the Reformed movement at home; they had even made isolated attempts to resist the Inquisition by freeing religious prisoners. But the ministers clearly needed a tangible focus for these aspirations, some means of expressing the ideology of the Reformed movement which would obliterate the disparities within the Reformed clergy and between the clergy and the nobility of the Netherlands. In the case of the Anglican ministers who had fled to the continent in 1553, this focus was provided by Elizabeth herself. Elizabeth welcomed the English ministers home, and they responded by exalting their queen as a kind of national messiah, a concrete embodiment of their spiritual destiny. The idea of the Church as a community of the Elect was extended to make England the community set apart by God for purposes of His own:[86]

More than ever the purpose would now be to identify the religion of the Word. . . with the cause of the national state, and the effect would be to give depth and range to the people's sense of being a people with an identity of their own, distinct from any other. The religion for which the martyrs in Foxe's book died was the religion of the Word in English.

In England, purely religious sentiments were transmuted into a kind of narrow chauvinism which gave the English Reformers a degree of ideological simplicity and unity which was denied the ministers who returned to the Netherlands in 1566. In the Netherlands, the national leaders were both foreigners and Catholics, and the native nobility, which under the tyranny of Alva would ally itself with the Calvinists, still tended toward an alliance with the Lutherans. Thus the Netherlands minister who wrote so confidently of the imminent triumph of the movement at home had, in this early stage of the Netherlands revolt, no actual focus for his hopes, and therefore no real hopes at all.

[86] W. Haller, *Foxe's Book of Martyrs and the Elect Nation* (London, 1967), pp. 72–3.

5
THE CONSCIOUSNESS OF THE REFORMED CLERGY

> . . .if only God had given me
> the soul of a prophet. . .
>
> Herman Moded

The subject of this chapter is the consciousness of the Reformed clergy: the ministers' perception of their rightful function, and of their rightful goals, as leaders of the Netherlands Reformed movement. It is not a portrayal of the ministers' collective mentality, for at least two reasons. In the first place, it is almost impossible to speculate on what the ministers 'really' thought about spiritual or political issues because their writings, with very few exceptions, were polemical in tone.[1] These pamphlets, letters to government officials and works of popular theology were published in an atmosphere of emergency; their purpose was to convince others of things which may or may not have been strictly true (e.g., the letters to magistrates which asserted the pacifism of the Reformers), and not as straightforward revelations of personal feeling or belief. Taffin's pro-Lutheran Confession was intended to win his admittance to a hostile German community; Junius' was written in haste at the request of the Confederate nobles, who wanted a declaration sufficiently bland to please both the Lutheran princes and the Genevan Calvinists; that of Guy de Brès was thrown over the castle wall at Tournai, in the hope that the magistrates who read it would be impressed by the Calvinists' lack of resemblance to more radical Protestant sects.

It is equally difficult to speculate about the ministers' individual personalities and their relationships within the Reformed community, because there are simply too few personal letters which might tell us what they were like as private men – whether, for example, the ministers were ascetics or lovers of comfort, guilt-ridden or well-adjusted, single-minded in their religious practice or flexible and tolerant. In short, the ministers' writings are of

[1] The writings dealt with here include some sixty published works, a body of private correspondence, and a number of utterances recorded in published consistory records, all composed before 1570. I have also referred to the Autobiography of François Junius, although it was published at a much later date, for the portion immediately relative to his activities in 1566.

interest to the historian as evidence of the ways in which they responded as actors in specific situations of pressure: pressure to conform to the practices of other Reformed sects, pressure to limit – and to extend – their authority within the Reformed consistories, pressure to cope with and somehow dominate the activities of lay preachers, who were often strangers to the orthodox Reformed movement, and pressure to succumb to physical and spiritual torture.

The second reason for my reluctance to consider the ministers' writings as evidence of a collective mentality is that, since the diversity of their background and experience has been emphasized throughout this book, it seems doubtful that such a collective mentality existed at all. What, for instance, could a young, noble French pastor, newly graduated from the Academy at Geneva, have shared with a much older, Flemish-speaking pastor with years of experience in refugee communities, other than the common commitment to achieve the public acceptance of Reformed worship and the common pressure to compromise with other Reformed groups in order to achieve that end?

The limited goal of my analysis, then, is to determine how Reformed theology and doctrines were mediated by the ministers' particular experiences at home and in exile, and how these experiences affected their perception of what was significant in the Calvinist movement, and of what was not. It should then be possible to estimate the effect which the ministers, as public men, had on the Netherlands Reformed movement during the Troubles. Since my interest is to clarify the ministers' own consciousness of their role as spiritual leaders, I have taken their writings at face value. I have assumed that what they conceived to be significant problems in defining their authority and propagating the movement were, in fact, significant problems. If, for example, the problem of the Real Presence in Communion was mentioned over fifty times – which it was – and the problem of the new bishoprics only once – which it was – then I have concluded that the ministers believed that the issue of Communion was more crucial than that of the status of the Catholic clergy. Claude Lévi-Strauss has remarked bemusedly about Villegaignon's Calvinist community in Brazil in 1566:[2]

Where they should have been working to keep themselves alive, they spent week after week in insane discussions. How should one interpret the Last Supper?... they went so far as to send an emissary to Europe to ask Calvin to adjudicate on certain knotty points.

On might safely assume, I think, that these Calvinists were not insane, and that if they had not considered the Last Supper to be of ultimate importance they would not have traveled to Brazil in the first place. And in fact, the

[2] Lévi-Strauss, *Tristes Tropiques*, pp. 87–8.

The consciousness of the reformed clergy

Reformers' beliefs about the meaning of Communion were of great importance in determining the character of the ministry. If transubstantiation
occurs in and of itself, then only the priest or minister can conduct the rite;
he is, in fact, a kind of magician. If, on the other hand, the efficacy of
Communion depends on the faith and morality of the communicant, then
the minister is no longer elevated above the congregation by virtue of his
office. His authority as a clergyman must come from somewhere else, and
this authority will rest not on his capacity to perform certain rituals, but on
his capacities as a moral and spiritual teacher. Thus the ministers' statements about the Real Presence, while they may appear repetitive and wholly
irrelevant to the 'real,' i.e. social history of the Reformation were actually
quite germane to the mentality of its leaders and to the evolution of the
Reformed community as a spiritual elite group.

PROPHECY

We shall understand 'prophet' to mean a purely individual bearer of charisma,
who by virtue of his mission proclaims a religious doctrine or divine injunction
. . .The enterprise of the prophet is closer to that of the popular orator or political
publicist than to that of the teacher.

Max Weber

According to Weber, the prophet always stands outside the established
social order.[3] Unlike the priest, whose authority rests on service to a sacred,
systematized tradition, the prophet's authority stems solely from his own
personal gifts. His existence is therefore always a challenge to priestly tradition and the magical elements surviving in priestly ritual. But the prophet's
own acceptance by the people is contingent on what Weber called 'charismatic authentication, which in practice meant magic.'[4]

It must not be forgotten. . .that the entire basis of Jesus' own legitimation. . .was
the magical charisma he felt within himself. It was doubtless this consciousness
of power, more than anything else, that enabled him to traverse the road of the
prophets. During the apostolic period,. . .and thereafter, the figure of the wandering prophet was a constant phenomenon.

Not only does the prophet stand in opposition to the spiritual order of the
priesthood; he also stands outside the economic order of society. The prophet
cannot be a salaried preacher, although he may receive alms and shelter from
his followers. The regularization of his economic status and the codification
of his teachings are both symptoms of the transformation of a prophetic

---

[3] On Weber's analysis of prophecy see *The Sociology of Religion*, trans. E. Fischoff
(Boston, 1963), Ch. IV.
[4] *Ibid.*, p. 47.

movement into an ecclesiastical institution. Weber claimed that men like Luther, Zwingli and Calvin were not prophets because they did not claim to offer a substantially new revelation or to speak in the name of a special divine injunction. But Weber also stated that both the prophet and the priest were ideal types; in real life, elements of the prophetic leader might co-exist in the same individual with characteristics of the priest, the magician – even the bureaucrat.

Clearly, the vocation of the Reformed minister contained elements of prophecy. The original Reformers upheld the doctrine of the priesthood of all believers, but instead of abolishing the ministry as a specialized priesthood, they made the vocation to preach originate in a summons from God; the formal summons of the congregation and the decision of the individual to join the ministry were contingent on this original inspiration. 'True pastors do not rashly thrust themselves forward by their own judgement,' wrote Calvin, '[they] are raised by the Lord...The government of the Church by the ministry of the Word is not a contrivance of men, but an appointment made by the Son of God.'⁵ The ceremony of ordination, however necessary as a means of organizing the new church, was fundamentally no more than a commemoration of this original summons. The pastor Guy de Brès wrote that ministers are called by the church and ordained: 'but each one must await the call of God, so that, having a witness of their vocation, they are certain of being elected by the Lord.'⁶

The chief function of the Catholic clergy had been to perform rituals for the living and the dead; a pamphlet of 1566 denounced the priests as 'sacrificateurs.'⁷ But the minister's duties were pastoral. His function was to educate the community to the true word of God, and he did this not by conducting ceremonies but by preaching. However the minister did not act as a teacher or rabbi, communicating his personal wisdom and knowledge of tradition to his followers. In order for his preaching to he efficacious, God must literally speak through the minister:⁸

There is no power and efficacy inherent in the physical voice, unless God has penetrated into the [ministers'] souls by the authority of His Spirit and...has inwardly taught the minds of the men, and has breathed on them with His unseen breath, by the which the mist of the blind mind having been driven away, their souls may be able to direct their gaze towards the blazing beams of the heavenly light.

⁵ Calvin, Com. Ephesians, iv, ii. Quoted in J. L. Ainslee, *The Doctrines of Ministerial Order in the Reformed Churches of the Sixteenth and Seventeenth Centuries* (Edinburgh, 1940), p. 8.
⁶ Confession of 1561, Article XXXI.
⁷ *Brief Recueil*, n.p.
⁸ Viret, Vol. 1, Bk. I, Ch. v, p. 2a, quoted in Ainslee, *Doctrines*, p. 47.

During the hedgepreaching, Nicaise van der Schuere once paused in the middle of a sermon and said to his congregation, 'Sing a psalm, brothers, and praise God, so that the divine spirit may come back into me, for without it I will never preach adequately.'[9]

In short, every Reformed minister was ideally a prophet in the sense that his vocation and effectiveness were based on inspired preaching, not on the possession of secret knowledge or on the authority to perform prescribed rituals and sacrifices. The minister was also heir to the specific prophetic tradition of the Old and New Testaments. He might conceivably view himself as a direct descendant of the Old Testament prophets, with the license to chastize kings and to predict the destruction of tyrants and the triumph of the Chosen People. Calvin had written that prophets and ministers were sent by God,[10]

...that they might reduce the world to order: they are not to spare their hearers, but freely to reprove them whenever there may be need; they are also to use threatenings when they find men perverse...prophets and teachers may take courage and thus boldly set themselves against kings and nations, when armed with the power of celestial truth.

The Marian exiles, a group which included many Reformed ministers, were much given to prophetic denunciations of this kind, directed against Mary Tudor, and to predictions of the calamities which would surely befall England under the pagan yoke. 'Albeit I never lack the presence and plain image of my own wretched infirmity,' wrote John Knox, 'yet seeing sin so manifestly abound in all estates, I am compelled to thunder out the threatenings of God against obstinate rebels.'[11]

The Reformed ministers in the Netherlands also viewed their mission as a prophetic one. Certainly they were hostile to the established priesthood and to the magical elements surviving in priestly ritual. It was common to identify the Roman clergy with the Pharisees and the Calvinist ministers with the apostles of Christ, who were also hostile to the legalism of religious bureaucracies. Pieter Dathenus compared the corrupt, pagan church to Babylon, while Guy de Brès pleaded that Philip protect the Reformers from his Catholic clergy:[12]

[9] Van Vaernewijck, *Troubles*, I, p. 267.
[10] Calvin, Jeremiah lecture, 2, I, 44, quoted in Walzer, *The Revolution*, p. 6.
[11] Knox, *Works*, III, p. 338, quoted in Walzer, p. 99. It is difficult to determine exactly how widespread this prophetic literature actually was, since, with one exception, all of the quotations in Walzer's account are from Knox.
[12] On Dathenus: *Een christelijcke verantwoordinghe op die disputacie* (Antwerp, 1582), fol. 39. The quotation from de Brès is from the Confession of 1561, quoted in Frossard, *L'Eglise*, p. 294.

They are, I tell you, successors of the Scribes and Pharisees, who, under this title of Church, of the great holiness of the temple of God...have given themselves license to corrupt the true service of God. And for this cause the prophets banded together against them...[and] destroyed their synagogues and assemblies at Sodom, Gomorrah and Babylon.

In at least one case, these attacks on ecclesiastical magic and the corrupt bureaucracy of the Church were motivated less by outrage against spiritual deviations than resentment against a privileged social group. Thomas van Til, formerly the abbot of a monastery in the neighborhood of Antwerp and an eminent figure in the Church, composed a public letter or Apology after his abjuration in 1567.[13] Van Til explicitly cited the new bishoprics as his chief reason for abandoning Catholicism. The bishoprics, he wrote, have incorporated into themselves the wealthiest abbeys of Brabant, including his own:[14]

And they want to help themselves to the disadvantage of the country, to the shame of the godly religion...In the time of the Apostles, to covet a bishopric meant only that one wished to die a thousand deaths a day for the name of Christ...and ...to roam the whole world in hunger and thirst, naked and cold...persecuted, cursed, banished, beaten, mocked, cast from one city to another...These bishops are like cruel wolves...and bloodthirsty tigers...these theologians and new bishops.

The ministers were also concerned to verify their own inward calling as God's messengers, and the idea of suffering as a means of 'charismatic authentication' pervaded the writings of even the ministers who had not faced martyrdom:[15]

For we are glorified in tribulation, knowing that tribulation engenders patience, and patience experience,...for, being captured we are not oppressed; being indigent, we are not destitute; being persecuted, we are not abandoned; being beaten, are not lost, because, always and everywhere, we carry in our bodies the mortification of the Lord Jesus, so that the life of Jesus may be manifested in our bodies.

The Reformers rejoiced in their suffering as proof that they have embraced the doctrine of the prophets and apostles: '...we abandon our bodies to the fire, to the cross, to death. For then we know that we are children and heirs

---

13 Thomas van Til, *Seynd-brieff* (1568), n.p. Also see Em. Steenackers, 'L'Abbaye de Saint-Bernard, à Hemixem, et Thomas van Thielt, administrateur du dit lieu 1544–1567,' *Bulletin du cercle archéologique litteraire et artistique de Malines*, xxii (1912), pp. 31–48.
14 Van Til, *Seynd-brieff*, n.p.
15 Letter of Junius to the Walloon church at Frankfurt, from Schoenau, August 11, 1569. Quoted in Cuno, *Franciscus Junius*..., pp. 291–3.

of God, true servants and disciples of Christ.'[16] Pieter Dathenus wrote that it was permitted for the Elect to sing during persecution. Describing Daniel in the lion's den and the sufferings of other martyrs, Dathenus noted that they praised God with psalms; 'so may all Christians in such a condition do the same.'[17] Jacques de Buzère, pastor of the community at Sandwich, wrote to a colleague in London that the brothers wanted to know who had started a controversy about the right of ministers to flee from plague. They maintained that it was legitimate to flee from plague or persecution if it was without serious harm to the church or to a neighbor; the minister might still consider himself a member of the Elect.[18] When Guy de Brès was imprisoned after the siege of Valenciennes, he composed a series of letters to his family and the Reformed community which were undoubtedly intended for publication by Crespin.[19] The minister counseled his mother to imitate a Jewish woman who, during the Maccabean revolt, joyfully watched seven sons tortured to death, exhorting them to remain firm: 'They are sending me along the road where all the prophets, the Apostles, even God's own son, have passed. . .'[20] For de Brès, the Reformers' suffering did not merely stand as proof of Election; it enrolled them in a spiritual tradition which included the Jewish prophets, Christ and the Apostles, and culminated in themselves. Thus the ministers' constant references to biblical martyrs were not simply literary conventions, but attempts to create a spiritual lineage of greater validity than the formal apostolic succession which they had already denied.

In denouncing the Roman priesthood as a pagan bureaucracy and in exalting their own, personal charisma as preachers of the Word, the ministers were no different from the Protestant clergy in other countries. What set these men apart was their perception of the prophet as a social and political figure. Unlike the Marian exiles who railed against tyranny, the Netherlands ministers were restrained, almost passive in relation to the political order. The element of prophecy which emerges from their writings was not that of the prophet summoned by God to chastize a sinful people, but of a prophetic leader who is despised by the world and independent of all social bonds; at

[16] Guy de Brès, *Histoire notable*, Preface, n.p.
[17] Preface to Dathenus' Flemish translation of the psalms, in *Documenta Reformatoria*, ed. J. N. Bakhuizen van den Brink, I (Kampen, 1960), p. 248.
[18] Letter to Wingius, December 14, 1563, in Hessels, *Ecclesiae*, III, No. 72. Charles Ryckwaert also wrote to Reformers in Ypres, assuring them that it was not sinful to flee during persecution (letter to Olivier de Keeuwere, from Norwich, July 4, 1567, quoted in H. Q. Janssen, 'De hervormde vlugtelingen van Yperen in Engeland,' *Bijdragen tot de oudheidkunde en geschiedenis, inzonderheid van Zeeuwsch-Vlaanderen*, II (1857), p. 216.
[19] 'Procedures tenues à l'endroit de ceux de la religion du Pais Bas,' *Bibliotheca Reformatoria Neerlandica*, VIII (The Hague, 1911), pp. 491–643.
[20] *Ibid.*, p. 372.

times he is even portrayed as independent of the Reformed community. Thus Guy de Brès wrote that the Reformers must imitate the prophets and apostles; they must be wanderers, alienated from all society, abandoning father and mother, home, inheritance and life itself to follow Christ.[21] Herman Moded also compared himself to an apostle, maligned and persecuted, wandering from city to city.[22]

The image of the minister as a social outcast was most vividly expressed in the only sermon which has survived from the period of the hedgepreaching. In the spring of 1567, when the Reformers were ordered to cease public preaching, Isbrand Balck addressed the Calvinist congregation at Antwerp for the last time before fleeing the city. Taking his theme from a passage of Mark, Balck compared the Reformed church to the mustard seed: poor, insignificant and harshly treated, the church has always been maligned by those in power, but the church, like the mustard seed, would some day blossom over the whole world. 'As Paul's faith spread to Asia, Italy and Greece, so ours has spread to Zeeland, Holland and throughout Europe. Christians are the poorest and most ignorant of men, but they have been chosen by God nonetheless.' The ministers of the church were also compared to the mustard seed:[23]

Yes, the world says, what sort of ministers or preachers are these? They know no Latin, they are tradesmen, weavers and shoemakers. Should I listen to such people? No! No! They must all be Masters, Doctors and Licentiates from great and noble families, before I will give ear to them.

The ministers of God are weak and despised, and work with their hands; yet they are chosen by God.

The life of Andreas Baerdeloos, an obscure Flemish preacher from the city of Hondschoote (as interpreted by another Flemish pastor, Adrien van Haemstede), approximated to perfection the prophetic image of the minister as inspired and alienated from society, even from his own friends, yet forgiving those who persecute him.[24] Baerdeloos had made public exhortations long before he was called to the Reformed ministry, but his vocation to preach was not merely independent of the institution of the clergy; it was actually a threat to the Reformed community, which nonetheless accepted him as a brother. As a young student, Baerdeloos was so passionate in his attacks against both Catholics and Anabaptists that he forgot his own desires, 'and held all things as filth in order to win Christ.' His disputations with the enemy eventually became so heated that he was prevailed upon to leave his

[21] Guy de Brès, *Histoire notable*, Preface, n.p.
[22] Moded, *Apologie*, 1567; printed in Brutel de la Rivière, *Het leven*, p. 33.
[23] *Leerrede over Marcus 4*, p. 20.
[24] Van Haemstede, *Historie*, fol. 420.

fatherland (Flanders) and to seek refuge in Antwerp, where he approached priests and monks in the street, exhorting them to abandon their idolatry and godless life. Having become a danger to the clandestine Reformed community, he was sent to England, where he remained until he again felt called upon to preach in the summer of 1566. Baerdeloos was captured and executed in November, forgiving his enemies with his last words. The Catholic burgher, van Vaernewijck was certain that Baerdeloos would go to heaven as a reward for the inspired quality of his behavior and preaching.[25]

All of this suggests an attitude which was closer to Anabaptist thought than to the mentality of the Calvinists, as it has been conceived by Walzer and Kingdon. Isbrand Balck spoke of the minister of God as obscure, unlettered and poor, and of the church as a wandering band of initiates, though Balck himself had been an educated and respected member of the Reformed movement for several years. Guy de Brès and Herman Moded also referred to themselves as wanderers detached from family and society, although both had been prominent in the organization of the Netherlands church for a decade. Several ministers also spoke about an imminent apocalypse, in which the Elect, who have passively accepted their suffering, would triumph.[26] The ministers were radically different from the Anabaptists in identifying their own cause with that of the Jewish people; but again, this identification was with the Jews as a pariah people, a people who embraced the doctrine of passive suffering rather than that of the downfall of tyrants.[27]

. . .and we believe firmly that God. . .has a wonderful concern for all His creatures, but especially for His Church, which is His heritage, His chosen people,. . .and as much as they fall in the cross and in suffering, they are resolved that this comes to them by the will and ordinance of God.

The reasons for this attitude are clear enough. The Reformed ministers, most of whom grew up in the Netherlands, were heirs to a popular evangelical tradition which had not existed elsewhere, and witnesses to the highly successful, pacifist Anabaptism of Menno Simons. Guy de Brès, who wrote

---

[25] van Vaernewijck, *Troubles*, I, p. 270.

[26] In his polemic against the Libertines, Dathenus urged all true Christians to abandon the Roman Church, just as the Jews fled when pictures of the Roman emperor were placed in the Temple. The Christian must flee Babylon before it falls, or consent to martyrdom (*Een Christelijcke*, fol. 45).

[27] Guy de Brès, *Histoire notable*, Preface, n.p. According to Norman Cohn, one of the salient characteristics of the millennarian sects was their anti-Semitism, but in the chapters dealing with the Reformation period, the Jews are not discussed. In another work on Anabaptism, the author describes a sermon delivered at Strasbourg in 1545, in which the minister preached on the flight of the Jews from Egypt, comparing the Anabaptists to the Israelites (C.-P. Clasen, *Anabaptism. A Social History, 1525–1618* (Ithaca, N.Y., 1972), p. 93.

the longest and most virulent polemic against the Anabaptists, had several works by Menno in his personal library. Moreover, the ministers *were* wanderers, persecuted by the authorities, their worldly goods confiscated, during this early period. But most important, the ministers' reluctance to imitate the prophet as a radical political figure was a function of their confused political circumstances. The ministers in France made no use whatsoever of this kind of prophetic rhetoric; given their alliance with the local Huguenot nobility, it would have made little sense for them to adopt the language of social outcasts or to denounce the existing political order, since they clearly hoped to coopt it. The radical Marian exiles, on the other hand, were ostracized not only from their own country but from the orders of the Anglican church, and they had fled a ruler whose intentions toward them were irrevocably hostile. They clearly had nothing to lose by attacking the English government and advocating the execution of the Queen. In Philip, however, the Netherlands ministers faced an enigma; and in the Netherlands itself there was no tangible villain to equal Mary Tudor, only a vacillating Regent. In fact, the Calvinists were actually optimistic about the possibility of convincing Philip to allow Reformed worship in the Netherlands, and not without grounds. The Inquisition, though severe, was intermittent, and Antwerp, an important center of Reformed heresy, was relatively immune from persecution. The ministers' relationship to the local nobility was also ambiguous. Before 1566 the Netherlands nobility was committed neither to the Catholic nor to the Calvinist cause; the majority probably considered themselves liberal, Erasmian Catholics or Lutheran sympathizers. Thus the Netherlands ministers were not wholly outcasts, as the Marian exiles were, nor were they wholly committed to an alliance with the nobility against the Crown, as the Huguenots were. And so they portrayed themselves as suffering innocents, and ignored Calvin's mandate to 'set themselves against kings and nations...'

Only when the political situation had become polarized, and it was clear that Philip's intention was to exterminate the Reformers, did the ministers abandon the image of the suffering outcast and embrace that of the Reformer as a prophetic warrior for the faith. In 1557, while he was still in the Netherlands, Herman Moded wrote an Apology in which the Catholic rulers – not the clergy – were denounced as tyrants; Philip had become Pharaoh. The reader could only assume that William of Orange, to whom the Apology was dedicated, was assigned the role of Moses.[28]

We say...that these troubled times, quarrels, and other hardships...do not stem from the pure teaching of the Evangile, as publicly given, but from Jesus, a mighty king who wishes to overthrow the kingdom of Anti-Christ...Oh, would that I had the spirit of a Prophet or an apostle, so that I might not only help to

[28] *Apologie*, pp. 38, 42–3; printed in Brutel de la Rivière, *Het leven*.

raise up the fallen house of the Lord, but to raise all the fallen walls and gates, and bring the kingdom of Anti-Christ under the feet of his Father.

Adrien Saravia, who remained in Britain during the Troubles, addressed a pamphlet to the government in 1568.[29] The polemic began as a plea for toleration and an end to tyranny. Saravia described Alva's persecution: the Spanish soldiers, doomed to perish with Babylon, were accused of sodomy and of intercourse with beasts, while Alva was depicted as a biblical tyrant whom God would smite through his servant Moses – again personified in William of Orange. 'It was clear in Antwerp that the Prince of Orange had no will to shed blood, but that he was sent as Moses was sent...'[30] Pieter Dathenus added a new Preface to his translation of a contemporary account of the Spanish Inquisition, in which he alluded to Philip as a biblical tyrant and made the same predictions of the imminent destruction of the Netherlands and the victory of the Chosen People.[31] Jean Micheus, a young Flemish pastor noted for his mildness during the hedgepreaching, wrote to a colleague from Antwerp about the arrival of Alva's troops; he had no illusions about the project of Brederode or the promised intervention of the Germans. 'Only God can break the head of the serpent, the monster Leviathan...'[32] Thus spoke the ministers' new heroes, the Jewish prophets of the Old Testament, 'boldly setting themselves against kings and nations...armed with the power of celestial truth.'

COMMUNITY

The minister's vocation did not rest simply on a personal assurance of grace; he had also to be accepted by the congregation as a preacher and ethical teacher. Since his religious functions were chiefly concerned with the moral regeneration of the community, it was of great importance that he be able to define precisely what the community was. The Netherlands ministers felt themselves to be members of a gathered church, a 'fellowship of holy beings' in the midst of a pagan society, but they were also aware that, according to orthodox Calvinism, the church was identified with civil society as a whole. Did this mean that the community was an elite group of initiates, those already in possession of grace, or was the community all those to whom the minister preached in the hope of bringing them to a state of grace?

Since his ceremonial functions did not guarantee the minister's authority

[29] Adrianus Zaraphya, *Een hertgrondighe begheerte, vanden edelen, lanckmoedighen, hoochgheboren Prince van Orangien,* 1568.
[30] *Ibid.,* p. 16.
[31] Gonsalvius Montanus, *Historie vande Spaensche Inquisitie,* 1569.
[32] Meylan, 'Lettres inédites,' pp. 73–85.

over his congregation, it was equally important to define the minister's exact relationship to the community and to the consistory. What were his pastoral obligations? Was he subject to the decisions of the consistory, or was his authority in matters of ecclesiastical policy higher than theirs? Guy de Brès had included a strong defence of ministerial authority in his polemic against the Anabaptists: 'The minister is summoned directly by God, through the Church; his office does not depend on personal good works; he is the sole means of educating the laity to the Word of God, since the Word is conveyed through preaching.'[33] But how could the minister be certain that he had received a godly vocation to preach in a certain area if he were not told to preach there by the consistory? If his life were in danger, how could he be certain that God had meant him to be in danger? In short, theological questions and questions of ecclesiastical government were conceived as problems of group organization and obedience – not of the individual's salvation and justification, but of the means of verifying that salvation had occurred.

These observations are, I think, generally applicable to early Calvinist Reformed movements everywhere.[34] But for the Netherlands ministers, questions of group organization and problems of vocation and authority constituted a far more serious and explicit problem. The congregations of Netherlands Reformers, whether at home or in exile, bore little similarity to that of Geneva, where the physical community equaled the community of believers and where the ideal of moral control and of the organization of the consistory preceded the installation of Calvin. The Netherlands ministers faced the problem of almost continual movement; hence Nicaise van der Schuere insisted that Reformers' attestations from other churches be no more than one month old, since it often happened that new members were accepted on the basis of testimonials from an earlier date, their faith and good behavior having declined in the meantime.[35] Other ministers were concerned about what to do with religious refugees who came to them for help. Dathenus' urgent calls for pastoral assistance from Emden have already been described. 'Where is Paul's daily concern for the community of Christ?' he asked. 'The apostles often summoned one another to aid in strengthening the new communities and you, in good conscience, should do the same.'[36] The minis-

---

33 Guy de Brès, *La racine, source et fondement des Anabaptistes* (n.p., 1565), p. 95.

34 See Walzer, *The Revolution*, pp. 23–4, and J. T. McNeill, *History of Calvinism* (New York, 1967), pp. 216f.

35 Letter to the London church in the name of the Maidstone community, Hessels, *Ecclesiae*, III, No. 138 (December 24, 1569).

36 Letter to the Emden church, February 27, 1557, printed in van Schelven, *De Nederduitsche*, p. 404. Herman Moded and Pieter Hazard also wrote several letters dealing with religious refugees (on Moded: Brutel de la Rivière, *Het leven*, p. 15, and WMV 3 ser. II, pp. 1–5; the letters were written in 1561–2. On Hazard: van Schelven, ed.,

ters also worried about the threat of competing sects and the need to unify the community against their blandishments. Gaspar van der Heyden wrote to Emden while he was still preaching informally at Antwerp about his tiny church, his 'kleine, Bruydt of Gemeente.'[37] He was concerned about pro-liferating heretical sects and had begun composing a Confession which would explain God's mercy, free will and the sacraments. He also asked for argu-ments to use against the Anabaptists and Lutherans: 'Not that I am confused in these matters, but I need your help against our antagonists...for on these questions I can give no clear answer without you...'

Because the Netherlands communities were more difficult to define and to control than those elsewhere, the ministers were intensely preoccupied with theological issues which related to this 'problem of the community,' par-ticularly the sacraments of communion and baptism. As orthodox Calvinists, the ministers defined communion as a seal of grace already achieved, not as a mystical rite which conferred a state of grace on the participant. It was also defined as a seal of the community's solidarity, a shared supper. Guy de Brès' Confession of 1561 stated:[38]

Christ has ordained and instituted the sacrament of the holy communion, to nourish and sustain those whom He has already regenerated...that which is eaten is the true, natural body of Christ and his own blood; but the manner by which we eat it is not by the mouth, but by the spirit of faith. This banquet is a spiritual table.

Antonio Corro also defined communion as a visible symbol of a spiritual event, a culmination of faith obtained through the Holy Spirit. More impor-tant, the rite was a symbol of communal grace – a reconciliation of individual faults in the community:[39]

...each of the exterior and interior members [of the body] accommodates its office and function to the healing of a sick arm, so that one sees a marvelous harmony and liaison of each part with the others. This is vividly represented to

---

'Een brief van Pieter Hazaert,' NAvKG, n.s. VIII (1911), pp. 202–4. Also see a letter of Jacob Pontfort from Norden to Utenhove in London (July 20, 1565), asking for money to aid a widowed Reformer (Hessels, *Ecclesiae*, II, p. 244).

[37] E. Meiners, *Oostvrieschlandts kerkelyke geschiedenisse*, I (Groningen, 1738), pp. 365–70; letter of December 17, 1555.

[38] Confession of 1561, Art. xxxv (printed in Frossard, *L'Eglise*, p. 287). Other Confes-sions by ministers echoed this belief: Balck wrote that the Host is spiritual, not corporeal (1566); de Messere, that the Host is a symbol and there is no transsubstan-tiation (van Haemstede, *Historie*, fol. 437).

[39] Antonio Corro, *Epitre et amiable remonstrance d'un ministre de l'Evangile* (n.p., 1567), n.p.

us...in the celebration of holy communion...in order that each one set himself diligently to conserve the unity of the body of Christ, we support each other, learning to cover the faults of our brothers, to pardon their injuries...in the celebration of this holy sacrament.

Since the purpose of communion was to define the true limits of the Church, the question of admission to the communion table was of the greatest importance; hence the ministers' reluctance to accept the Lutheran dictum that sinners might receive the body and blood of Christ.[40] During the Troubles, when Calvinism supposedly became a mass movement, Jehan Leseur told his inquisitors that new members of the Reformed church were not required to take an oath of allegiance or to renounce Catholicism, but that at communion they must undergo an examination or catechism of faith, '...in order to know if they believe that spiritually and by faith...they receive or will receive the body of Jesus Christ without which confession they are not admitted.'[41]

The ministers viewed baptism not simply as a rite which cleansed the individual of all previous sins, but as a ceremony comparable to circumcision, in which the individual is distinguished from the world at large and is claimed as a member of the community:[42]

We believe and confess, that Jesus Christ... by his spilled blood has put an end to all other effusion of blood, and abolished circumcision which was made by blood; and in place of this has ordained the sacrament of baptism, by which we are received into the Church of God, and separated from all other peoples and foreign religions in order to be entirely dedicated to Him; bearing His mark and His sign...

In the baptism controversy which disrupted the refugee churches in Germany (described in Chapter 4), the ministers had to decide whether or not the children of Calvinist refugees might lawfully undergo Lutheran baptism rather than forego the sacrament altogether; they had to decide how broadly they might define the boundaries of the Reformed community without risking assimiliation into the larger community of the Lutherans. Dathenus

---

[40] On their reluctance to accept the new definition of communion in 1564, see Braekman, *Guy de Brès*, pp. 196–8. The ministers also argued with the Lutherans at Antwerp on the issue of communion in 1566; see the *Epitre* of Corro. Pieter Carpentier accused another Reformer of being too 'Lutheran' on the question of communion. Taffin and Bacquereel presented a pro-Lutheran Confession at Worms, but insisted that the Host must be received 'dignement' to be more than bread; they were told to leave the city at once (C. Sepp, *Drie evangeliedienaren uit den tijd hervorming* (Leiden, 1879), pp. 7–8).

[41] Desilve, *St. Amand*, p. 234 (Leseur's interrogation).

[42] Confession of 1561, Article xxxiv (Frossard, *L'Eglise*, p. 284).

maintained that compromise was not unorthodox in this emergency, and Calvin, as we have already seen, agreed with him.[43]

The baptism controversy in the London Dutch church was also a struggle to define the nature and limits of the community; but here the problem was conceived not as a threat to the integrity of the group from the outside, but as a threat to the authority of the group coming from above, in the person of the minister. The conflict began when the pastor Godfried Wingius ruled that a father, in order to baptize his child, had to submit a declaration by two prospective witnesses or godparents. The measure was intended as a guarantee that the parents were indeed orthodox Reformers and had a right to baptize their child into the community; given the continuous stream of refugees, it was not an unjustifiable proposal. Wingius was opposed by the deacons, who argued that all church offices, including that of minister, were charismatic; since they originated in God, they carried no intrinsic personal authority – therefore the minister had no spiritual mandate to impose his personal will on the community. In London, they maintained, the church council had set itself above the deacons; the consistory demanded unconditional obedience, and the deacons had been degraded below their rightful status; the ministers wanted to rule as men over the hearth of Christ, not as guardians of the community, and they used church discipline as a means to expand their own power. The deacons finally resigned *en bloc* and the matter was submitted to the English bishop, who favored Wingius. Three years later, in a final effort to reconstitute the community, two Flemish ministers, opponents of Wingius, submitted a proposal for the reconciliation of the London church on the question of godparents:[44]

As no peace or unity in religious affairs can be effected with any one before he is reconciled to God...we request everyone to accept and approve a basis of the doctrine of Christian liberty...preservation of Christian ceremonies, and polity in public worship and assemblies, power of the ministers and rulers of the community, of the obedience of subjects, or unity with the community, founded on the Bible and the opinion of all reformed communities...

The Reconciliation then stated that because the eldership and deaconship

[43] Ruys, *Pieter Dathenus*, p. 37, and *Calvini Opera*, xix, No. 3777. Dathenus also heard from the Antwerp Reformers on this question; they wanted to know if believers might have their children baptized by papists when no one else was there (*Calvini Opera*, xvi, No. 2963). Dathenus also participated in a dispute on baptism with Petrus Bloccius (see the letter to Bullinger of September 11, 1560, NAvKG, n.s. x (1913), pp. 328–43).

[44] The account is in Lindeboom, *Austin Friars*, pp. 47–8. Also see A. Sprenger-Ruppenthal, 'Ausdehnung und grenzen der befugnisse der diakonen in der Londoner Niederlandischen gemeinde 1560–1564,' *Sonderdruck Aus dem Jahrbuch der Gesellschaft für Niedersachsische Kirchengeschichte* No. 63, Bd. 1965. The proposal of 1569 is printed in Hessels, *Ecclesiae* ii, No. 93. Letter of April 26, 1569.

were apostolic offices entrusted by God alone, they could not be resigned except for very weighty reasons. Wybo also sumbitted a proposal for the government of the London Dutch church. No decisions were to be taken on matters of importance without the knowledge and consent of the assembly; the minister should conform to the vote of the consistory; finally, the church should adopt the English custom of having three people explain each text, the minister serving as a moderator.[45]

The ministers' involvement in theological controversies concerning communion and baptism was certainly not unorthodox; the point is that as orthodox Reformers they might have focused on other issues – predestination, for example. But although Weber believed that predestination was the most characteristic dogma of Calvinism, it was not mentioned in the 1566 edition of de Brès' Confession of Faith, which had been adopted for national usage.[46] In fact, given the complexity of orthodox Calvinist doctrines, the ministers might easily have focused on a great many issues other than communion or baptism. According to one modern scholar,[47]

The simple effort to utter the truths of the Bible may have made Calvin hesitate to force its meanings to a consistent pattern. If we try to represent the sovereignty of God as the ...principle of his theology, we have difficulty with his views of sin and evil...If we attempt to make his thought begin and end with pre-destination, we have to contend with a constant stress upon human responsibility... Indeed...we have been invited...to understand [his theology] as essentially composed of inharmonious elements...or conjunction of opposites.

Thus it was not so much a concern to define the mechanism of salvation that motivated the Reformers to quarrel about communion and baptism in London, in Frankfurt, in Metz and at home. Nor were the ministers simply imitating the behavior of Calvinists in other countries or indulging in factional disputes because they wanted power within their own communities. Their theological arguments were, I think, evidence of an anxiety to define, and to test the boundaries which set them apart from the rest of the world, and to maintain a balance between their desire to propagate the movement in the world, and their commitment to protect their own spiritual integrity.

It was certainly because of the Reformers' anxiety to define and to preserve

---

45 Hessels, II, No. 94. Wybo was one of those who advised the deacon party in 1564. He also opposed Wingius in the iconoclasm controversy. In fact, both quarrels were partly a function of a conflict between older and younger generations in the London community. But as we have seen, the generational split did not always parallel the split between radicals and moderates in the Reformed movement.

46 Oppenraaij, *La doctrine*, p. 70.

47 McNeill, *History*, p. 202. According to Walzer, the Puritans focused on the sovereignty of God and the presence of Satan; they were also strictly predestinarian (p. 103).

the community that they turned with such vehemence on one of their own ministers, Antonio Corro. Corro was a Spanish pastor, trained in Geneva, who had preached in Antwerp during the Troubles, where he had tried unsuccessfully to mediate between Calvinists and Lutherans on the issue of communion.[48] The following year he settled in London and attempted to reconstitute the Spanish refugee community. He was immediately prosecuted by the French and Walloon Reformers as heterodox and denied permission to preach, despite his attestations from churches in France and Antwerp and the support of Bishop Grindall. The actual evidence of heterodoxy was fragile, to say the least. Three years before, Corro had written to his compatriot in London, Cassiodoro de Reina, not knowing that de Reina had already been expelled for heterodoxy and immoral behavior. Corro's letter was confiscated, and it was found that he had requested certain religious works of an equivocal nature. Corro's own writings were also used against him; phrases like 'The true temple of Jesus Christ is. . .the heart of a faithful man' were interpreted as tending to the deification of humanity and the dilution of the Calvinist doctrine of the Elect.[49] Finally, having been declared a heretic and expelled from the Calvinist ministry, Corro actually did repudiate Calvinism; he later became a successful Anglican academic.

Why was Corro persecuted? The real issue, according to his biographer, was that Corro rejected the Church's claims to supervision and pressed for the creation of a Spanish conventicle within the larger congregation. Although he was attacked as a heretic, he was really excluded because he refused to become assimilated into the established Reformed community. When the pastor Etienne Marmier wrote to the bishop of London, asking for his intervention in the Corro case, he had less to say about Corro's spiritual deviance than the threat which he posed to the existence of the group. Corro's writings threatened 'the public repose of our whole church. . .for if. . .it is licit for a particular member to conspire against the whole body of the church. . .of what use in the world is the magistrate? What would be the use of laws? What would become of the public peace, and the repose of churches?'[50]

Wingius and Corro were not the only ministers who attempted to assert their personal authority over that of the consistory. Joris Wybo, a respected

---

[48] An account of Corro's life is in Hauben, *Three Spanish Heretics*, pp. 25–57.
[49] The works were the *Epitre*, and the *Tableau de l'oeuvre de Dieu* (1569). The *Epitre* dealt mainly with communion; the *Tableau* emphasized God's good will toward men. Wybo, accused of leniency in accepting the work, later published an attestation that it was read to him from a bad Flemish translation while he was ill, and that he was distressed at the emphasis on human action as a means to salvation; he also suggested that a special consistory be held to forgive him (Sepp, *Geschiedkundige nasporingen*, III (Leiden, 1872–5), pp. 165–7. The citation was dated July 15, 1569).
[50] July 22, 1569. Hessels, *Ecclesiae*, III, pp. 81–2.

minister of the Antwerp church for several years before the Troubles, refused an offer to become pastor to the London church in 1568, because he felt neither adequate for the task, 'nor inwardly moved to accept it.'[51] In Norwich, three Flemish ministers, Algoet, Ryckwaert and Balck, carried their disputes so far that all three were expelled from the community and forbidden to hold church offices in England.[52] Herman Moded traveled to London to submit the question of the legality of prison breaks to the consistory; when London disapproved of violence, Moded stopped corresponding with the London church.

Other pastors, trained in Geneva or Emden or London, clearly found it difficult to submit to the dictates of local consistories in the Netherlands which they themselves had founded. Thus Adrien Saravia, who had studied theology in London, left his community at Antwerp in 1563 without informing the consistory. Still other ministers resolved this problem of authority by deferring entirely to the consistory. Gaspar van der Heyden refused to take any important action without the approval of the mother church at Emden, 'so that we have no false prophets.' And Jehan Cubus, when he was asked to return to the Antwerp church, responded, 'I think with you that Antwerp should be provided with a minister, but in my opinion *you* ought to send me, for if I went of my own accord, and encountered any danger, I could not sufficiently console myself and feel sure that the Lord had sent me.'[53]

LANGUAGE

According to Weber's ideal type, the prophet was never a member of the priestly class or, indeed, of any part of the social establishment. But many of the Netherlands ministers had been humanist clerics or academics before their conversion. As educated pastors, they did not cease to identify themselves as intellectuals; they did not choose to stand apart from the cultural establishment as the biblical prophets had done. In their few serious theological works the ministers tried, as it were, to beat the Catholics at their own game. The *Baton de la Foi* by Guy de Brès was an exercise in erudition, '. . .composed and gathered faithfully from the ancient doctors' own books. . . Now [you can] see which of us are the enemies of the fathers.'[54] The ministers also corresponded with theologians of far greater eminence than themselves. Dathenus and van der Heyden both wrote to Calvin on matters

[51] *Ibid.*, II, No. 86; letter to the elders of the London church from Emden, March 2, 1568.
[52] Burn, *The History*, p. 198, and Moens, *The Walloons*, p. 31.
[53] Letter of May 11, 1575. Hessels, *Ecclesiae*, II, No. 336.
[54] *Baton de la foi, Epitre*, pp. 75, 80.

of church discipline and theology, while Antonio Corro felt that his literary activities were even more important than preaching; in 1563, while a refugee pastor in France, Corro wrote to a colleague in England that he required proof of their progress on a Spanish translation of the Bible in order to mollify the local Reformers, who had accused him of neglecting his pastoral duties.[55]

In short, the ministers continued to write in Latin, to attend book fairs, to discuss the problems of publishing, and to gossip.[56] In 1566 Antonio Corro addressed a polemic to his colleagues at Antwerp, accusing them of intellectual vanity in publishing so many books:[57]

...I fear that your intention is...to have the occasion to send your books to the next fair at Frankfurt, rather than zeal for the pacification of our afflicted Church ...wanting the world to know that you have such a great facility in composing books, that in one evening after dinner you can scribble more pages than the printer can turn out in a week.

Herman Moded was certainly vain; he always carried with him a testimonial letter from the University of Copenhagen in recognition of his services as chaplain.[58] This sort of humanist conceit was also evident in the poetry produced by the former librarian Jean Taffin, 'Aux seigneurs gouverneurs des Pays-Bas.'[59] A sample:

> Est-ce sédition que le Placcart du Roy
> N'est sy bien observé que la divine Loy?
> Le Peuple est-il mutin que le salut de l'âme
> Ne veult assubjectir à l'édict de Madame?

Like other humanists, Taffin enjoyed puns; witness the motto he adopted after his conversion – 'A Dieu ta vie; à Dieu ta fin.'

But these humanist activities formed only a part – in fact the lesser part – of the ministers' literary vocation. The ministers believed that the Word of God was to be made accessible to all; hence they rejected Latin and, like Luther, helped to create the vernacular as a literary language. They translated the Bible and the psalms into French and Flemish and wrote public letters

---

[55] Hauben, *Three Spanish Heretics*, pp. 14–16. This happened in 1563.

[56] e.g., Dathenus' letter to Utenhove from Frankfurt, April 11, 1560, (Hessels, *Ecclesiae*, II, No. 41): 'I'm being brief because I'm busy with the fair. The French broils are gradually settling down; but François [Perussel] surpasses himself by daily impudence. Calvin wrote to me this fair and depicted this wretch in his true colors. I congratulate Gisbet Wolff on his money, and hope that, by his continuous integrity, he will show that it has not been stolen.'

[57] Corro, *Epitre*, pp. 75, 80.

[58] Moded, *Apologie*, p. 33.

[59] Printed in the *Bibliophile Belge*, IV (1879), pp. 37–42.

and songs which were peddled at the hedgepreaching.[60] Wingius wrote about the difficulties of publishing his translation of the New Testament in 1557:[61]

There is nothing but misery here. I am weary with the blindness and ingratitude of men, and nearly all my hope that the purity of the Gospel, to which we have contributed so much, could be promoted in the Netherlands, has fallen to the ground. The printing of our New Testament has caused me great and uninterrupted vexation, to such an extent that it has made me seriously ill...

Everyone complained of its long title, which deterred the Anabaptists, who 'had been waiting here for our sale, as well as others, from buying our version.' Wingius fretted that over one thousand copies having been sent to the borders of Flanders, the sale was damaged by a page being printed upside down. '...then again everybody complained that the language was patchwork;...others considered it obscene; others said it was unintelligible on account of its readings differing from all other versions.'[62] Jean Taffin, who had been in contact with the Plantin publishing house while still the librarian of Granvelle, also published works of popular theology: psalms in translation, a *Briefve Instruction Pour Prier*, treatises on the sacraments and sermons, all printed in French.[63]

What was the effect of the Reformers' preoccupation with language? On the one hand, their interest in the vernacular made them and their congregations more parochial, for although the Reformers might travel and live abroad, their lives did not become more cosmopolitan. On the contrary, language differences, accentuated by the insistence of the ministers on preaching and writing in the vernacular, meant that the Reformers lived in a cultural ghetto. The variety of local dialects made this true even in Germany, whose language was similar to Flemish. Pieter Dathenus wrote to Emden from his refugee church in Frankfurt in 1557, complaining that the members of his congregation 'know no Latin, nor even any French; whenever I must have dealings with the Government, or with the ministers of the French church or the English church, I find myself completely alone.'[64]

---

60 The most influential of these works was Dathenus' Flemish translation of the psalms (1566), taken from the texts of Marot and Beza. Dathenus also translated the Heidelberg catechism and a new version of the Calvinist liturgy with van der Heyden. The catechism was accepted for general use at the Emden synod of 1571 (Ruys, *Pieter Dathenus*, pp. 244, 247–8).

61 Letter to Utenhove from Emden, April 13, 1557, Hessels, *Ecclesiae*, ɪɪ, No. 21.

62 *Ibid.*, ɪɪ, No. 25.

63 C. de Clercq, 'Jean et Jacques Taffin, Jean d'Arras et Christophe Plantin,' *De Gulden Passer* xxxvɪ (1958), pp. 125–36.

64 Letter of February 24, 1557, printed in Meiners, *Oostvrieschlandts*, p. 378. Dathenus' reason for composing a new liturgy was that he felt alien from the one used in the London Flemish church, and wanted one for his own community. He also found difficulties in uniting with the French church in the use of the psalms, even though

Antonio Corro's main purpose in going to France was to constitute a Spanish-speaking Reformed community; the French ministers were in turn hostile to the Spanish Reformers, and everyone else was hostile to the French.[65]

The Netherlands ministers thus found themselves in a difficult and para-doxical situation. As authors and as leaders of refugee churches abroad, they were members of an international ecclesiastical elite, and – as intellectuals and elitists – they stood somewhat apart from their communities, whose members could understand neither their neighbors nor the local ministers. In this sense the ministers formed a sort of international priesthood, privy to a secret language and to secret knowledge about the Reformed movement as a whole. But because of their own preoccupation with the vernacular and because of the needs of the refugee communities, the ministers were also forced to be narrow-minded and chauvinistic, preoccupied with their own national group rather than the ecumenical church. Thus the effect of exile was not to estrange the ministers from their homeland, but to bind them more closely to it; they would, I think, have disavowed the statement made by an English exile: 'Oh Zurich, Zurich, I think more of Zurich in England than ever I thought of England while I was in Zurich.'[66] On the contrary, the existence of language as a barrier between groups probably contributed to the Reformers' success in maintaining their sense of national identity during the years of exile and in making them all the more eager to return to the Netherlands in 1566.

In another sense, the ministers' preoccupation with the vernacular made them more broad-minded. They wanted to create a genuinely popular move-ment – not merely a popular following, but an audience capable of participat-ing in the Reformed cult by singing, receiving the Word, and studying Scripture and the catechism. Hence the bulk of their writings were anti-elitist and geared to a popular audience. Dathenus asserted that all the essen-tials of true belief were contained in the Psalms, and Guy de Brès, in his *Remonstrance*, defined the Reformed movement in the simplest possible manner: 'And those who declare that they have such an intention and desire, and are held to be virtuous people, believing in God, are recognized for

the two churches agreed on theological questions (Ruys, *Pieter Dathenus*, pp. 49, 228). At a much later date, Isbrand Balck wrote from Danzig to the Dutch church at London, complaining that the Flemish Reformers could not understand high German (Hessels, *Ecclesiae*, II, p. 843, No. 244, Dec. 12, 1590).

[65] Letter of Beza to Johannes Cognatus, March 11, 1569, referring to the writings of Corro: 'You see that Satan endeavors to ruin you by the same wiles by which he has destroyed other French refugee churches, namely by the opinion rooted in some people that wherever the French go they bring discord and tumult with them.' (Hessels, *Ecclesiae*, II, No. 92).

[66] Walzer, *The Revolution*, p. 116.

members of our Church, and admitted to the holy Communion...' In his 'Oraison au Seigneur' de Brès composed a most eloquent disparagement of worldly education and worldly wisdom:[67]

Give us, oh Lord, not the wise men of this world, nor those who teach things which do not aid in the salvation of souls, and who seek to speak pompously, searching for themselves, but...true...ministers...who propose to us Jesus Christ...who dwell only on the preaching of the cross of the Evangile, which is the folly which surmounts and confounds all the wisdom of the world.

POLITICS

The ministers accepted Calvin's definition of the state as a repressive institution, ordained by God as a means of bridling the sinful nature of the individual. 'I recognize the civil magistrate,' wrote Godfried Wingius, 'and I believe that it is a divine ordinance that, by the labor of chiefs, the good are defended and the wicked repressed, and thereby piety, honesty and peace preserved among men.'[68] Pieter Dathenus devoted the first chapters of his polemic against the Libertines to a defense of law: he admitted that there is no law that can ensure salvation; but, he insisted, law exists in order to give man knowledge of his own weakness.[69] Guy de Brès maintained that a repressive government is indispensable at all time. 'Don't we know well enough that men naturally love themselves...looking out for their own convenience...?'[70] The ministers also embraced the Calvinist principle of obedience to the magistrate. 'Everyone should render obedience, honor, reverence, assistance, taxes, tributes...to the magistrate,' wrote Wingius. 'Subjects owe all this to wicked as well as to pious magistrates.'[71] De Brès thought that the magistrate obeyed God's will when he imposed the death penalty to protect law and order; in 1567, on the scaffold, he uttered a prayer for the public authorities.[72]

But the ministers qualified this doctrine of total allegiance to the magistrate, as Calvin had done, by claiming that the magistrate was obligated to protect the true religion. De Brès asserted that just as it is the duty of a good Christian to participate in public life, so it is the duty of the governor to be a good Christian. He also reserved for the consistory absolute authority in matters of

---

[67] Guy de Brès, 'Oraison au Seigneur,' printed in E. Braekman, *Guy de Brès: Pages Choisies* (Brussels, 1967), p. 20.

[68] Confession of Wingius, August 6, 1570, printed in Hessels, *Ecclesiae*, II, No. 102, pp. 341f.

[69] Dathenus, *Een Christelijcke verantwoordinghe*, fols 10–19.

[70] Guy de Brès, *La racine*, p. 813.

[71] Wingius, Confession of 1570.

[72] 'Procedures,' p. 639.

ecclesiastical discipline. Conversely, pastors were to remain aloof from politics; only the lesser magistrate had the right of resistance to the government.[73] Wingius agreed:

If anyone constitutes himself a lord or magistrate, against the laws and privileges of his country, or, being a magistrate, robs his subjects of their privileges and liberty or oppresses them, the ordinary magistracy should resist him, but in a legitimate way, so that there may be no occasion for sedition or rebellion.[74]

All of this was a straightforward adaptation of Calvin's political doctrines. What set the ministers apart from their orthodox colleagues in other countries was not their political ideology, but the unique political circumstances which affected their behavior. In France, as we know, the Reformed clergy was closely allied with the Huguenot nobility, and Huguenot writings emphasized the 'ordinary right' which the nobility had, as an alternative power to the crown, to fight for the Reformed cause.[75] But if the Huguenots were saints in office, the Marian exiles were, as Walzer put it, saints out of office, and the English ministers did not defer to the nobility as they did in France. As free men, under no jurisdiction, holding no office either in a church or in public life, the politics of the English ministers were more radical than those of their French colleagues.[76]

Enough has been said about the experience of the Netherlands ministers at home and in exile to show that they were in no way free men. Their communities in Germany and France were physically insecure, and even in England, where the local Reformers were benevolent, the refugees were in no position to advocate revolutionary activity unless they were willing to risk expulsion by the bishop of London. Their attitudes, in the political sphere at least, were therefore more complex – and more confused – than those of their colleagues elsewhere. My impression is that the apparent contradictions which appear in their writings are less a function of our lack of available sources, or of duplicity on the ministers' part, than of simple hedging, an absence of any clear political stance. Thus de Brès' letter to the Tournai magistrates, following the *chanteries* of 1561, deplored both the persecution and the public demonstrations; it was not the Reformers' place to revenge themselves on the inquisitors, but God's.[77] The letter also contained what seemed to be a veiled threat to the magistrates: 'If the people are not treated with greater gentleness. . .we fear that a terrible confusion will occur in all the cities of the realm.'[78] But the 'veiled threat' was actually an expression of de Brès'

[73] On de Brès' legalism, see his *Remonstrance*, n.p.
[74] Wingius, Confession of 1570.   [75] Walzer, *The Revolution*, p. 88.
[76] *Ibid.*, pp. 106–7, 185.   [77] Moreau, *Histoire du protestantisme*, p. 183.
[78] Braekman, *Guy de Brès*, p. 154.

inability to come to an agreement with the local consistory in formulating a policy regarding public demonstrations.

The ministers also hedged on the important question of religious toleration. De Brès maintained that the government had a duty to protect the true religion, but he was unwilling to advocate the execution of those who opposed the true faith, even the Anabaptists; the church would do better to extirpate idolatry and institute public preaching of the true word of God, and so win the simple-minded Anabaptists back to the fold. Elsewhere de Brès wrote eloquently, if somewhat vaguely, of his desire for religious toleration:[79]

And with regard to our neighbors. . .what do we ask, but to. . .live in quietness and friendship with them, wishing them true prosperity? All. . .that we desire, is that we have the holy word and that we be able to live according to it.

But in *La racine*, de Brès advocated a policy of clemency toward religious deviance only as a means of discovering what the true word was; public preaching and public debate by all sects would, he asserted, make this unequivocally clear. And once idolatry was banished, 'those who were raising the sword one against the other, when they are converted and have been received in the communion of the Church, will meet together in a true unity.[80] Religious toleration as an ultimate goal was therefore inconceivable.

De Brès' biographer tells us that the minister was unique in possessing an irenic spirit; in his political attitudes, de Brès was more an Erasmian than a Calvinist.[81] Another minister, François Junius, expressed similar views in his *Brief Discours*: public disputations would make the true word of God evident to all and obviate the need for the persecution of heretics – one historian credits Junius with the spirit of a *politique*.[82] But while both ministers were certainly Erasmian in spirit, neither was convincing in his espousal of religious toleration. De Brès believed that public disputations were useful not to control conflict but to end it, while Junius, despite his weak arguments for toleration (the Turks had it), could only conceive of the triumph of the Reformed cult; the thrust of his argument was that Calvinist preaching should be accepted as God's exclusive word. Certainly no minister openly asserted that the Reformer should serve both God and Baal. Jean Taffin, another moderate pastor, expressed this fundamental refusal to compromise with the Catholics in a poem addressed to the governors of the Netherlands:[83]

[79] *Oraison*, n.p.
[80] de Brès, *La racine*, p. 826.
[81] Braekman, 'La pensée politique de Guy de Brès,' BSHPF, cxv (1969), p. 18.
[82] J. Lecler, *Toleration and the Reformation* (London, 1960), p. 198. Lecler thinks the pamphlet was by François Baudouin; but he gives no evidence, and it is elsewhere attributed to Junius.
[83] *Bibliophile Belge*, iv, p. 38.

The consciousness of the reformed clergy

Si l'Eternel est Dieu, sy ne le suivez vous?
Et sy Baal est Dieu, rengez vous à luy tous.
Vous ne pouvez servir tout d'un coup à deux maistres,
Ny advouer ensamble et ministres et prêstres:
La Messe Romanesque et Cène du Seigneur
Jamais ne marcheront d'une égale teneur.

The Reformers were not only uncertain about the question of toleration by Catholic governments; they also expressed confusion on the question of their own toleration of other Reformed sects. Dathenus wrote an account of the persecutions at Frankfurt in 1563 after his expulsion from the city, in which he supported co-existence with the Lutherans and maintained that he was not hostile to the Augsburg Confession.[84] But his longest polemical work was written against compromisers, and in 1567 another Netherlands minister, Rhetius, agreed with Dathenus in *opposing* Orange's position that the Calvinists should accept the Augsburg Confession.[85] In fact, the only polemical work which was a genuine advocacy of religious toleration, whether among Reformers and Catholics or Reformers and other Reformers, was the *Epitre* by Antonio Corro, published in 1567. Corro wrote that the pulpit had become a place of dissension; 'there are some among you, who in full assembly with injurious and angry words, call the other ministers of the Evangile heretics, sacramentarians, rebels against the magistrate, and people unworthy of being supported in a republic...' But Corro's pamphlet, which his biographer rightly described as 'quasi-*politique*,' had absolutely no influence either with Orange, who sympathized with the Lutherans, or with the Calvinists, who later used it as evidence of Corro's heterodoxy.

Given the Reformers' experience in exile, where disputations had not only served to obscure the true Word but to lead to physical expulsion from the community, it is understandable that the ministers' advocacy of toleration was less than strident. It becomes even more understandable when we remember the attempt of de Brès and several other ministers to reach an accord with William of Orange in 1564; having finally convinced the Netherlands consistories to accept the project of unification with the Lutherans, the ministers were opposed by Beza and the project came to nothing.

Iconoclasm was another issue which confounded the ministers. All agreed with Calvin, and with many humanists, that the use of images was dangerous; but when it came to their actual destruction, the ministers were divided in opinion. Herman Moded denied personal responsibility for the

---

[84] Dathenus, *Kurtze und wahrafftige erzehlung* (1563), quoted in Ruys, *Pieter Dathenus*, pp. 260f.

[85] Ruys, p. 66. In 1566 Dathenus cited the polemic against compromisers (*Een Christelijcke verantwoordighe*) as proof of his orthodoxy, and maintained that he had never advocated baptism in the Roman church (p. 258).

iconoclasm of 1566, reserving that honor for the biblical prophets; 'Thus did God, not from my commands, but from the express summons and witness of His bold words, ...command obedience.'[86] Other ministers, Taffin and Junius among them, opposed the image-breaking as seditious, and their arguments continued even after the ministers' expulsion from the Netherlands and the arrival of Alva. During the Engelram affair (see Chapter 2), Philip Garcia was cited before the consistory for declaring in a prophecy that Christ had driven the money-changers from the temple on his private authority, and that his example should be followed by the Reformers.[87] Wingius countered that the duty of the subject is to obey the wicked magistrate, that those who opposed the inquisitors were seditious, and the subjects who attempted to assume the magistracy by the destruction of images and statues were also seditious. 'For it is the Lord's to alter and reform kingdoms, to exalt or humiliate kings, to convert the wicked or to substitute pious magistrates.'[88]

If there was one theme which characterized the ministers' attitude with regard to politics, it was less the desire to become the dominant religious cult by challenging the secular and ecclesiastical powers, than to achieve a sense of legitimacy within the larger society. Hence the thrust of almost every political polemic, whether addressed publicly to Philip or privately to the consistory, was toward the importance of maintaining law and order and a hierarchy of political authority within the community. Dathenus' defence of law, quoted earlier, was typical of the Reformers' attitude on this point; nowhere could we find a statement which paralleled that of Knox:[89]

...neither the consent of the people, process of time, nor multitude of men, can establish a law which God shall approve...It appertaineth to you, therefore, to ground the justness of your authority, not upon that law which from year to year doth change but upon the eternal providence of God...

The Netherlands ministers could not conceive of violence outside the context of law, even when they were sympathetic to the idea of freeing prisoners or breaking images. In 1561, Wingius wrote to the London church from Flanders, asking for advice on the legality of using violence to aid Reformers.[90] He also wished to know whether inquisitors and their officers should be recognized by prisoners as magistrates who are not to be resisted.

[86] Moded, *Apologie*, p. 38.
[87] Garcia later retracted his statement, and said in the consistory that Christ had done this as King and high priest (WMV, I, I, pp. 186-7).
[88] Wingius, Confession of 1570.
[89] Knox, *Works*, IV, p. 49. quoted in Walzer, *The Revolution*, p. 102.
[90] Hessels, *Ecclesiae*, II, No. 100.

You could perhaps also send us some maxims from imperial law whereby we might warn the blind magistracy as to their duty and office, and induce them to greater reflection regarding religion and the like from papal law, wherewith we may encounter the papists, and remove their unjust sword.

During the iconoclasm, François Junius was approached by a local Reformer in Ghent, who asked his advice on the legality of the image-breaking. Junius replied that the Reformers must act according to their vocation: Since they were not magistrates, they had no mandate to act as public officials, and as private persons the Reformers had no right whatsoever to break images. Junius added: 'The fact that you came to me for advice proves that God has not given you any extraordinary right to commit violence.'[91] A more radical pastor, Peregrine de la Grange, was interrogated on the contacts of the nobility and the Valenciennes rebels in 1567.[92] He was asked why the Reformers insisted on the convocation of all the Knights of the Fleece or of the Council of State; '[He] answered that it was a matter which concerned the entire country and, as such, must be resolved by the governors of the country in common...'

The ministers' concern for legality also explains their obsession with the Anabaptists, whom they viewed not only as religious deviants but as political anarchists – enemies of law and order. De Brès wrote that the purpose of the Confession of 1561 was to convince the magistrate that the Calvinists were both orthodox and orderly, unlike the Anabaptists. And de Brès' longest work, a tract of over eight hundred pages, was a polemic against the Anabaptists. Here the minister assumed the role of an outraged cleric, fearful of the Anabaptists' power to seduce the ignorant and to level wholesale attacks against existing institutions. In fact, the arguments of *La racine* are reminiscent, both in tone and in content, of those uttered by the Catholic Peter Frarin against the Calvinists in his oration of the same year: the Anabaptists appeal to the ignorant; they deny legitimate political authority; they quote Scripture indiscriminately, 'just as if they had eaten the Bible,...the

---

[91] Junius, *Autobiography*, quoted in Fris, *Notes pour servir à l'histoire des iconoclastes à Gand* (Ghent, 1909), p. 49. In a quarrel in the Frankfurt church (1569) on the improper use of church funds, Junius wrote that parties should consider whether this was a civil or ecclesiastical matter, 'car si elle est civile...ilz n'ont point d'occasion de s'en mesler...' (Cuno, *Fraciscus*, p. 293).

[92] Ch. Paillard, 'Interrogatoires politiques de Peregrine de la Grange,' BSHPF, xxviii ser. 2 (1879), p. 228. Dathenus, another radical minister, wrote to the magistrates of Ypres after the Reformers had already taken over the churches in 1566: 'I have been to the houses of several notables and found no one at home. Having taken oaths at Antwerp and Ghent, and protesting that I am not a rebel, I proceeded to preach.' (Diegerick, p. 8). The most explicitly radical minister was Ambroise Wille, who tossed a letter to the crowd at Tournai, threatening 'un apparent sedition' if a minister was harmed (Hocquet, *Tournai*, p. 320).

poor people...being ravished in admiration to hear so much Scripture...'[93] They accuse the Calvinist clergy of immorality, and they seduce the ignorant by their capacity for martyrdom :[94]

...(the Anabaptists) secretly insinuate themselves with a marvelous appearance of sanctity, and of mortification of the flesh, walking as if they were in the religion of the angels...they assail...those who are not greatly versed in Holy Scripture, and all this in the absence of ministers...

Other ministers echoed these denunciations of the Anabaptist as anarchist. 'And there are no more seditious people in the world,' wrote Junius, 'than those who have been seen as Anabaptists in Münster...'[95] Dathenus gave a long account of the Münster uprising in order to contrast the Anabaptist heresy with the orthodox Reformed church; 'The Anabaptists are a new church. They use the Bible, but so do all heretics. They fool simple people.' 'Watch out for false prophets who come to you in sheep's clothing, when they are really wolves.'[96]

In short, while the Netherlands ministers embraced the political doctrines of orthodox Calvinism, their political attitudes were more complex, less one-sided and fanatical than those of their colleagues elsewhere. For the Netherlands ministers, the Calvinist doctrine of obedience to the government was a buttress for their position as defenders of the conservative virtues of obedience to authority and to existing institutions, while the doctrine of resistance through the lesser magistrate was perceived by the ministers not as a justification for revolution, an opportunity to begin questioning the distinction between the duties of the public figure and the private individual, but as an excuse to condemn violent activities by private persons. Certainly their writings do not indicate that Calvinist political ideology inspired the uprising of 1566; rather, it seems that the repression of Alva's new regime forced the Reformers to adopt a more openly revolutionary stance – a posture which some found difficult to sustain even after their exile to foreign churches and the beginning of the Dutch Revolt.

II

Max Weber believed that there are a number of social and spiritual values, like those of the Confucian literati and the biblical prophets, which are absolutely irreconcilable; there can be no ultimate synthesis, either spiritual or practical, between the type of tolerant educator and the religious fanatic. Many studies of Reformed movements have also assumed the existence of ultimately irreconcilable values. Their authors have distinguished between

[93] de Brès, *La racine*, p. 5.   [94] *Ibid.*, pp. 4–5.
[95] Junius, *Brief discours*, p. 19.   [96] Dathenus, *Een Christelijcke*, fol. 65.

apostolic, sectarian religious cults, whose relationship to the political authority ranged from indifferent to hostile, and the 'magisterial' Reformation, comprising those members of the educated Establishment who had the economic and intellectual wherewithal to create a disciplined movement capable of infiltrating the political structure – or of challenging it. Thus Walzer described the Calvinist saint:[97]

...the elective affinity of aristocrats, ministers, gentlemen, merchants and lawyers with the Calvinist and Puritan ideologies did not lie only in the anxiety they all shared, but also in the *capacity* they all shared to participate in those 'exercises' that sainthood required. They were the 'sociologically competent'...The Calvinist faith did not appeal to men, however anxious, below the level of such competence. Laborers and peasants were more likely...to adopt some more pacifistic or chiliastic faith whose promise did not depend upon their own hard work...

But the mentality of the Netherlands clergy, as I have described it, comprised a whole series of paradoxes or opposed values. The ministers were educated in the tradition of the Erasmian humanist – and in that of the biblical prophets. Their writings convey an image of the minister as a cosmopolitan intellectual – and as an unlettered exile. They carried on an international correspondence, and they were certainly conscious of their participation in a movement of international proportions – but they were also narrow-minded and chauvinistic. They spoke in authoritarian, conservative tones – and in the tones of the apostles. Their literary images were reminiscent of ancient Judaism, of Anabaptism and of established Roman Catholicism. One might even venture to say that the only image which is missing from the ministers' early writings is that of the Calvinist revolutionary saint.

In fact, there was nothing new in the appearance of self-styled prophets harking back to biblical legends, nor in the fact that these modern prophets were also educated, nor in their emphasis on language – the communication of the pure Word of God – nor in their attempt to gain the patronage of the lay nobility. What *was* new, and what caused the ministers immense difficulty, was the potential, chiefly through printed literature, of generating a wide-spread popular Reformation, while preserving the integrity of the original, elitist Reformation. The original prophets were elitist; the millennarian movements were popular; the Anabaptists were sectarian. The Reformed ministers, in trying to maintain their integrity as elitists and as popular leaders, were less decisive and, in the short run, less successful than their predecessors – above all, they were contradictory in their behavior. One finds van Haemstede defying the consistory in order to preach independently and, after his excommunication, trying for the rest of his life to be reinstated by the consistory. One finds the ministers in England ruling that communicants

[97] Walzer, *The Revolution*, p. 309.

must enter the church by a special door, and then organizing mass meetings in Flanders for group singing and communion. But there is one theme which seems to characterize each of these contradictory elements: the search for a new authority.

The problem of authority, whether it was expressed as the need for patronage, for proof of Election, or for a standard of church discipline, was fundamentally an existential problem. The Reformation reopened the question, 'How am I to know I am saved?'; and since the believer had to supply the answer himself, through his own faith, the Reformation obviously led to a form of individualism. But this new condition must have resulted not only in a new freedom of conscience, but in a crisis of conscience; the desire to entrust the responsibility for assuring one's salvation to something outside oneself. The letters of martyrs written in prison often betrayed this fear of not possessing the internal strength to remain calm under torture, and the need to derive assurance of Election through membership in the group.

This question of authority was not only a spiritual one. For Reformed ministers everywhere, the Reformation also raised the problem of finding physical protectors. But the problem of establishing a position vis-à-vis the political authority was surely more acute in the case of the Netherlands ministers, because external circumstances did not force them into an unequivocal position either as adherents or as opponents of the local magistracy. In every sense, then, the ministers were confronted by this problem of finding and defining a new authority; they more than anyone, because it was the authority of the clergy which suffered most in the Reformed cult. Hence the minister looked to mother churches in Emden, London and Geneva, attempted to placate local magistrates even as they took over their churches, and quarreled about the legality of the iconoclasm long after it had been accomplished in fact, and the ministers had been exiled as rebels.

The ministers articulated this problem of authority in legalistic terms; they perceived issues which were fundamentally spiritual as legal issues. The subject of iconoclasm was raised in consistory meetings solely for the purpose of asserting that private persons had no legal mandate to break images; according to the London consistory, Christ himself expelled the money changers from the temple in his capacity as a public figure. While the Reformers in Zurich discussed iconoclasm as a theological issue, relating it to the cult of saints and to the notion of ecclesiastical art as the bible of the illiterate, the Netherlands ministers viewed it as a problem of legality, not of religion.[98]

98 Garside, *Zwingli*, pp. 130–56. The humanists and Puritans in England argued on the basis of necessary vs. unnecessary images and of the possibility of using the image as a spur to meditation (Surtz, *The Praise*, p. 194, and J. Phillips, *The Reformation of Images: Destruction of Art in England, 1535–1660* (Berkeley, 1973), p. 202).

Likewise the ministers discussed the sacraments not as they related to the salvation of the individual, but as they related to the problem of authority within the religious community.

This problem of authority was equally striking in the ministers' reaction to the Anabaptists. In their prophetic writings they identified with the image of the Anabaptist as a social pariah, a despised apostle; but as political conservatives they condemned them as seditious and anarchistic, enemies of a legitimate order which included both Calvinists and Catholics. In fact, the actual relations between the Reformed ministers and the Netherlands Anabaptists were at least as pacific as those between Reformed sects in other countries; conflicts between Reformers and Mennonites consisted of public disputations similar to those conducted between Lutherans and Calvinists in Germany, while the Münster episode, which had been condemned by Menno himself, was exploited as propaganda a quarter of a century after the event.[99] Clearly the ministers' portrayal of the Anabaptists as monsters had little to do with their actual experience of that sect. It was more likely a reaction to their experience in Germany, where every Netherlander was treated with suspicion after the Münster uprising, and to the very real success of the pacifistic Anabaptists in the Netherlands. Thus the popular and outdated image of the Anabaptist as a dangerous anarchist helped to form the consciousness of the Reformed ministers, who chose to portray themselves as ordinary good citizens – not saints – who were irreconcilably opposed to sedition of any kind, for any reason.

In short, the consciousness of the Reformed clergy was formed as much by their position in the larger society as it was by Calvinist theology. This was equally true of the Netherlands Anabaptists, who adhered to a very different theology, but who shared the status of the Reformers as a religious minority; and in fact, the attempts of the Anabaptists to legitimize their own movement paralleled those of the Reformers.[100] Originally, the Anabaptists had asserted that the efficacy of the sacraments depended on the morality of the

---

[99] Wingius wrote to Utenhove that the Anabaptists were awaiting his new version of the New Testament: 'The Anabaptists are said to examine our text for something to calumniate – in vain. They, perceiving the opinion of the learned is with us, have vainly tried to persuade Menno to condemn our version publicly' (Hessels, *Ecclesiae*, II, No. 21, 25). Dathenus complained that Hermes Bacquereel was disputing with Menno instead of coming to assist the refugee church in Frankfurt (van Schelven, *De Nederduitsche*, p. 405). In Bruges, Calvinists and Anabaptists had considerable contact; Decavele denies that the hostility depicted in the martyrologies was really true, and cites one family with members from both churches (*Dageraad*, p. 355). Certain ministers did carry on violent disputes with Anabaptists: de Lesenne and Baerdeloos were reported by van Haemstede to have indulged in heated public arguments.

[100] Keeney, *The Development*, pp. 46, 99–117.

minister, who traveled as an apostle with no formal church affiliation. But as the movement became more firmly established in the Netherlands, the Mennonites recognized the need for a more rigid corporate structure of the church and a more formalized relationship between the individual and the religious community. In 1554 the Mennonites ruled that 'no one [had] the right to go from congregation to congregation teaching and preaching unless he [had] been sent or ordained by the church or an elder.'[101] Thus the Anabaptist ideal of the individual's communion with God and the capacity of every man to be a witness or evangelist was curbed as the need for legitimacy became more pressing.

It is also interesting to compare the Netherlands Reformed ministry to that of the Anabaptists settled in countries with Reformed governments. Here the Anabaptists bore a relation to the Reformed church which paralleled that of the Netherlands Reformers to the Roman clergy, and Anabaptist conventicles and secret religious meetings were similar to the Reformers' conventicles and outdoor preaching.[102] The Anabaptists in S. Germany expressed great resentment against Lutheran and Calvinist pastors, calling them hypocrites and Pharisees.[103] In Switzerland, the Anabaptists believed that the Calvinist pastors had incited the government to drive them out and confiscate their property. The pastors, they said, attended universities in order to learn heathen fables, but Christ's words were clear and could be preached by simple men. 'The old priests shat on us, and the new ones do the same.' They also criticized the pastors for disagreeing on theological points and for viewing their activity as a business, not a calling: the pastors lived on salaries, cut themselves off from the people, and demanded titles like 'doctor' or 'rabbi.' The Anabaptists' acts of violence – shouting, upsetting the chalice, trampling the Host – 'these were the result of a hatred of pastors and established churches that had been stirred up by the Anabaptist leaders.'[104] It would be foolish to wholly identify the Netherlands Reformed clergy with the Swiss Anabaptists; they certainly bore no resentment against the priesthood for its greater education! But the Netherlands ministers surely had as much in common with these Anabaptist leaders as with their colleagues in Puritan and Huguenot churches.

Max Weber distinguished between charismatic leaders and bureaucratic officials, between prophets and priests. If we were able to ask the ministers

---

[101] C. Krahn, *Dutch Anabaptism* (The Hague, 1968), pp. 230–1. In 1565 the Emden church ruled that a minister required a commission from his home congregation in order to preach elsewhere.

[102] Clasen, *A Social History*, pp. 95, 112.

[103] *Ibid.*, pp. 77, 79.

[104] *Ibid.*, p. 88.

themselves where they belonged in Weber's schema, I imagine they would have given as complicated a reply as that offered here. The ministers did have a sense of their office as charismatic, inspired directly by God, and they certainly had a sense of the destiny of the Reformed movement as more exalted than that of mere human institutions. But the ministers also sought to legitimize this movement in the eyes of their enemies, to create a new institution. One might say that they occupied a highly uncomfortable position somewhere in transition between Weber's charismatic prophet and his bureaucrat.

But the usefulness of Weber's analysis lies not so much in his 'ideal types' as in his conception of the reciprocal effect of individual inspiration and group interest in forming group values and ideologies. The ministers were heirs to the inspired teaching of the original Reformed leaders. They also embraced the prophetic tradition of the Old and New Testaments. Moreover, they shared the conviction that true religious experience could only occur within the context of an established church, and that the church in turn had an explicit relationship to the political order. But their political and social problems, and therefore their interests as a discrete group in Netherlands society, affected their perception of these original convictions. And so they identified with the prophetic tradition of the suffering outcast, and not that of the chastizer of kings, because of their peculiar and uncertain status in society. Thus it was the ambiguity of their social and political situation, not the *Institutes*, which determined the particular elements of the Reformed tradition which they would embrace at a particular time, and which determined that they would seek a greater sense of legitimacy within the larger society instead of fomenting revolution against it.

6

THE MINISTERS AND THE TROUBLES

They are thieves that come in the windowe...Satan's ministers...they doe the Commons wrong, they conspire againste Princes, they divide the Churche with Sectes, they provoke God himselfe with horrible Blasphemie. By flatterie, and bearinge themselves a lofte like grave bearded goates they currie favor with the simple people, and studie to be in credit with the commons and basest sort, by clawing them where they itche, and telling them faire tales of liberty, looseness and light burdens, such as they know the people are glad to heare.

Peter Frarin, 1565

Pious burghers of Antwerp...you have such great hunger and thirst for the Word of God, as men for one hundred miles around.

Cornelis Huberti, Lutheran
preacher, 1565

Having learned something of the ministers' experience in the years before the Troubles, and something of their perceptions about the nature and goals of the Calvinist movement, we should be in a position to speculate on the relationship of the ministers to their audience. What was the source of their charisma during the summer of the hedgepreaching? What did people expect to gain from their participation in the *prêche*, and why did they refrain from participating in the more drastic ritual of the iconoclasm? To put the question more abstractly, what was the relationship between the restricted, usually clandestine Reformed movement which had persisted in the Netherlands for over twenty years, and the mass movement of 1566? Were these really two separate movements, with basically different perceptions and interests, or did the Calvinist elite finally and briefly get a mass constituency?

Weber described charismatic authority as something imposed from above: the charismatic leader stands above and outside the social order, and he changes the course of social development by his introduction of a unique and original message:[1]

---

[1] H. H. Gerth and C. Wright Mills, ed., *From Max Weber: Essays in Sociology* (New York, 1971), pp. 245-7, 'The Sociology of Charismatic Authority'.

The natural leaders in distress have been holders of specific gifts of the body and spirit; and these gifts have been believed to be supernatural, not accessible to everybody. . .The holder of charisma seizes the task that is adequate for him and demands obedience and a following by virtue of his mission. . .It is the duty of those to whom he addresses his mission to recognize him as their charismatically qualified leader. . .

Thus the audiences at the hedgepreaching were somehow *forced* to recognize the authority of the ministers; they did not choose their own patterns of behavior.

I can find no resemblance between Weber's description of charismatic leadership and the character of the ministers who preached during the Troubles. In the first place, the ministers had no clear sense of what their mission was to be once they returned home in 1566. Certainly they were not shock troops dispatched by Calvin to foment religious revolution, as the Huguenot ministers in France were said to be. On the contrary, the Netherlands ministers were divided on almost every conceivable issue. They had been educated in different countries and they turned for guidance to different mother churches who often disagreed among themselves. Calvin advocated compromise with the Lutherans, while the Emden church opposed it, and Beza's intransigence in matters of theology paralyzed the ministers even after they had managed to formulate a unified policy toward the Lutherans in 1564.[2] At home the ministers were forced to rely on lay preachers to assist their efforts, preachers whose activities sometimes jeopardized the entire movement; the persecution of 1563 was a result of public demonstrations conducted chiefly by these lay preachers, without the approval of the leading pastors. In exile the ministers were treated with hostility by both Lutherans and Catholics, who identified them with the radical Netherlands Anabaptists at Münster; but while they were united in their adherence to the Reformed movement and in their eagerness to return home, the ministers were uncertain whether they were returning as loyalists or as rebels, for like everyone else, they were ignorant of the king's real intentions toward religious dissidents. Thus it would have been impossible for the ministers to form a united party with a single mission as loyalists to the Crown, as insurgents or as outright revolutionaries (like the Anglicans, the Huguenots or the Puritans respectively).

And so the ministers became defensive. They argued incessantly among themselves about questions of authority – their authority to punish members of the community, their authority to act independently of the mother churches, and their authority to commit violence. The ministers' public

---

[2] On the ministers' attempts to compromise with the Lutherans, see Ch. 4. Beza opposed the ministers, and the project came to nothing.

behavior was also defensive. Their pretensions to membership in an international elite made them strive to be dignified rather than theatrical, and they were supremely concerned to assert their moral superiority over both the priests, whom they regarded as corrupt magicians, and the Anabaptists, whom they feared as anarchists. This concern for moral legitimacy was reinforced by pressures from outside the Reformed community. In exile, they had little claim to the loyalties of the Netherlands nobility and no claim to the favor of the Crown, and yet their wish remained that both the nobility and the Crown should welcome them home.

In one sense, this concern for legality was characteristic of Calvinist ministers everywhere. In France and England the clergy tended to be fatalistic; they were unwilling to take the initiative in challenging the legal authority and in fomenting war, but once war had been declared they accepted the violence as a sign from Providence and participated with greater zeal – and greater stubbornness – than their allies.[3] But this general fatalism or reluctance to initiate violence was greatly magnified in the case of the Netherlands ministers, who felt the absence of clear lines of authority, and of a mandate to take violent action, more acutely. Hence it seems very unlikely that the ministers hesitated to condone violence against the magistrates and the churches in 1566 simply because they calculated that the moment to act had not yet arrived. What they also needed was a sign from Providence – and perhaps they interpreted Alva's arrival in that light.

But even if the ministers had succeeded in finding an ideological focus for their religious aspirations, they had no disciplined organization to compare with the system of consistories which existed in France, which they might have used to 'demand obedience by virtue of [their] mission.' In many cases, Calvinist consistories were introduced only after the Troubles had begun and the Calvinists had been accorded the right to preach in public. If this was true in an important city like Ypres, it was undoubtedly true in those smaller communities whose connections with the Reformed movement had been so sporadic. In these instances, it seems, Calvinist organization did not cause the success of the hedgepreaching and the iconoclasm; on the contrary, the success of the hedgepreaching and the iconoclasts enabled the Reformers to introduce the structure and practices of organized Calvinism into numerous towns and villages where Calvinist discipline was known only by repute.[4] This does not mean that the Reformed movement was unpopular,

---

[3] Kingdon, *Consolidation*, pp. 149, 153, 165.

[4] At Ypres, 2 ministers settled in late August and set up a consistory (Diegerick, *Documents*, II, pp. 117–19, 121). At St Amand, Jean Leseur committed iconoclasm and set up a consistory on the following Sunday (Desilve, *Le Protestantisme*, pp. 221–2). Van der Heyden did the same at Axel and Hulst (Decavele, 'Axel en Hulst,' p. 20). At Turnhout, Pieter Carpentier organized the consistory; at Renaix, the magistrates

nor that the ministers were incapable of leadership; the eagerness of local Reformers to welcome ministers from Antwerp or Tournai is clear evidence of the movement's early success outside the main centers of Calvinist worship. It does mean that the organization of Calvinist churches in the Netherlands was less extensive than contemporaries supposed, and that the degree of organization and discipline which existed was not sufficient to explain the sudden success of the public preaching in 1566. Calvinist discipline does not explain why Reformed services were found to be so inspiring by so many people, why the popular, clandestine Reformed movement became a mass movement. Indeed, by voting to hold services after public preaching had already begun in Flanders and Antwerp (by the Lutherans), the Antwerp consistory could hardly claim to have led a Calvinist conspiracy to introduce Reformed worship in the Netherlands.

What about the ministers' *personal* charisma, their 'specific gifts of the body and spirit,' as Weber put it? What did people see when they looked at the Calvinist preachers? By all accounts, the ministers were subdued, never eccentric or flamboyant in appearance. Jean Leseur was described as tall and stout, habitually dressed in black; Guy de Brès was also tall, with a long thin face, wearing a black coat; Peregrine de la Grange was of middle stature, pale, also dressed in black.[5] Some ministers undoubtedly seemed exotic to their audiences because they were foreigners. Herman Moded had traveled in Germany and the N. Netherlands, where he was rumored to have two or three wives; Pieter Dathenus arrived at the city hall in Ghent with letters of introduction from Frederick of the Palatinate; Peregrine de la Grange, a French nobleman, was said to have participated in the siege of Rouen.[6] But the ministers' charisma did not seem to depend on lack of familiarity. Jean Rudsemelis and Nicaise van der Schuere were both well-known in Ghent, where they preached. Rudsemelis was the son of a lawyer and *procureur* who had sent him to study in Geneva; van der Schuere was the son of a

heard in September that the Calvinists were planning to create deacons and sub-deacons (H. Raepsaet, ed., 'Mémoire justificatif du magistrat de Renaix 1566–1567,' *Messager des sciences historiques* (Ghent, 1853), p. 214). In Holland the consistory was often the culminating process of organization; it was preceded by an inchoate body with an almoner and a leader who guarded the preacher (A. C. Duke and D. H. A. Kolff, 'The Time of Troubles in the County of Holland, 1566–1567,' TvG, LXXXII (1969), pp. 316–37).

[5] Desilve, *Protestantisme*, p. 48; Braekman, *Guy de Brès*, p. 136; Ch. Paillard, 'Les grands prêches Calvinistes de Valenciennes (Juillet et Août, 1566),' BSHPF, XXVI (1877, p. 34. An exception was Pieter Hazard who, when he preached before the Troubles, wore a high silk hat (de Coussemaker, *Troubles*, I, p. 55).

[6] de Schrevel, *Séminaire*, p. 361; F. de Potter, ed., *Dagboek van Cornelis en Philip van Campene* (Ghent, 1870), p. 118; Paillard, 'Les grands prêches,' p. 33.

wine merchant. 'One saw his mother, the simpleton, going to hear him, as if she were obeying a movement of great devotion.'[7]

More important, the ministers' appeal did not seem to depend on a particular type of 'charismatic' behavior. Some ministers were aggressive and heroic: Ambroise Wille preached at Tournai for two hours with an injured leg which had been crushed by a horse; Pieter Hazard was transported to a *prêche* in Flanders on a wagon filled with armed men; Jean Leseur arrived at a *prêche* at Cateau on horseback, brandishing a pistol, and then departed across the French border. And when the Regent offered a reward for capturing a preacher, Herman Moded appeared before the President of the council of Flanders and announced, 'Well sir, here I am; do you want to earn a hundred Flemish pounds?'[8]

But the ministers were also unpretentious and informal. Herman Moded preached at Ghent sitting on a pile of coats; Nicaise van der Schuere, 'young, small, and of a sickly appearance,' was so short that he preached at Turnhout standing on a stool, and so timid that he often had to pause in the middle of a sermon.[9] Martin de Smet wept as he apologized to his congregation for misleading them during the time he had been a priest.[10] Van Vaernewijck, who was quite willing to acknowledge the virtues of the Calvinist preachers, wrote of Rudsemelis that he was 'more scatterbrained than wise, and certainly did not have the capacity to preach.'[11] In fact, the only quality which the ministers seemed to have shared was an almost prophetic eloquence. At Tournai, Etienne Marmier prevented a riot during the execution of a Calvinist simply by speaking to the mob. And at Ghent, after the execution of the preacher, Andreas Baerdeloos, a Catholic official wrote,[12]

It was badly done to have let him talk so much, for he magnified himself for having served God despite his youth, searching for the way to arrive at the truth and announce it to everyone. They should have gagged him. . .

What was this truth which the ministers announced to their followers – their 'unique and original message'? Since only one sermon from the hedge-preaching has survived intact, our information comes second-hand, from

---

[7] Van Vaernewijck, *Troubles*, I, p. 25.

[8] On Wille: Pasquier de la Barre, *Mémoires*, I, p. 90; on Hazard: de Coussemaker, *Troubles*, IV, p. 242; on Leseur: Desilve, *Protestantisme*, p. 219; on Moded, Brutel de la Rivière, *Het leven*, p. 24.

[9] E. van Autenboer, 'Uit de geschiedenis van Turnhout in de 16ᵉ eeuw,' *Taxandria*, n.s., XLI (1969), p. 15, and van Vaernewijck, *Troubles*, I, p. 25. The Reformers made him a stool or platform of earth and wood.

[10] Van Vaernewijck, *Troubles*, I, p. 321.

[11] *Ibid.*, II, p. 347.

[12] M. Poullet, ed., *Correspondance du Cardinal de Granvelle, 1565–1586*, II (Brussels, 1877), p. 70. Letter of Morrillon, November 2, 1566.

contemporary witnesses whose perceptions were often clouded by prejudice.[13] The friar Cornelis, who loathed the ministers and often slandered them in his sermons, said that Moded preached standing 'on a pile of bones' (i.e., in the Bruges cemetery), against the resurrection of the flesh; nearby, Pieter Carpentier preached that Mary had given birth to other children besides Jesus, while a third minister preached in French against the doctrine of free will.[14]

See and hear how, outside Antwerp, that great Babylon. . .they all stand and preach and rant and gesticulate against each other. Here stands a cursed Calvinist or Sacramentarian, there stands a damned Lutheran or Martinist or Confessionist, there stands a cursed Anabaptist, there a devilish Libertine, each trying to outdo the others. One says that Christ's true flesh and blood is not in the Host. . . Another says we are only required to have faith, without doing any good works . . .Another says that there is no God. . .

What is worse, said Cornelis, the Reformers wanted to destroy all morality. They advocated only two sacraments; 'Thus the marriage bans are dissolved, so we may each leave the wife we now have for another – even better, we might each take several wives as the Turks do.'[15]

A more objective account of the substance of Reformed preaching may be inferred from the Confession of Faith which was read after the sermon at Antwerp on July 28:[16]

I believe in God as He is depicted in the Bible, rejecting all other doctrines. I believe that all is created by God, and that nothing escapes His Providence. I condemn all means of salvation besides Christ's death and resurrection. The church of Christ is all those elected and predestined to eternal life. God ordained the preaching of the Word and two sacraments to confirm our faith. These are the marks of the true church. The Host is neither purely symbol nor is there transsubstantiation. We must honor the magistrate in all that does not conflict with God's will.

The Reformers placed great emphasis on the purity of Scriptural text as they presented it, in contrast to Roman superstition, which they constantly ridiculed. On baptism,[17]

[13] Specific information about the sermons is difficult to find, even in the interrogations of witnesses or the reports of spies; usually the government official wanted to know how many attended the meeting, where the preacher lodged, the names of participants, and indications of seditious intent – not the content of the sermons.

[14] Janssen, *Bruges*, p. 56.

[15] Quoted in Blenk, 'Hagepreek,' p. 26. Also see Broer Cornelis, *Historie*, pp. 49, 50, 57; he reported that Carpentier preached that Mary was not a virgin and had had children by other men.

[16] *Sommaire de la confession de foy. . .leu apres la prédication publique, faite près d'Anvers, le 28 de Julet 1566* (n.p., n.d.) [paraphrased].

[17] Van Vaernewijck, *Troubles*, I, pp. 40–1. In Antwerp, a minister preached that God is not physically present in the Host: 'Si Dieu en personne est dans ce pain. . .où est

[The ministers] said that our priests juggle with their dolls, turning their fingers in their ears, slobbering and spitting on them with much crossing and affectation, anointing, salting and rubbing, adjuring the demon to depart from them, as if the mother had carried an unclean spirit in her breast for nine months, and all with ceremonies and superstitions unknown to the holy apostles.

Van Vaernewijck, who reported the first sermons with scepticism and condescension, could not help but agree that, in a sense, the Reformers were right.[18]

But whether or not the Reformers were right, they certainly were not unique or original in preaching about the power and mercy of Christ or in attacking the cult of saints and the Catholic clergy. Indeed popular Reformed theology, as it was purveyed in catechisms, psalms and in the hedgepreaching itself, was probably indistinguishable from the anti-clerical, Erasmian sentiments which had been presented for years in the plays of the Chambers of Rhetoric. Almost every play written during the 1560s was anti-Roman, and several were openly sympathetic to the Reformers. One playwright criticized the Mass, where wine is withheld from the laity; the author also defended the Calvinist (or Anabaptist) doctrine that only those who are already worthy may participate in the Mass. In another play the allegorical figures 'Search for Truth' and 'Understanding' appeared as teachers or ministers.[19] In still another, the Jewish nation was identified with the Church and the heathens with Catholic idolaters, and the words of the prophet were spoken by a 'preacher.' Artistic creations were portrayed as gifts from God, worthwhile only if they were dedicated to His honor.[20] In one production the curtain opened on a scene of a painter finishing up his work. A man entered,

donc alors passé le sang; où est resté le sang?' (R. van Roosbroeck, ed., *De kroniek van Godevaert van Haecht* (Antwerp, 1929), p. 169. At Maastricht, Kackhoes preached that the bread cannot become flesh; he also said that the apostles baptized only with water, and attacked the doctrine of free will (Bax, *Het Protestantisme*, p. 128). Another preacher at Maastricht spoke against the clergy and against free will (*Ibid.*, p. 110). At Bruges, the ministers attacked the idolatry of communion and church councils (Cornelis, *Histoire*, pp. 49, 50, 57). The bishop François Richardot accused the ministers of preaching that they had the authority to interpret Scripture, of maintaining the doctrine of justification by faith, attacking the vocation of the priesthood, the cult of saints, relics, etc. (*Epistre d'un evesque, aux ministres des églises nouvelles* (Paris, 1566), n.p.).

18 Van Vaernewijck, *Troubles*, I, pp. 65–6. Van Vaernewijck defended the symbolism of the ritual, but said it was too complex to discuss.

19 Enno van Gelder, 'Erasmus,' p. 308. The author argued that the plays were Erasmian, not Calvinist: less concerned with a sense of evil and the need for Grace than with lessons on social behavior (pp. 295–7, 316, 330). But he also said that those who attended the plays saw no reason not to attend Reformed conventicles or to read heretical literature.

20 *Ibid.*, p. 310.

obviously a Protestant, who became violently angry about 'these paintings which God forbids.'[21] Several of the more notorious plays were either printed whole or transformed into popular ballads. In printed form, they provided an excellent indoctrination of the principles – and the slogans – which were later applauded with so much enthusiasm at the hedgepreaching. After the Troubles, the Englishman Richard Clough wrote to Thomas Gresham:[22]

In these times were done plays which cost the lives of thousands; for the first time the word 'God' was discussed in public. And the texts of these plays were and are as severely forbidden as the books of Martin Luther. They were one of the principal causes of the devastation of Ghent.

Thus the theology presented by the Reformed ministers did not burst upon the average layman with the force of prophecy; nor was it noticeably different from the doctrines preached by the Lutherans. In both cases, popular preaching centered positively on the omnipotence and mercy of Christ and negatively on the evils of the Roman clergy.[23] In 1563 the priest at Kiel, later condemned as a Lutheran, spoke to his congregation about the sins of man. By trusting in the priests, he said, the sinful man has only half of God; he must give himself wholly to Christ, for only Christ – not the sacraments – can save him.[24]

Christ is the honest shepherd. It is He we must follow. There are many wolves and tyrants who would lead us from Him to idolatry...Jezabel persecuted the truth and the prophets of truth...There are the Jesuits or Jezabelites, who hide behind the pillars with their books and paternosters...to keep our Lord from hearing anything else.

[21] Liebrecht, *Les chambres*, p. 117.
[22] *Ibid.*, p. 113. Performances of the Chambers took place in nearly all of the towns where hedgepreaching took place in 1566 (*Bibliotheca Belgica*, I, pp. 483–538).
[23] François Alard, a Lutheran preacher, wrote a catechism which, according to his biographer, contained no specifically Lutheran teachings; it stated that government was an ordinance of God, and defended justification by faith and the symbolic nature of communion; it was also fervently anti-clerical ('Die catechismus op vrage ende andtwoorde gestelt door Franciscus Alardum,' 1568, printed in *Jaarboek der vereeniging der Ned.-Luthersche Kerkgeschiedenis* (Amsterdam, 1909). Elsewhere Alard wrote that the unworthy also receive Christ's flesh – but the Calvinists were also willing to say this under pressure (*Een cort vervat van alle menschelycke insettinghen der Roomsche kerke* (Antwerp, 1566). The list of signers of the Confession of May, 1566, included both Lutherans and Calvinists; it consisted of biblical quotations (van Schelven, 'Het "Scriptum de Fide" van Franciscus Junius (Juli 1566),' BMHGU LI (1930), p. 107).
[24] *Antwerpsch Archievenblad*, IX, pp. 144f. Van Haecht reported that the Calvinists preached iconoclasm, while the 'Martinists' told the people to let images stand as art (*Kroniek*, p. 97). But whether or not the Calvinist ministers preached more radical sermons, the effect of Lutheran preaching could be just as volatile; the incident at Antwerp, where the crowd almost attacked a priest who debated with a minister, involved a Lutheran.

The preacher compared the lambs of Christ, who need no other advocate, with priests and Pharisees; many heathens wear the clerical habit, he said, but they are all hypocrites.

The theology of the Anabaptists was certainly different from that of the Calvinists and Lutherans concerning the doctrines of baptism and the incarnation of Christ. But the Anabaptists in the southern provinces *were* similar to the 'magisterial' Reformers in their rejection of chiliastic beliefs and in their emphasis on ethical behavior. 'Through the Word of God you receive godly senses that are exercised to discern both good and evil, for the Holy Scriptures testify to God's goodness, and make the ignorant. . .wise to fear God. . .and do good.'[25] Their notion of the priesthood was radically different from that of the Catholics, but not from that of the Calvinists. According to one Anabaptist minister, Jacob de Rore, Christ was the only high priest; before Him all men are equal in authority.[26]

It would be foolish to belabor the similarities of theology among Protestant groups in the Netherlands; certainly the Anabaptists themselves gladly went to the stake to affirm the integrity of their doctrines against the challenges of both Catholics and Calvinists. My point, however, is that the theological doctrines of the Mennonites would not have impressed outsiders as radically different from those of other Protestant groups. These Anabaptists were not anarchistic, nor did they prophesy the coming of an apocalypse.[27] And to the average Catholic layman, the idea of spiritual regeneration by adult baptism probably appeared a good deal more palatable than the Calvinist doctrine of predestination. Or perhaps the average layman was merely indifferent to these theological differences; the Catholic van Vaernewijck certainly thought so.[28]

[25] Letter of the martyr Matheus Bernaerts (van Braght, *The Bloody Theater*, p. 948). He also denied that everyone may receive the Host (p. 948). Another martyr – also a preacher – said that Christ was born out of Mary, not by her (A. L. E. Verheyden, *Anabaptism in Flanders* (Scottsdale, 1961), pp. 7–8).

[26] van Braght, letter of Jacob de Rore, p. 776.

[27] Verheyden, *Anabaptism*, p. 59. Their mildness was reflected in their request presented at Antwerp in September; in it they asserted their obedience to the magistrate and their ideal of tolerance ('Request der Doopschgezinden te Antwerpen aan Prins Willem I in 1566,' *De Navorscher*, XII (1862), p. 366). Anabaptists in other countries were more radical (see e.g., C. Christensen, 'Iconoclasm and the Preservation of Ecclesiastical Art in Reformation Nuernberg,' AGR XVI (1970), pp. 205–21, for the influence of the iconoclastic writings of Ludwig Haetzer).

[28] van Vaernewijck, *Troubles*, I, p. 80. Van Haecht reported that on August 12 the Calvinists did not preach in the afternoon, so many attended the Lutheran prêche at Kiel, where they objected to the difference in the psalms which were sung. The chronicler observed that there was no great difference between the two religions, except in the use of the sacrament (p. 97). In Armentières a band of Calvinists who rescued a prisoner delivered an Anabaptist as well (van Vaernewijck, *Troubles*, I, p. 34).

If the Anabaptists. . .the Martinists or the Libertines had come here to spread their propaganda, they would surely have attracted as many partisans as the Calvinists. One can see this at Antwerp, where some follow Calvin [and] some Luther. . . The Calvinist preachers haven't produced any new doctrines. . .only the lesson of the Apostles.

When the Calvinist pastor Gaspar van der Heyden arrived in Antwerp as a religious refugee, he saw his host reading the Bible late at night and knew immediately that he was a member of the Reformed community. This adherence to Scripture was probably the most obvious and popular definition of Protestant worship, particularly since the ministers of every Confession continually challenged each other to public debates in which the one with the greatest knowledge of Scripture would be declared the 'winner,' the bearer of religious truth.[29] Surprisingly, most observers did not suggest that the ministers' sermons were politically revolutionary.[30]

The minister exhorted the people to peace, forbidding them to make any uproar, and he prayed for the king, the Regent and her Council, the government of the city of Ghent and also for their enemies.

The ministers did not promise an apocalyptic reversal of fortune or the coming of an earthly or heavenly utopia; on the contrary, they asserted that true believers would be persecuted until the end of time.[31] Nor did the preachers titillate their audiences with miraculous demonstrations of their superior powers, as the Anabaptists had done at Münster.[32]

Sometimes one observed to the partisans of the Calvinist *prêches* that their ministers did not accomplish miracles. . .The Calvinists affirmed that miracles were of no use to them because, in spite of the denials of the Catholics, their doctrine went back to the source of Christianity.

It is worth emphasizing that the ministers' attacks on the Roman clergy, which seem so provocative to the modern reader, were entirely familiar to lay audiences, not only from the plays of the Chambers of Rhetoric, but from

---

[29] Van Vaernewijck said that the presence of so many Bible-centered doctrines made people sceptical that any one of them had the truth (*Troubles*, I, pp. 31–2).

[30] Quoted in van Deventer, *Het jaar 1566*, p. 25. Cornille de Lesenne preached that the time had not yet come for the triumph of the Reformers; but that if they were imprisoned for their beliefs – not sedition – they would receive aid (EA Vol. 282, fol. 203r). At Valenciennes, spies reported that there was no non-religious content in the sermons, only repeated exhortations to obedience (Clark, 'An Urban Study,' p. 188).

[31] Van Vaernewijck, *Troubles*, I, p. 248.

[32] *Ibid.*, I, p. 31. One exception was at Limbourg, when Junius was reported to have cured a madwoman; but even here, the cure was done by telling her that she had only to do good and she would be saved.

Catholic reformers as well.[33] This is not to say that anti-clericalism was an unimportant issue in 1566; only that it was not a new or original issue – also that it was not necessarily anti-Catholic. What impressed van Vaernewijck far more than these attacks on the clergy was the respect shown by the ministers for their audiences. Catholic preachers, he said, made no attempt to enlighten their auditors, merely to teach them to lead pious lives. 'By such discourses they instantly impressed the hearts of good and ignorant people who declared themselves ready to sacrifice their goods and even their life in order to confess the evangelical doctrine and the name of Jesus Christ.'[34]

II

How then, and to what degree, did the Reformed ministers influence mass behavior during the Troubles? Granted that the Calvinists were better organized than the Lutherans and Anabaptists, and granted that they possessed greater unity and fervor than either of these groups, it is still fair to say that the image which has been presented of the Netherlands Calvinist elite – both by contemporaries and by most modern historians – is an exaggerated image of the Reformers' actual unity and power. These exaggerated claims for the authority of the Reformed leadership have been sustained, I think, largely because of the basic assumptions which have been made about the relationship between charismatic leaders and their followers. Most observers have accepted Weber's notion that charisma is somehow embodied in an extraordinary leader, a man of apparently supernatural gifts, and they have tried to account for the success of the Calvinist movement by discovering what these gifts were; hence their interest in Calvinist theology and methods of organization, and their willingness to attribute greater powers of communication and discipline to the ministers than they actually possessed. Our own observation of these leaders has shown us that the interests of the ministers seemed to parallel the behavior of the crowd, but we have been unable to determine in what way the ministers actually caused this behavior.

A more recent and, I think, more useful theory of the nature of charisma has been advanced by the anthropologist Peter Worsley.[35] Worsley rejects Weber's notion that the exercise of public authority is a one-way process, a

[33] On Catholic preaching in the Netherlands, see J. J. Altmeyer, *Les précurseurs de la réforme aux Pays-Bas*, i (Brussels, 1886), pp. 145–6: Catholic preachers, members of the Brethren of the Common Life, preached against image-worship, church wealth and papal abuses. On France, see A. Renaudet, *Préréforme et humanisme à Paris*, 2nd ed. (n.p., n.d.); preachers attacked the vices of the clergy, the sale of sacraments, salvation by works, (pp. 167, 209).

[34] Van Vaernewijck, *Troubles*, i, pp. 30–1. Van Vaernewijck did criticize the preachers for preaching sedition, but this was after the iconoclasm.

[35] Peter Worsley, *The Trumpet Shall Sound*, 2nd edn. (London, 1957).

charismatic leader acting upon a passive audience. In many cases, he argues, charismatic authority may be diffused among several leaders. More important, in order for the message of the leader to be accepted, it must reflect what people already hope to hear; in a fundamental sense, the message is imposed from below, not from above. 'Followers. . .cleave to an appropriate leader because he articulates and consolidates their aspirations. . .'[36] Worsley uses the example of soapbox orators in Hyde Park; one becomes a popular leader while another is called a crackpot, but this is only partly because the first man is a better speaker or conveys a more valid message; it is also because he speaks to some need already present in the minds of his listeners.

Can Worsley's theory of charisma be applied to the phenomenon of the hedgepreaching? Instead of simply assuming the charismatic superiority of the Calvinist ministers over other potential leaders, we should rather assume that people listened to the Calvinists because they saw in the Reformed movement something which they wanted very much to see. If the hedgepreaching was not hysterical, if the ministers were not flamboyant, if there was no revival of the apocalyptic millennarian craze of the 1530s, this was only partly because Calvinist theology forbade such practices. It was also because the people sought other means of self-expression; they accepted Calvinist leaders, and not other leaders who were more or less radical, because the Calvinist 'message' was an articulation of their own anxieties and aspirations. In this context it becomes less important to examine the ministers' objective qualities – their theology, their connections, their methods of organization – and more important to examine the society in which everyone, both leaders and followers, lived and tried to survive.

At the beginning of the Reformation, people 'objected not to the church's power, but to its weaknesses. . . Their movements against the church. . .were movements not for release from a religious control, but for a fuller and more abundant religious control.'[37] H. G. Wells was probably not thinking about the Netherlands when he made this remark, but it perfectly expresses the situation there in the period before the hedgepreaching, with this difference: whereas in other European countries it was merely ecclesiastical power that had weakened, in the Netherlands authority of every kind – ecclesiastical, social and political – had broken down. Not that the Netherlands had ever had a rational system of political authority. On the contrary, in the Netherlands individual cities had their own charters which defined their privileges vis-à-vis the central government, and the armed rebellion of

[36] *Ibid.*, p. xiv.
[37] H. G. Wells, *The Outline of History*, quoted in Eric Hoffer, *The True Believer* (New York, 1951), p. 41.

a city against its monarch was an established tradition. Because the machinery for systematic government was lacking, the exercise of political authority in the Netherlands depended on an informal system of personal patronage. In order to function successfully, the Regent or *Stadhouder* or town magistrate had to have a party of those below him who depended on his favors and who believed that his superiors were, in turn, receiving favors which guaranteed *their* authority. Traditionally, the town magistrates had looked to the local *seigneurs* and to the provincial governors, members of the high nobility. They, in turn, attended meetings of royal councils where they discussed matters of 'national' policy with the Regent, who communicated to them the policies of the highest authority, the king. But while Philip's predecessor, Charles V, had catered to the pretensions of the nobility and governed in what appeared to be their own interests, Philip openly by-passed the noble governors by establishing a *consulta* headed by his personal spokesman Granvelle, and by refusing to summon the States-General; the king was also suspected of subordinating Netherlands foreign policy to Spanish interests. But the greatest source of tension between Philip and his subjects was his religious policy. Philip's ultimate goal was to reform the administration of the Church and to extirpate heresy, and to this end he had re-organized the system of bishoprics and attempted to enforce the authority of the Inquisition. The new bishoprics aroused anger, among other reasons, because the salaries of the newly-appointed bishops were paid from revenues confiscated from many noble-held abbeys; this severed old patronage connections among church officials and between the Church and regional noble families.[38] The major trading cities also fought the bishoprics because they feared that increased supervision would lessen their ability to circumvent the government's edicts against heresy. Certainly it was Philip's insistence on prosecuting heretics that made a government based on any degree of good will impossible – a fact which Margaret and Granvelle fully realized. The officials of the Inquisition were loathed by Catholics and Protestants alike, not only on humanitarian grounds, but also because the magistrates resented the intrusion of the ecclesiastical authority into their municipal jurisdictions and feared the effects of persecution on the economic life of the cities.

Philip's Spanish advisers saw the problem of heresy not as a religious issue, but as a breakdown in the chain of authority and in the administration of justice.[39] And in fact, many noble governors simply refused to act as mediators between the royal government and the cities. In June, 1563, the Marquis de Berghes informed Margaret that he intended to abstain from offering

[38] Clark, 'An Urban Study,' p. 220.
[39] P. D. Lagomarsino, 'Court Factions and the Formulation of Spanish Court Policy towards the Netherlands (1559–1567),' Diss., University of Cambridge, 1973, p. 50.

advice on the religious situation at Valenciennes since Brussels ignored it. Instead of functioning as a governor, de Berghes became a mechanical transmitter of royal edicts; he would submit them to the local magistrates, saying that they emanated from another authority than his own, and leave their enforcement to a lower official.[40] The city magistrates, in turn, often refused to enforce the penalties against heretics, either because they were sympathetic to the Reformers or because they had no confidence in their ability to prevent a riot at the execution. Thus at Valenciennes the magistrates allowed two victims about to be burned at the stake to be liberated by the crowd; at Antwerp they remained passive when the crowd witnessing the execution of a minister began throwing stones; and at Bruges, two officials of the Inquisition were actually imprisoned by the magistrates in 1564.[41] The result of this resistance – intentional or otherwise – was that the Inquisition was never introduced into the province of Brabant, and in Flanders, the chief inquisitor Titelman could recall only three heresy trials in the past thirty years.[42]

After Granvelle's departure in 1564, the activities of both the noble and religious wings of the opposition increased. Since the Netherlands belonged to the Burgundian circle of the Holy Roman Empire, the nobles were theoretically entitled to the protection of the Emperor in their dealings with Philip; in the summer of 1565 a delegation from the Netherlands met with Louis of Nassau at Spa, the first step toward an alliance of the Confederate nobles and the German Lutherans. In December, an emissary of the Calvinists was sent to Germany, his powers signed by three ministers at Antwerp. Contacts were also established between the Confederates, the Calvinist clergy and a group of wealthy Antwerp merchants who formed an association to finance these negotiations; their ultimate plan was to recruit an army in Germany, should Philip prove to be intractable. Meanwhile the most eminent members of the higher nobility, Orange, Egmont and Horne, had withdrawn from the Council of State after Philip had again refused to summon the States-General or to mitigate the religious persecution. By the spring of

[40] Clark, 'An Urban Study,' p. 272.

[41] Magistrates and bishops often quarreled over their right to judge a particular prisoner. After the iconoclasm at Bois-le Duc, the Count of Meghem was sent to install a garrison, but he had a history of quarreling with the city over seigneurial rights to neighboring properties, so even the Catholics would not admit him (Dumont, *La vie*, pp. 81–4). At Axel and Hulst, the magistrates could not prosecute Reformers because the bailiff never came to church (Decavele, 'Axel en Hulst,' pp. 11–13). At Audenarde the magistrate was unable to act because many Calvinists lived under the jurisdiction of a local aristocrat who was indifferent to religion (Russe, 'Hans Tuscaens').

[42] Lagomarsino, 'Court factions,' p. 213. The Inquisition differed from the royal edicts on religion. The edicts of the Council of Trent, published in 1534, were not accepted until after 1564, in Antwerp not until 1570.

1566, the popular terror of the Inquisition was such that thirty thousand people were thought to have fled to England, and the destiny of local privilege, the national interest, and the principle of religious toleration seemed to rest with the nobility, which was viewed as the ultimate source of social and political authority in the Netherlands.[43]

But in fact there was no commonly accepted 'national interest.' It was Philip who had actually sought to standardize ecclesiastical government by reforming the bishoprics; the nobles and local magistrates, virtually autonomous within their own spheres of jurisdiction, were inevitably divided among themselves as they sought to protect their charters and privileges. There was also a division between the more conservative, Catholic high nobility and the militant Confederates who forced Margaret to issue the Moderation in April, 1566. Unless the nobles were prepared, not only to unite among themselves but to go to extremes in their opposition to the king, it would be the king who held ultimate power in the Netherlands. But the king had not set foot in the Netherlands since 1559, his letters came sporadically, and when he did send instructions to the Regent she had no means of enforcing them, for she in turn depended on the noble governors, whom she was clearly unable to trust.

This virtual absence of political and ecclesiastical authority in the period before the Troubles was even more painfully evident during the hedgepreaching, when local magistrates found themselves utterly unable to intimidate the Reformers. 'Those of the religion were in wonderfull great numbers, and armed, who according to the weake government that was in the towne, might have made themselves masters thereof. . .if their designs had been other than good.'[44] When the Prince of Orange arrived in Antwerp to restore order, he found the city full of mutual enemies:[45]

For the magistrates did put no trust in the burgesses, much less in them of the [Reformed] religion. On the other side, the inhabitants in general. . .distrusted the Court (fearing the garrisons which they would give them) and much more their magistrates. Then they of the religion feared and distrusted, not only the Court and the magistrate, but also the members of the town, and what is more, they were jealous of one another, they of the Confession of Augsburg on the one side, and those of the Reformed religion on the other.

But when Orange wrote to Margaret asking for authorization of a lieutenant to take his place, she deferred the matter. And during the iconoclasm, as we have already seen, the magistrate fled to the city hall while the cathedral was sacked; as a witness tersely put it: 'The Margrave came into the church with

---

[43] On the opposition of the Antwerp merchants to the Inquisition, see E. Trachsel, *De colomban aux gueux* (Brussels, 1949), pp. 79–84. On the activities of the nobles and the German Lutherans, see van Deventer, *Het jaar 1566*, pp. 16f.

[44] Petit, *A General History*, p. 394.   [45] *Ibid.*, p. 394.

half a dozen men, who being willed to leave, stayed not.' Whether or not the magistrates were Calvinist sympathizers seemed to be irrelevant; the Catholic magistrate of Antwerp left a church door open out of fear and impotence, while Pasquier de la Barre was accused of opening a church door in Tournai in order to help the image-breakers. In both cases the churches were sacked.

In desperation, Margaret pleaded with the high nobility to assert their authority against the preachers:[46]

...the moment has arrived when...you can no longer let sleep your sword... The government of the provinces which has been entrusted to you, the oaths which you have taken as knights of the Golden Fleece, the fidelity to the king, of which you must give an example...impose on you the duty to maintain...the supreme authority...Will you suffer the peace of the cities and the cult of religion to be ruined in front of you...?

But the response of the Catholic nobility to the hedgepreaching and icono-clasm was even less strident than that of the local magistrates. In October, the Count of Hornes wrote to the king that he simply had no idea what to do.[47]

In short, the Calvinists were active in a society where the breakdown in the lines of authority was so extreme that van Vaernewijck, himself a magistrate of Ghent, believed that it was a sign from God. 'When God...wishes to inflict some calamity on a country, city or village or family, he blinds the wise and experienced leaders, and makes them grope about in broad daylight as if they were in shadow.'[48] A Spanish advisor, writing to Philip about the breakdown in the chain of authority between the king and his subjects, called the Netherlands 'a body without a head.'[49] And Peter Frarin, speaking in 1565, already envisioned the collapse of universal order:[50]

[How is it] that all things are done in a confused tumulte, nothinge advisedly and in order? That the highest and lowest without distinction are mingled and ruffled together? That colde and heate, drowthe and moisture strive and contend with continual discord?...

At the annual *ommegang* at Antwerp in August, 1566, several new tableaux, entitled 'The Present Time,' were added to the usual display of allegorical and religious subjects.[51] The first tableau, 'The Theater of the World,' showed the suspicion in which each nation holds the other. Then came

[46] Kervyn de Lettenhove, *Les Huguenots*, p. 371, letter of August 22.
[47] *Ibid.*, p. 365–6; van Deventer, p. 25.
[48] Van Vaernewijck, *Troubles*, II, p. 124.
[49] Lagomarsino, 'Court factions,' p. 293. Letter of Villavicencio, May 1, 1566.
[50] Frarin, *Oration*, n.p.
[51] Fl. Prims, *De Antwerpsche ommeganck op den vooravond van de beeldstormerij* (Antwerp, 1946).

'Earthly Avarice,' 'Disorderly Nature' (depicted as both an old woman and a man with a huge belly), and finally 'Discord,' a figure spinning a tangled fabric which was labeled, 'Insatiable Desires.'

What was the significance of this breakdown of authority, this 'continual discord' which contemporaries perceived in society, in religion, in government, and in nature itself? Two things are obvious. First, there was a surprising similarity in the behavior exhibited by Catholics and Calvinists. Both groups seem to have felt inhibited about the use of violence; the Calvinists, much as they valued the opportunity to effect a spiritual revolution, were unwilling to kill priests, while the Catholics, much as they dreaded the destruction of the established order, were unwilling to massacre Protestants. Thus it was not simply a matter of the Calvinists choosing to behave peaceably because of their theology or their leadership; probably the Calvinists would have been far more violent in their behavior if the Catholic soldiers who appeared at the *prêches* had simply fired into the crowd or actually arrested the ministers – but this almost never happened. In France, the Huguenots at Sens held a public *prêche*, having obtained letters of safeguard and a captain to protect them; the crowd was massacred by Catholics.[52] At Tournai, the crowd attending a *prêche* on July 3 returned quietly to the city,

...and the other workers gave them no hindrance, nor did they pour forth insults or sharp words, which was much the contrary of what happened to them ...[in] France...where similar *prêches* were held in the fields and outside the cities...

The witness goes on to remark that in France the Huguenots were often massacred on the way home.[53]

Some observers have explained this passivity on the part of the Catholics as evidence of their indifference to the fate of the Roman clergy and their sympathy with the Reformed movement; but if this were so, then it is hard to understand why the Calvinists were not doubly successful in taking over the churches and obtaining official and exclusive recognition of the Reformed cult. Certainly our original hypothesis – that the behavior of the crowd was determined by the policy of their charismatic leaders – is even less useful as an explanation of this general behavior, since the Catholic bystanders were presumably not affected by the ministers at all. It would make far greater sense to assume that if the behavior of Catholics and Protestants differed so little, then the two groups must have been acting from similar motivations.

The second observation which should be made about the behavior of Calvinists and Catholics is that the ideal of legitimacy was tremendously im-

52 Claude Haton, *Mémoires*, I (Paris, 1857), pp. 189–92.
53 Pasquier de la Barre, *Mémoires*, I, pp. 75–6.

portant to both groups. I have already discussed the ministers' desire to establish their authority both within the Reformed community and in relation to the larger society. But the Calvinists were not the only ones talking about the duties owed to the magistrate or the need for a legal mandate to take violent action; the Catholics also expressed anxiety about questions of public authority – but in their own case, the question was not so much of establishing their relationship to the government as of discovering why the sources of public authority seemed to have evaporated.

Many observers, both contemporary and modern, have offered excellent explanations for the violence which occurred in 1566: the spiritual goals of the Calvinists, the popular hatred of the Catholic priesthood and the Inquisition, and increasing economic hardship. But the expression of this violent activity seems to have been constantly inhibited on both sides; and this *absence* of extreme violence can only be explained if we grant that the desire to act legitimately was more important to most people than the desire to express anger against the Catholics or allegiance to the Calvinists – or simply to attack the rich. The behavior of contemporaries during the Troubles becomes understandable if we take them at their word, rather than assuming that their protestations of loyalty to the government were rationalizations for more devious or radical motives. For the fact is that while all groups may have been willing to acquiesce in the destruction of the churches, none of these groups was willing to assume the initiative and exercise public authority in a crisis; the magistrates because they had no noble mandate to do so; the nobles because they were unsure of Philip's position; the ministers because they had based their entire authority to act as spiritual leaders on their alliance with the nobility and their loyalty to the Crown.

But what about the average man or woman? Surely the ordinary person was far less affected by the breakdown of local government and the absence of the king than those groups in society who were actively involved in government and social control. Since our object is to understand the Troubles as a mass movement, how can we suggest that political factors actually determined *popular* behavior more than, say the rising cost of food? My argument is that this breakdown of political authority had a very great negative effect on every person in the Netherlands, simply because society had not become polarized into hostile parties; it had become fragmented into an infinite number of groups with confused loyalties, and hence it was impossible for the adherents of any one group – whether political or economic or religious – to amass a large, united following or to view the other half of society as an enemy to be exterminated. Thus the political breakdown of Netherlands society effectively short-circuited the attempts of isolated groups – whether workers, nobles or Calvinist radicals – to incite a violent mass movement, and the very real economic hardship which the average person suffered was not articulated in any strong collective action. We could say that economic grievances created a general disposition to engage in some form of collective activity, but in fact there was little reflection of that kind of concern in the religious violence which did occur. Indeed we could go farther, and say that the evidence of popular behavior during the Troubles indicates that even the ordinary person was simply not willing to do violence against his enemies, even when these were made of wood, without the apparent sanction of the constituted authorities.

Hence the strangely limited character of the iconoclasm. On the ministers' side, the violence was always defended as legitimate – dictated by the nobles or by the Court.[54] At Hulst, Gaspar van der Heyden sent two delegates to the city hall with a list of thirty people assigned to break images; the magistrates were asked to cross off those who were considered rebels.[55] At Ghent a Calvinist appeared before the high bailiff and announced that his people were armed and ready to destroy idolatry under the express charge of Egmont and the Confederate nobles. The mob proceeded to a church, where one of the bailiff's delegates made a short speech: only those with a mandate to break images might do so, and looting was forbidden. One of the group then knocked down a statue of Christ and someone cried, 'That's clear enough! In breaking images like that, one is executing the orders of the high bailiff!'[56] At Poperinge, the minister Sebastien Matte stood before his congregation with a letter which sanctioned acts of iconoclasm; the letter, he assured them, bore the seal of Philip II.[57] At Tournai, Ambroise Wille destroyed the archives of the cathedral chapter of Notre Dame in order to absolve the king and the magistrates of the oath which they had taken to preserve the privileges of the Order. After the iconoclasm the ministers declared that since they were under the protection of the Confederates, and the Confederates were in turn protected by the great nobles, 'that therefore their actions must be attributed

---

[54] The only exception I have found was at Bois-le-Duc, where Cornelis Walraeven said that his only commission to break images was from God (Cuypers van Velthoven, *Documents*, p. 49).

[55] van Lennep, *Gaspar van der Heyden*, pp. 47–8. The minister told the magistrates from Hulst, who had requested that he avoid the town, that he had orders 'from above' to go there and invited all the magistrates in Axel to accompany him there. The magistrates removed the ornaments and opened the gates (Decavele, 'Axel,' p. 17).

[56] Justification of the magistrates, quoted in Fris, *Notes*; Van Vaernewijck's version was slightly different. He wrote that the Calvinist leader said that he could not stop the people from acting, that he had a valid commission, but had no time to display it (*Troubles*, 1, pp. 105–7).

[57] Dierickx, 'Beeldenstorm,' p. 1044. This also happened at Ypres. A witness saw letters addressed to the community at Hondschoote, saying that Egmont was coming to help the Calvinists and that he forgave all the iconoclasm that had been done (Des Marez, *Documents*, pp. 125–6).

to the said nobles...'[58] Of course the ministers had no royal mandate to break images. But whether or not they believed they were telling the truth is irrelevant; the point is that they were regarded by the general public as emissaries of the government.[59] 'Things reached the point,' wrote van Vaernewijck, 'that, of one hundred persons, there was barely one who did not imagine that the iconoclasm was ordained and determined by the magistrates.'

On the Catholic side, little was done to stop the violence. The majority of the populace may have been horrified by the image-breaking, and certainly the magistrates and bourgeois citizens would have been reluctant to destroy church property which they themselves had donated.[60] On the other hand, many were unwilling to compromise themselves in order to help the Catholic clergy unless they were certain of the government's real relations with the Calvinists. Van Vaernewijck, describing the iconoclasm in W. Flanders, observed that a number of Catholics passively watched the burning of an important relic because they believed that since the authorities did nothing, the Court must have supported the Reformers in secret.[61] The nobles themselves contributed to this misconception simply by being passive. Egmont left Ypres two days before the iconoclasm there; two days before the iconoclasm at Antwerp, William of Orange left the city.[62] Moreover, certain nobles *had* assisted at the iconoclasm; the most notorious was the Count of Culembourg, who fed the Host to his parrot.

Perhaps more important, the actual violence committed in the churches showed almost no evidence of hostility toward the upper classes. The facts indicate that the opposite was the case; the iconoclasm was, among other things, an affirmation of popular respect for the nobility. Almost no one proposed to attack the sepulchres of the nobles or the houses of the rich. Tombs were certainly damaged, but there was, to my knowledge, only one instance of a noble corpse being disinterred and mutilated.[63] At Ghent the iconoclasts,

[58] Pasquier de la Barre, *Mémoires*, I, p. 138; II, p. 203.

[59] Jean Leseur was certainly lying. When asked why he had boasted of a mandate to commit iconoclasm, he replied that someone had come from Valenciennes with a placard ordering the iconoclasm. He said, putting his hand in his pocket, 'I have it also,' and they both laughed (Desilve, *Le Protestantisme*, p. 231).

[60] This was different from the situation at Nürnberg, where the magistrates followed a strict policy of surveillance and discipline because they themselves had donated the art (Christensen, 'Ecclesiastical Art,' pp. 212–13).

[61] Van Vaernewijck, *Troubles*, I, p. 75.

[62] At Ypres, the magistrate told Egmont that the people had gone to the iconoclasm at Poperinge, and asked permission to retaliate if they used force when they returned to do the same at Ypres; Egmont replied that he had no such charge, and left the city (Paillard, *Huit mois*, p. 238).

[63] This took place at Tournai, against a noble whose family had been particularly hated (Motley, *The Rise*, p. 501). A Catholic polemic mentions insulting nobles in their

like executioners, broke off the heads of the statues, but no one dared to touch the pedestal which supported the lions and insignia of the *Toison d'Or*; 'and by this they testified to their greater respect for the emblems of temporal princes than for the insignia and representations of the holy spirits and of God Himself.'[64] Compare this to the behavior of the image-breakers in France, who systematically desecrated the bodies which they uncovered in the churches.[65]

Thus the primary motivation for tolerating the violence of the iconoclasts was not class hatred; on the contrary, the people allowed the iconoclasm because of their desire to believe in the ministers' assertions of a legal mandate for restrained violence. This was equally true during the autumn, when the soldiers at the battle of Wattrelos–Lannoy returned home after they learned that the ministers' promises of noble leadership would not materialize.[66] At Valenciennes and elsewhere, the people withstood a siege by royal troops to defend the Reform; but the revolt of individual cities against the Crown for the sake of its privileges was by no means unheard of in the Netherlands.[67] There is no reason to think that the magistrates of Valenciennes intended their gesture as part of a national revolution. There, as elsewhere, the emphasis of the ministers was on legality, on the promise of moral and physical support by the high nobility; at the height of the siege, de Brès and the con-

---

graves, but the example is the same noble from Tournai (Willem Verlinde, *Een clair betooch vanden oorspronck der Lutherie. . .tot den jare duust 1566* (Bruges, 1567), p. 286). Van Vaernewijck says that noses were broken off the statues of a former bailiff and his two wives (*Troubles*, II, p. 133). He also mentions numerous sepulchres turned over, but no mutilation of bodies (*Ibid*, I, pp. 132–5, 137). Kervyn de Lettenhove says that the cadaver of Duke Adolphe of Guelder was thrown in the river – he had once tortured a minister (*Les huguenots*, p. 369).

64 Van Vaernewijck, II, p. 128. At Antwerp the iconoclasts accidentally damaged the insignia of the Toison d'Or while knocking down a crucifix; 'The magistrates and townsmen began to be moved thereat, and being somewhat better encouraged, repulsed those that sought to have done the like. . .and three that were found doing the deed. . .were hanged' (Petit, *A General History*, p. 402).

65 In France the iconoclasts took the image of King Louis XI and cut off the arms, legs and finally the head. Then they opened the tomb and burned his bones (de Sainctes, *Discours*, p. 387). As a Catholic, he was probably exaggerating in this and in other accounts of violence. The point is, Catholic chroniclers in the Netherlands did not mention these atrocities.

66 See de Coussemaker, *Troubles*, II, pp. 251–60, on the promises of the ministers that they were supported by the nobility.

67 At Valenciennes the ministers assured the people of the nobles' protection, and public prayers were offered for Brederode (van Langeraad, *Guido de Bray*, p. lxix). At Hasselt the siege was supported by a local noblewoman, Catherine de Bronckhorst de Batenberg. She appeared in the city and declared that taxes were imposed unjustly, and publicly defended the preachers (A. Hansay, *La dame de Vogelzang et les Calvinistes en 1566–7* (Hasselt, 1932), pp. 17–18).

sistory overruled the Calvinists who wanted to accept French aid, and affirmed their loyalty to the government.[68] In short, the upper classes played an important role, both practically and symbolically, in the iconoclasm and in the military ventures that followed, but as heroes – not villains.

Popular anxiety about questions of authority not only determined these negative aspects of the Troubles; it also determined why people looked to the Reformed minister as the ideal type of public leader. Everyone, both friends and enemies of the movement, believed in the invincibility of the Reformed clergy. After the iconoclasm, van Vaernewijck observed that the ministers, instigators of all the evil, were not arrested; like everyone else, he attributed this to high influences protecting the preachers – influences emanating from the Court.[69] Clearly people exaggerated the power of the Reformed ministers because they wanted to believe in the existence of a genuine center of authority. But they also wanted to believe that this authority was legitimate; they did not idealize their leaders as revolutionaries. The fulfillment which the ministers offered their followers was not a new theology or the promise of liberation from political oppression or from the taxes of the Catholic clergy; least of all was it the possibility of revolution. The ministers offered their audience a sense of restored authority, of the ideal re-integration of society at a time when society seemed to be falling apart. And the reason people saw the *Calvinist* preachers as the providers of this new spiritual, social and political authority was not that the Calvinists were really able to take control, either through the inspiration of their theology, their advanced methods of organization, or through their alliance with the Protestant nobility; it was that the Calvinists themselves were extraordinarily concerned to assert their own authority, both within their own consistories and in relation to the outside world. The Calvinists, as we have already seen, were preoccupied with questions of legality, and they were concerned above all to present themselves as members of a legitimate, orderly reform movement. This concern was reflected in their propaganda, which was legalistic in tone; the ministers demanded the removal of the Inquisition because it was an outrage against local privileges.[70] More important, the ministers went to great lengths to publicize their connection with the nobility and with Reformed leaders abroad. Thus, while the Lutherans actually had more ties to the centers of political power in the Netherlands, the Calvinist ministers communicated an image of importance and legitimacy much more effectively.

In analyzing the popularity of the Reformed ministers, we should remember

[68] Clark, 'An Urban Study,' pp. 385–6.
[69] Van Vaernewijck, *Troubles*, I, p. 188.
[70] Clark, 'An Urban Study,' p. 297.

Calvinist preaching and Iconoclasm in the Netherlands

that the choice of these men as leaders of a mass movement was not inevitable. The ministers and their consistories were simply not powerful enough to organize and sustain a movement of this kind, and even if they were, it is certainly possible that other, more radical leaders could have appeared on the fringes of the movement as time went on. It is in this context that we should consider the behavior of the one hundred forty-nine lay preachers who were active in the southern provinces during the Troubles. The lay preachers were not members of the Calvinist elite, trained in a particular theology and discipline. By far the greatest number had never preached before and the great majority, according to contemporary records, never preached again.[71] These were obscure priests or laymen, mainly from the Flemish working class, who responded spontaneously to Reformed propaganda and to the preaching of the Reformed ministers; many were actually part of the ministers' audience during the early summer.[72] Hence their behavior as preachers

---

[71] See Appendix C. The asterisk indicates those who preached before 1566, a total of 13. The following preachers were martyrs: C. Traisnel, Vrancq, de Meyere, van Maeldegem, de Hollandère, de Smet, de Hongère, Pluquet, Bonniel, de Messere, du Rieu, de Meen, Coomans, Pyllian, Ruvart, Carbon, Carlus and de Hase. These were active later in a Reformed church; *Rhetius*, van den Driessche, Lems, Slabbaert, *Woundanus*, *Daniel*, *Schoonhove*, *J. de Pourck*, *Escaille*, Thevelin, *Savary*, *van Til*, *Walraeven*, *Kok*, *Munt*, N. Panquert, *Algoet*, *de Bestère*, *Brunink*, *Habosch*, Moyessone, Houvenagle, van der Thomme, Schuddematte, J. de Bois, de Wilde, *Happaert*, *van Hernen*, *Callewaert*, Tardif, *de Meester*, *de Monnier* (those italicized were also in the Netherlands during the Revolt). 3 preachers abjured: Willem Florin van Lommersen (Bax, *Het Protestantisme*, p. 84); van den Driessche was accused of requesting a pardon from Alva in order to recover his property; he later served the church in London (WMV, I, 1, p. 323 and Hessels, *Ecclesiae*, II, p. 440). Denis de Hasque abjured in 1586; this may have been the same who preached in the Liège area in 1566; he was again accused of heresy in 1619 (Bax, *Protestantisme*, pp. 334–5 and Daris, *Histoire*, p. 399).

[72] Twenty-two were artisans or laborers, 43 priests and 16 bourgeois or in the liberal professions. As for the remaining 66, it is safe to assume that most were lower class (see G. Moreau, 'Corrélation'; most information concerns confiscations, fines, etc. Those not mentioned in the records were probably poor. Also, several of the bourgeois preachers – Bourlette, Rhetius, van Vyve – were mentioned as important lay Reformers by several sources, and only once as preachers. Either the source was mistaken, or – like Lopez and Traisnel, they preached on only one occasion.)

As for education: J. Coomans and J. Louchard were literate; Coomans wrote letters from prison (Crespin, *Histoire*, p. 602), while Louchard used books to catechize (de Coussemaker, *Troubles*, II, p. 213). R. Damiseau ran a Reformed school at Nivelles, (Chambre des Comptes, III, fol. 65r). M. de Messere studied for a time before preaching (van Haemstede, *Historien*, fol. 437). L. Callewaert wrote to Jean Micheus in Latin (Meylan, 'Lettres inédites,' p. 77). P. Bert was cited as one of the most gifted brothers in the London Dutch church in 1569 (BWK Prot., I, p. 434). Of the priests, M. de Smet and C. Walraeven had humanist educations (van der Laar, 'Wie cibe'). Three others, C. Daneel, A. Algoet and T. van Til were known for their erudition, BN, I, p. 220). Three were somewhat educated in Reformed doctrine (de Bestère, S.

162

may be viewed as a reflection of the attitudes of Netherlands society – more accurately, of the more discontented elements of that society. It may also be viewed as an indication of the kind of fulfillment that many ordinary people hoped to gain by their participation in the Reformed movement.

Judging from their outward behavior, the lay preachers were not attracted to the Reformed movement from a desire for personal attention, or to express their hostility to the government or to the Catholic clergy. In the first place, they were not outrageous exhibitionists. There are no reports of eccentric or hysterical behavior by the preachers; on the contrary, their impulse was apparently to imitate the behavior of the pastors in Antwerp or Tournai or Valenciennes. Thus Maurice Watelet, a weaver's son, attended a communion service conducted by the pastor François Junius. Later he was arrested for holding a *prêche* in the woods near his home; he had recited and then explained a psalm of David, led prayers, and read from a book of martyrs printed in England.[73] Jehan Louchard attended several meetings in Artois, where he sat as close as he could to the minister; later he went to live in La Gorgue, to 'instruct and entice the people.'[74] Martin Lopez, a prominent bourgeois and member of the Antwerp consistory, suddenly felt moved to preach in the Calvinist *temple* in the autumn of 1566.[75] A few months earlier, one Leonard Xhoka, a vicar of Limbourg, announced to his congregation that he would no longer hold Mass, saying, 'that he had abused the good people for a long time, praying their forgiveness, saying that he had received the holy spirit and that they must rejoice with him for the gift that he had received, preaching from then on the doctrine of Calvin.'[76] Another Catholic vicar, Gilles de Meyere, was suspended from the priesthood in October, 1566; he moved to a private room where he held religious meetings

---

Habosch, L. Bruninck). Two possessed heretical literature (G. de Meyere, J. van Houte). I have assumed that those who came from monasteries in the large cities were literate (Kok, de Hollandère, Robrecht, Lievyn, Savary, Cools). Judging from the cases of de Smet and de Meyere, who lived in tiny villages, the number was probably higher. 7 others belonged to the liberal professions.

[73] Interrogation printed in Rahlenbeck, *L'Eglise de Liège et la révolution* (Brussels, 1864), pp. 277f. He may also have administered communion. One Denis de Hasque, a rope-maker, held a secret service in a house on Christmas day, 1566; he made the people fall on their knees and pray to prevent evil and to increase their number. He also ordered the secret election of a deacon and sub-deacon (Daris, *Liège*, pp. 399–400). The preacher later disavowed this testimony.

[74] De Coussemaker, *Troubles*, II, p. 213.

[75] Christophe and Antoine Traisnel, father and son, were also bourgeois members of a consistory before 1566 who preached only once – this time immediately after committing iconoclasm in the church at Sailly (de Coussemaker, *Troubles*, II, p. 284).

[76] Bax, *Het protestantisme*, p. 79.

and 'evangelized' from house to house.[77] Martin de Smet was converted to Calvinism on the example of a fellow priest. In 1566 he preached a farewell sermon to his parish; weeping, he asked their pardon for not sincerely fulfilling his ministry and offered to return the money which he had collected from them.[78] Other members of the Catholic clergy preferred to preach Reformed doctrines in their parishes, if they could get away with it, instead of making an open break with the church.[79]

Contemporaries described these lay preachers as vagabonds, implying that they were both poor and itinerant. But the records indicate that while they were certainly poor, they actually moved very little; most preachers appear to have been active in only one community, or in the area of one major city.[80] More important, the most active lay preachers were also the ones who had established some contact with the organized Reformed movement. Guillaume de Hollandère left the Augustinian cloister at Ypres in August, 1566, and began to preach in the area; two months later he had become *pasteur en titre* at Rousbrugge, where he stayed for several months, building his own *temple* with materials donated by the congregation.[81] Martin de Smet offered his services to the Antwerp church, which sent him to Mechelen in November, 1566. De Smet held outdoor services and conducted negotiations with the local magistrates until February, when he was arrested and hung without trial.[82] Often the preacher was recruited by a lay Reformer who brought him to a community, or he acted as a sort of back-up to a more important Calvinist

---

[77] De Meyere was vicar of the village of Vinderhoute, near Ghent. He had been cited ten years before for his sermons and suspect books, again in 1566 for refusing to say Mass, preach in Latin and preaching against purgatory, the saints and the Real Presence (H. van Nuffel, 'Gillis de Meyere, pastoor van Vinderhoute en martelaar voor de Hervorming,' BSHPB ser. 4, x (1967), pp. 440–50).

[78] Van Vaernewijck, *Troubles*, I, p. 321. He had been in Italy as secretary to a cardinal, and had a large collection of Latin inscriptions. He, de Meyere and A. van Maeldegem were all converted on the example of another priest, Jean Castelius.

[79] The pastor of Hedel preached Reformed doctrines for over a year in his parish church, with the patronage of the local count, and to the irritation of the parishioners. He received Walraeven in his own house (J. G. R. Acquoy, *Jan van Venray en de wording en vestiging der hervormde gemeente te Zaltbommel* (Bois-le-Duc, 1873), p. 14). The vicar of Lathem, about 22 years old, suddenly started preaching the Reform in his church; his audience then took him to a tavern and got him drunk – the officials let him ride away (van Vaernewijck, *Troubles*, I, p. 576). Another monk in Ghent preached that there were only two sacraments – he later paid a fine (*Ibid.*, I, pp. 318–20). Also see de Coussemaker, *Troubles*, IV, pp. 359–60 on priests in Flanders preaching Reformed doctrines.

[80] See Appendix C.

[81] Heinderycx, *Jaerboeken*, II, pp. 30–1. He was hanged in 1567 and his *temple* demolished.

[82] Van Haemstede, *Historie*, fol. 421.

minister.[83] After the iconoclasm at Limbourg Leonard Xhoka moved into the parish church. When the pastor Junius arrived in October, Xhoka preached in the fields outside the city; when Junius fled, he resumed his activities as the preeminent preacher in the town.[84] Another preacher, an apostate monk called Kackhoes, had been active in the neighborhood of Maastricht for several years before 1566. During the Troubles he preached alongside the pastor Herman Moded.[85] Jan Munt, a preacher in Bruges, attended a Calvinist meeting in Ghent in order to recruit a French-speaking pastor for the community; he succeeded in bringing François Junius to Bruges for several days as a visiting preacher.[86]

But the most interesting fact about the behavior of the lay preachers is that only forty-five committed any violent acts during the Troubles, and of this number, thirty-nine had also established contacts with the orthodox Reformed movement.[87] One of the most notorious preachers was a young man whom we know only as Julien. On August 10, 1566, Julien conducted a public service in the church cemetery at Richebourg, in French Flanders, accompanied by an armed guard of five-hundred men playing tamborines and fifes. When the priest entered the pulpit to deliver his sermon, the Reformers entered the church and began to insult him – it was said that he died a month later of the shock. 'And as [the priest] was consecrating [the Host], the *sectaires* pronounced execrable words, saying that he held and ate Jean le Blanc; and after the presentation they came to take the altar to divest it of its ornaments.'[88] Now Julien was certainly no Calvinist; the Reformers who accompanied him admitted that since he was young and ignorant, one had to have patience with him.[89] But he was proud of his attachment to the Reformed community, and boasted to his congregation that he had been summoned to court by the princes. After the iconoclasm he preached regularly in the church at Sailly, alternating with two other preachers; he also attended the synod at Ghent in October and fought in the battle of Wattrelos.[90] Martin Lopez, who aided in the recruitment of troops from Germany, had been a

[83] e.g., Jan van Diest was recruited by the Bruges consistory (de Schrevel, *Seminaire*, p. 334). L. van Baecx and L. van Thorn by that of Wessem (J. Kleijntjens, 'Bijdrage tot den beeldenstorm. Beeldenstorm te Wessem, *De Navorscher*, LXXXIV (1935), p. 146). M. Loysier came to Ypres after the important ministers had left in the autumn of 1566 (Leblanc, 'Les prédicants,' p. 6).

[84] Bax, *Het protestantisme*, p. 79.

[85] *Ibid.*, p. 131.

[86] P.-C. van der Elst, *Le protestantisme Belge avant, pendant et après les troubles du XVIe siècle* (Brussels, 1856), p. 149.

[87] See Appendix C.

[88] The priest's testimony is printed in van Vloten, *Nederlands opstand*, pp. 170–1.

[89] De Coussemaker, *Troubles*, II, p. 273.

[90] *Ibid.*, II, pp. 197–212.

leading member of the Antwerp consistory for years; he attended the presentation of the nobles' request in April, the meeting at St Trond in July, and the synod at Ghent in October.[91] Jan de Vlameng broke images in Hasselt under the direction of Herman Moded. And Mailgaert de Hongère, who led an abortive invasion of the city of Ypres, was consecrated in 1566 by Pieter Hazard.[92]

This general absence of violent behavior on the part of the lay preachers is certainly curious. One would expect that the popular response to the Calvinist ministers would have triggered a second, more unrestrained movement led by the lay preachers, many of whom were described as very young men, and that as a result of their activities the iconoclasm would have become more violent, more formless, certainly more prolonged, than it actually was.[93] But we would be wrong to assume that the restraint of the lay preachers derived from their dedication to Calvinism. The lay preachers may have attended synods, dealt with local magistrates and helped to organize consistories, but few had any prolonged training in Reformed doctrines.[94] Indeed, in many cases the consistories seemed to have controlled the lay preachers. Julien's relationship to the Reformers who accompanied him was probably of this nature; at any rate, his knowledge of Reformed doctrine was perhaps less than that of his 'congregation.'[95] What did motivate these lay preachers, aside from religious conviction, was less the desire for personal attention than the opportunity to operate in a group, and to assume a share of what many felt to be a genuinely legal, not personal authority. This hypothesis is supported by their overall patterns of behavior. There was really much less movement from place to place than contemporaries supposed; even though the preachers did not all join churches, they did tend to preach in one community, if only for a short time. And, as I said before, their general behavior was not hysterical or original but restrained and imitative; Adrien, the vicar of Oostwinkel,

---

[91] J. A. Goris, *Etude sur les colonies marchandes méridionales...à Anvers de 1488 à 1567* (Louvain, 1925), p. 587.

[92] Diegerick, I, p. 107.

[93] Twenty-three were cited as young men, 7 as old; the rest were unknowns. In France the pastor Lucas Hobé wrote to Geneva about acts of iconoclasm started by two lay preachers, which had led to riots, murders and beatings, after which the monks escaped. Hobé wanted to know how to control this kind of behavior (Kingdon, *Geneva and the Coming*, p. 44).

[94] Also the relations which many established with Reformed churches were superficial; e.g., an anonymous preacher ate lunch with Reformers, held a service in a church, and left town (van Vaernewijck, *Troubles*, I, p. 82). Thomas van Til entertained Reformed ministers at his abbey; M. of Oudenberg was married by Pieter Dathenus.

[95] At Bois-le-Duc the consistory actually instructed the preachers in the content of their sermons (W. Meindersma, 'De Reformatorische beweging der XVIe eeuw te 'S-Hertogenbosch,' NAvKG n.s. VII (1910), p. 383).

broke images in his own chapel because he had seen the Calvinists in Ghent do the same.[96]

The lay preachers thus enjoyed a borrowed charisma. They copied the behavior of the Reformed ministers instead of parading as demagogues or eccentrics; while some, like Julien, were undoubtedly exhibitionists, they did not, like John of Leyden, wear robes and crowns.[97] Certainly they ridiculed the Catholic clergy, as did the pastors, but they did not molest them. This general restraint explains why the most active lay preachers were also accepted as members of the orthodox Reformed movement. It also explains why they were accepted as popular leaders by local communities. If people had been inclined to violence or revolution, they could have rejected the preaching of the Calvinist ministers and followed other leaders, or they could have created their own leadership – lay preachers who ignored the pastors' exhortations to peaceable behavior and committed violence on their own authority. Thus the charisma of the ministers cannot be understood in the conventional sense of manipulating an audience or inciting a certain type of behavior. Charisma really meant popularity: the ability to articulate the sentiments of the congregation in a manner of which they themselves were incapable but with which they could completely identify. If people chose to identify with leaders who adhered to the example of more prominent ministers and who, by and large, avoided personal violence, then we may infer that they did not view the hedgepreaching as a prelude to the destruction of social institutions and political authority. For both pastors and lay preachers, and for their audience as well, the hedgepreaching was a ritual which symbolized the ideal, peaceful re-integration of society.

The *prêche* was essentially a socializing experience. In a sense, it was also a levelling experience, a ritual which invited the participation of all members of society on an equal footing.[98] The physical form of the *prêche* was usually

[96] M. Ryckaert, 'Een beeldenstorm in de kerk van Oostwinkel op 23 Augustus 1566,' *Appeltjes van het Meetjesland*, VIII (1957), p. 109. Adrien of Oostwinkel witnessed the iconoclasm in Ghent, returned home, met with local magistrates that night, and broke images the next day (van Nuffel, 'Gilles de Meyere,' p. 443).

[97] There was little emphasis on reversing social roles; poor weavers who became preachers did not dress up in the robes of priests and, unlike popular millenarian movements, only one woman became a lay preacher (van Vaernewijck, *Troubles*, II, p. 324).

[98] All classes attended: reports of spies at Valenciennes said that most came from the peasantry or were week-workers. One *prêche* was attended largely by unmarried young people or children. Whole families went, including relatives and servants. The males represented 91 trades: merchants, artisans, weavers, etc. Many of the cloth-weavers were probably masters, since the spies recognized them. Many had arms or horses. A few échivinale families attended, more from the merchant class – in short, a distribution roughly proportionate to actual society (Clark, 'An Urban Study,' pp. 181–7). On Ghent, see van Vaernewijck, *Troubles*, I, p. 42.

a circle: At Ghent the 'pulpit' was mounted on a wagon in the center of a field, and the congregation was entirely surrounded by wagons, carrying pikes and weapons, and by pedlars of forbidden books.[99] The general atmosphere was informal, even festive. At a *prêche* held at Bruges one could hear cries of 'Ghent! Ghent!' or 'Eekloo! Eekloo!' as groups from different towns gathered under their own banners, while wagons of food were prepared and beer was served.[100] Two pulpits were set up in the open field, and the people camped overnight and listened for two days to sermons by four ministers, speaking in both French and Flemish. The ceremony itself was also co-operative and informal: at Axel, after the sermon, a child was baptized with water carried to the pulpit from a nearby stream.[101] At St Amand, the communion table was set with a plate of coarse bread, sliced 'as if to eat eggs with,' and two glasses of wine, similar to the glasses used at ordinary meals.[102] At Antwerp, the preacher distributed bread and wine to an assembly of several hundred, who stood around the communion table, passing the sacrament from one to the other.[103] At Ghent, people formed groups of two or three hundred and walked through the streets arm in arm during the evenings to sing in unison psalms which the preachers had taught them.[104]

Not only did the ministers create an atmosphere of community; they also directed their attention to the poor, the uneducated, and the degenerate members of society. At Valenciennes, the poor could receive alms which were denied them by the city charity laws.[105] At Ghent, benches were set aside for the children's catechism, and during the evenings there was instruction in psalm-singing. At Antwerp the taverns were deserted; 'people of dissolute habits, notably a number of married women whose misconduct had caused a scandal, and men whose vices had caused them to be cast out by their families, threw themselves into the new party.'[106]

But the ritual of the *prêche* also served to reinforce social differences. In almost every case, the congregation was seated according to sex or status in the community. An eyewitness at Ghent wrote, 'The Calvinists have a certain order in their *prêches*: the women sit in the middle in a circle, fenced in

---

99 Brutel de la Rivière, *Het leven*, p. 25. The *temple* built after the iconoclasm at Ghent was round with a straw roof.

100 Janssen, *Bruges*, pp. 49–50. At a service at Ghent, 4 barrels of beer and 2 baskets of bread were brought from the city (van Vaernewijck, *Troubles*, I, p. 52).

101 Brutel de la Rivière, *Het leven*, p. 26.

102 Desilve, *St. Amand*, p. 225.

103 Van Haecht, *Kroniek*, pp. 121–2.

104 Van Vaernewijck, *Troubles*, I, pp. 67–8.

105 Clark, 'An Urban Study,' pp. 188–9. There was also charity at the *prêches* at Eekloo, and at Deinze (Conseil des Troubles, Vol. LV, fol. 70r).

106 Van Vaernewijck, *Troubles*, I, p. 27. The absence of drinking is especially strange because the ministers often drank with their followers in public.

by stakes. . .around them soldiers hold watch. . .'[107] Or else the seats directly under the pulpit were reserved for rich tradesmen and their wives, while the entire group was surrounded and protected by armed men on horseback who were often members of the nobility. In the town of Reckheim, near Maastricht, the minister was provided with the use of the church by the local nobleman, who attended the service, while the burghers from the city sat with their backs to the altar, like chairmen at a meeting, and remained seated even during the elevation of the Host.[108] At Culembourg the count and his family sat next to the raised pulpit, apart from the congregation, and left by a separate door.[109] At Ghent there was a hierarchy of preachers as well: the elite of the city followed Jean Micheus and Pieter Dathenus, who preached in the new temple, while the other ministers spoke in the open air to satisfy the crowd.[110] Even the group singing was sometimes organized according to status: van Vaernewijck noticed a group of shoemakers returning from a *prêche*, singing and marching in unison.[111]

Clearly, the function of the *prêche* was not to give people a sense of equality, a feeling that social and economic barriers between them had been dissolved, as they might have felt at a mass rally where the consciousness of the group is surrendered to the preaching of a demagogue. Nor did the *prêche* function as a ritual in which social roles were symbolically inverted, as in the French *charivaris*, where those in power or their effigies were ridiculed by those who were ordinarily deprived of power. On the contrary, at the preaching of 1566 the traditional position of social and economic groups was upheld and, with few exceptions, the personality of the minister was de-emphasized; many were not even known by name.[112]

The relationship of the phenomenon of the hedgepreaching to the larger society was ambiguous. Whether they were motivated by religious commitment or by simple curiosity, many people were willing to attend the *prêches* because they believed that they were doing something that was

[107] Blenk, 'Hagepreek,' p. 24.

[108] Bax, *Het protestantisme*, p. 128.

[109] O. J. de Jong, *De reformatie*, pp. 102–3. Services were held in a room of the castle, with the arms of the count cut above the door, painted on chairs, etc. The count ordered that the area where he sat be made more spacious, more apart 'from the ordinary people.'

[110] Van Vaernewijck, *Troubles*, I, p. 409.

[111] *Ibid.*, I, p. 42.

[112] Thus the hedgepreaching was not a manifestation of 'communitas' as Victor Turner describes it. It was not an affirmation of the equality of all men before God, or against the king. Turner describes such movements as involving equality in dress, conventional behavior – he includes both the hippies and monasticism under this rubric (*The Ritual Process* (Chicago, 1969). The anonymity of the preachers poses a considerable problem of research; Herman Moded, for example, was often referred to as 'Master Herman.'

legitimate. Once there, they enjoyed a sense of participation in activities which were peaceful, communal, and sanctioned by the nobility; one might say that the ritual of the *prêche* – the seating arrangement, the variety of activities, both mundane and spiritual – was a microcosm of society as a whole, but a society which was ideally integrated, as the real society of the Netherlands certainly was not. Thus Herman Moded boasted in his *Apologie*:[113]

> Haven't we seen how drunkenness, banquets, great excessive expenditures...
> have decreased? Then there was quarreling and disunity between man and wife
> ...then there was quarreling and disunity between friends...with judging,
> haggling, deceiving...Haven't we seen this wickedness stopping everywhere?...
> Where does one hear now of so many homicides, murders, robberies and thieveries,
> outside as well as inside the cities, as we have seen and heard of everywhere
> before the public teaching and exercise of the holy Evangile?

At the Antwerp *ommegang* of August, 1566, the new tableaux began with scenes of 'Discord' and 'Disorderly Nature.' There was also a third display, entitled 'God's Providence,' which consisted of three horsemen, 'Wise Counsel,' 'Prudent Inquiry,' and 'United Community.' These were followed by an orator who recited a poem, telling of God's power to reconcile differences between men. Then another figure appeared, holding in one hand a flaming sword, 'The Word of God,' and in the other a book, 'Evangelical Teaching.' Then came several figures bearing biblical quotations and, finally, the figure of Grace itself.[114]

Conversely the *prêche* was also a display of power. The message of the sermons, clearly reminiscent of Old Testament prophecy, was implicitly hostile to the social order, both in its anti-clericalism and its opposition to the repressive policies of the royal Inquisition: there was also an element of class hostility against the wealthy clergy, who 'dress their wooden blocks in velvet suits.' The impact of this message was intensified by the atmosphere of violence which coexisted with that of the general camaraderie, so much so that the group singing must have often reverberated like hymns of battle. Indeed, the scene of the hedgepreaching, wrote van Vaernewijck, looked like a battle-field; 'Everywhere the eye was struck by trophies of arms as for a troop in the field.'[115]

But the violence remained implicit. It was expressed visually, in the aspect of weapons and armed horsemen, and verbally, in the threats uttered by both Catholics and Calvinists; but in most cases the violence was symbolic, not real. It seems that most people were quite willing to express their hostility to the priesthood and their attraction to the new faith, but they were only will-

[113] Moded, 'Apologie,' p. 144. (Printed in Brutel de la Rivière, *Het leven*).
[114] Prims, 'De Antwerpsche ommeganck.'
[115] Van Vaernewijck, *Troubles*, 1, pp. 67–8.

ing to express this hostility in a form which demonstrated the fundamental unity of society as it had existed before the breakdown of public authority. Once aggression became overt there was less enthusiasm for the Reformed movement. In this sense the *prêche* expressed a feeling of passivity as well as violence. Brother Cornelis expressed this double nature of the *prêche* when he preached to his Catholic community at Bruges:[116]

Bah, see how they come here with wagons and carts, with baggage, with food. . . with pot and kettle;. . .bah, hear now how they call Ghent, Ghent, Eekloo, Eekloo; bah, see how they stand there in order, as if going to the slaughter, [*slacht-ordenen*]. . .bah, see [their] weapons,. . .hear how they call *vive les Geus*. . .

Of course the enemies of the movement saw the hedgepreaching as seditious, and individual Reformers certainly contemplated a transference of political power from the Catholic magistrates to the Calvinists. But the *prêche* itself did not represent a symbolic alternative to the existing political hierarchy; on the contrary, for the majority of the ministers' adherents, political reality had not changed at all.

How could people have believed that the *prêche* was not seditious? In the first place, the ministers did not behave violently. Because of the magistrates' inactivity, there was no need for any minister, whether moderate or radical, to consider taking violent action to defend the faith, nor were the ministers ready to take aggressive action to preach in the cities and force a confrontation with the Catholic church. The ministers also showed themselves to be remarkably able in avoiding confrontations with the local authorities. They took advantage of the complex system of local jurisdictions by holding services chiefly in areas whose jurisdiction was in dispute, or in the lands of Reformers. Services were held regularly in cities like Antwerp, where the Inquisition was not in effect, or Valenciennes, where permission to hold public meetings had been granted by the local council and nobility, or Tournai, where the number of Reformers was said to exceed the number of Catholics. From these cities the ministers and their followers traveled to other towns, held public services, and immediately returned home, making it difficult for local magistrates, who knew of these events only by rumor, to make arrests.

Thus the Reformers were allowed to preach unmolested, and people invariably took this to mean that, whatever the placards might say, the nobles did indeed support the Reformed movement. The Confederates' actions in Brussels and their occasional presence at the *prêches* gave a further stamp to the Reformers' claim to legitimacy; Herman Moded, it was said, wore the Confederate emblem on his hat.[117] Most people did not know that the ministers had been unable to obtain a written contract with the nobles at St

[116] Cornelis, *Historie*, p. 53.
[117] Brutel de la Rivière, *Het leven*, p. 29.

Trond, that Junius left the meeting saying that the Reformers had accomplished nothing, or that William of Orange had written privately that the Calvinists were not to be trusted. They saw only that the ministers were preaching peacefully, that they seemed to be having a positive effect on social behavior, and that they, more than the municipal authorities or the Regent, seemed to know what they were doing. Thus it seemed that the mutual suspicions and misconceptions of both the government and the people had combined to render the preachers inviolable; the people believed that the preaching was legitimate because the government and the high nobility did nothing to stop it, while the government did nothing to stop it because they feared that the people would riot if they acted against the preachers. In Tournai, Ambroise Wille ridiculed an edict of July 1, forbidding the public preaching. Wille assured the congregation that the edict did not emanate from the king and the high nobility; it was an old proclamation on which the magistrate had changed the date. Wille then announced that he preached on the authority of the high nobility and the Confederates and that the courts were therefore powerless against him. Margaret, who was convinced that the preachers were deliberately lying, issued a placard on July 11 which stated that the ministers had boasted of their authority in order to deceive simple people. Evidently the credibility of the ministers was greater than that of the Regent, for the letter was posted in several cities, without effect.[118]

We should also remember, in this context, that the government actually seemed to be behaving more sympathetically toward the Reformers in 1566 and that Philip was, as yet, an unknown quantity, so that even if there had been a popular impulse toward rebellion, there was simply no tangible enemy to rebel against. Moreover, while many people saw the preachers as prophets of a new spiritual order, there is no reason to believe that they viewed their attendance at the preaching as a heretical act, since the ministers' sermons invariably praised the king, and since Reformed doctrines so closely approximated those of the Catholic Chambers of Rhetoric. In short, many people found it possible to ignore the seditious elements in the hedgepreaching, and to accept the presence of the nobles as 'proof' that the *prêche* was, in fact, a restoration of genuine order and might even be tolerated by the Court; even the Catholic van Vaernewijck became more, not less sympathetic toward the preachers as the summer wore on.

But the hedgepreaching was an illusion; the social and political conflicts which we have described were muted only temporarily. The Confederates, for their part, made the situation potentially explosive by pursuing their aggressive alliance with the Germans and alienating themselves from the conservative high nobility; during the autumn they issued a Beggar's seal,

[118] Pasquier de la Barre, *Mémoires*, 1, pp. 84, 92–3.

stamped with a picture of the iconoclasm. More important, the situation was explosive because of the absence of political authority and of recognized social norms. Whereas the English ministers returned home at the beginning of a period of stability, the Netherlands ministers returned home to a political vacuum. Any innovative action on their part, even a new seating arrangement at a worship service, inevitably increased the anxiety of the magistrates, who knew that they were incapable of controlling the people if violence should occur. Thus the ministers' preaching excited both fear and hope; fear that any open clash with the Roman church or the officials of the Inquisition could not be controlled, and hope that Margaret's partial acquiescence to the Confederates' demands and her failure to execute the ministers meant that the Reformers might actually be able to elevate religious life and protect the people from the Inquisition. Finally, the situation was aggravated because of the Reformers' own beliefs. The ministers conveyed a sense of restored authority, but their ultimate goal was not to defend the sanctity of the renovated Catholic church but to restore a godly society which had no need of Roman Catholicism. It is by no means certain that the thousands who attended the preaching perceived this, or that they would have accepted the formal institution of Calvinist worship even if it were approved by the nobility. The people might have felt both comfortable and exhilarated at the *prêches* – but they were not all Calvinists.

The Reformers appeared to be at the height of their power in the period following the iconoclasm. At Antwerp, a temple was built with contributions from churches in Tournai, Armentières and Valenciennes. At the local *bourse*, Calvinist books were more plentiful than Catholic works, and rumors multiplied about the preachers' seditious intentions: one merchant reported that three Calvinist merchants from Tournai had told him that they were sorry the iconoclasts were so pressed as to begin their exploits on a Wednesday, for if the violence had been postponed until Sunday, when everyone was at Mass, the whole city would have been theirs. At a synod held in December, delegates from Ghent, Ypres, Valenciennes and the northern provinces discussed the issue of resistance to the magistrate and decided to offer the command of their forces to William of Orange.[119] At Valenciennes the Reformers coopted the essential functions of local government and commenced regular preaching in the churches. At Axel and Hulst they broke

[119] L. van der Essen, 'Les progrès du Lutheranisme et du Calvinisme dans le monde commercial d'Anvers,' *Vierteljahrschrift für Sozial- und Wirtschaftsgeschichte*, XII (1914), pp. 197–8; van Roosbroeck, *Het wonderjaar*, pp. 211–15. They also wrote to Frederick, asking for support and offering to submit to a Christian free synod A. Kluckholn, ed., *Briefe Friedrich des frommen, kurfürsten von der Pfalz*, I (Braunschweig, 1868), pp. 730–1, No. 389.

into a prison after the arrest of two iconoclasts and besieged the city hall, crying, '*Vive les Gueux*! Let the bailiff and the papists come, we will kill them all...We will see the bailiff dead if we have to sit in front of the city hall for three days.'[120] The consistory then sent to nearby communities for help against the magistrates and spoke about throwing the Catholics out of town. Many of these activities appear to have been coordinated by Jean Crespin, who had come to the Netherlands from Geneva. Crespin and the pastor Jean Taffin drafted a request to be given to the king after the fall of Valenciennes; in his interrogation, Peregrine de la Grange named Crespin as one of those in Antwerp who counseled Valenciennes not to accept an immediate truce; Crespin also visited several cities to guide consistories in their negotiations with royal officials.[121]

But the iconoclasm not only gave the Reformers an opportunity to take over the churches; it also revealed the conflicts which existed between the ministers, the nobility and the conservative Catholic populace – and among the ministers themselves. Many people who had acknowledged the attractiveness of the ministers at the hedgepreaching backed away from the Reformers after the image-breaking. Van Vaernewijck, who had written favorably of several pastors, and wonderingly of the people's devout behavior at the *prêches*, became an enemy of the Reformed movement after August. Many nobles also backed away from the movement after the iconoclasm, either because they disapproved of the image-breaking on principle or because they considered the violence premature. Egmont, who had been half-hearted in his opposition to the preaching, severely punished the iconoclasm on his own lands. Even the Calvinist Marnix of Thoulouse, who defended the iconoclasm on principle, was irritated at the behavior of some ministers: 'They can advise, but they cannot command. They cannot dominate; they must leave man's conscience free.'[122] And the Lutherans, who had willingly discussed proposals for unification with the Calvinists, made every effort to disassociate themselves from the Reformed movement after August; during the riots of March, 1567, the Lutherans sided with the Catholic magistrates against the Calvinists.[123] When the mob at Axel and Hulst called for assistance in their siege of the city hall, too few people came and the siege was ended.[124] In short, the iconoclasm proved effective in the short run, since it enabled the ministers to preach for a time in the purified Catholic churches and, in a few cities, to assume control of the functions of local government.

[120] Decavele, 'Axel,' p. 22.
[121] Ch. Paillard, 'Note sur Jean Crespin,' BSHPF xxvii (1878), pp. 382–3.
[122] Léonard, *Histoire*, p. 89.
[123] J. W. Pont, *Geschiedenis van het Lutheranisme in de Nederlanden tot 1618* (Haarlem, 1911), pp. 86–8.
[124] Decavele, 'Axel,' p. 22.

But in the long run the iconoclasm destroyed the power of Calvinism as a mass movement.

It also aggravated the conflicts which had always existed within the ministry itself. At the period of their greatest power, the ministers were unable to formulate a unified policy toward the local magistrates despite their attempts to do this at the October synod in Ghent. When foreign preachers were instructed to leave the cities, Junius left Antwerp, while Marmier refused to leave Tournai. The ministers certainly made aggressive gestures – gestures which were bound to impress outsiders as manifestations of an organized, revolutionary conspiracy. But their actions in the autumn of 1566 were no more unified or consistent than their behavior in the period before the Troubles, when they were spread over several countries, not least because Beza himself refused to provide the Reformers with a mandate for action; his letters of 1566 counseled against compromise of any sort, but also against aggressive action.[125] And so Guy de Brès pursued an alliance with the nobles, and was instructed by them to keep the people quiet; yet it was de Brès who decided to hold a public communion service at Valenciennes at a sensitive point in the negotiations with Noircarmes. François Junius, who appeared at Antwerp fresh from Geneva in 1565, was a member of the original noble league to oppose the Inquisition and to ally with the Germans. It was Junius who opened the first meeting of the Confederates with prayers for their success; it was also Junius who vetoed the iconoclasm and who got out of town as soon as he was told to do so by the Regent. And Andreas Baerdeloos, who was considered a danger to the early Reformed movement because of his unrestrained preaching, instructed his congregation to depart from a *prêche* in Flanders: 'Dear brothers, let us obey: respect is due to the magistrates.'[126]

III

The observer who hopes to interpret the Troubles must try to bridge the gap between abstract ideas and concrete behavior; specifically, between the doctrines of Calvinism and the rituals and violence which occurred in the

---

[125] On August 19 Beza wrote that a worse time could not have been chosen to act (presumably referring to the negotiations with the Germans), and that having advanced little by little for so long, the Calvinists should do nothing to jeopardize their situation. He also counseled against the 3 million guilder project and an alliance with the Catholics. 'You know what our intention is, but what should I have done. Ministers are requested of us. They turn to me as if I were fully aware of all these things...I have many reasons for ambiguity.' (Letter to Jean Crespin, de Vries de Heekelingen, *Genève*, II, pp. 156–65). See also letters §484, 589, 516 in the *Correspondance de 1566*.

[126] Van Vaernewijck, *Troubles*, I, p. 269.

Netherlands in 1566. Both contemporaries and historians have perceived this relationship of ideas and behavior as an either/or situation: either Calvinist ideology inspired the Troubles and the Dutch Revolt, or it did not. Some historians have observed that the presence of Calvinist ministers had been a theme in Netherlands history since 1544, and that the leaders of the Dutch Revolt were Calvinists – and they have concluded that Calvinist ideology became an element in the formation of Dutch nationalism in the same way that the Enlightenment doctrine of individual happiness is supposed to have inspired the leaders of the American Revolution. According to these historians, Calvinist ideas were secretly introduced by the early ministers, spread underground despite persecution, burst upon the national consciousness during the hedgepreaching and found ultimate expression in the iconoclasm. The image-breaking would thus appear as the symbolic inauguration of the Dutch Revolt, when religious ideology was fused with nationalist sentiment; another storming of the Bastille. The alternative to this interpretation has been to reject the influence of ideas altogether, and to view the preaching and the violence as evidence of social and economic discontent: the preachers used Calvinist doctrines as slogans, but they might just as well have used the slogans of the Anabaptists or Catholics.

Enough has been said to demonstrate that Calvinist ideas did not cause the Troubles in the sense I have just described. People were not moved to applaud the hedgepreachers and to commit violence because they believed in a revolutionary ideology which had been imposed on them from above by an organized, international elite. In fact, it appears that Calvinism was not perceived as a revolutionary ideology even by many of its own leaders. But this is not to deny that popular behavior was influenced by ideas. Attendance at the hedgepreaching and participation in the iconoclasm was at least partially determined by what people thought about the Calvinists and their powers of self-discipline and organization. The events of 1566 were 'Calvinist' phenomena in the sense that Calvinism was perceived by most people through the prism of their own anxieties and expectations. But the ritual of the *prêche* was not the result of a Calvinist conspiracy; it was the product of the people's need to believe in the stability of a higher social and spiritual authority, and of their belief that the ministers had the practical and spiritual capacity to provide that authority.

It was also a political gesture. The nobles and magistrates of the Netherlands had a vision of something called the national interest, but they conceived of that ideal in terms of their own traditional privileges – their personal right to legislate on religious matters and dispense patronage within their own spheres of jurisdiction. It was clear that some sort of overall political authority was needed, but every attempt to impose administrative and

political order had failed by 1566. Philip's efforts to centralize the government and reform the bishoprics had failed because they depended on the
acceptance of the Inquisition and the sacrifice of provincial authority; the
nobles' efforts to deal collectively with religious matters in the States-General
also failed because of Philip's insistence on submitting the religious edicts to
each provincial council separately – to control the people by fragmenting
them. 'The meeting of the States-General was considered by all sensible
people to be the only remedy against the Troubles,' wrote an Antwerp
official.[127]

What else could be concluded when neither the supplication of the nobles, nor
the desire of various provinces and towns...had succeeded in persuading the
court to do it? There seemed to be nothing left to give them hope that the
promises to the nobles might be kept, or that the inhabitants might be released
from the hated persecutions and odious inquisition...Despair made those who
dissented in religion more obdurate...This was the reason why they started to
hold their meetings and services each day more openly, thus getting so many
adherents.

The failure to call a meeting of the States-General was commented on and
resolved in the *prêche*, where the main thing achieved and noticed was order-
liness, restrained enthusiasm, and the synthesis – not the disappearance –
of disparate elements: different social groups, localities, languages. In symbolic terms the *prêche* accomplished what the States-General had been meant
to achieve; it was a statement of collective solidarity against the Inquisition
and the foreign government, and a defence of the separate identity and authority of local magistrates, guilds and nobles. Both as worshippers and as
citizens, the people would have liked real life to reflect the *prêche*: organized,
hierarchical, harmonious, with the ministers and nobles as the guardians of
the spiritual and political integrity of the country.

But if the ministers and their adherents were willing to act as public
authorities during the *prêche*, why were they also willing to defer authority
during and after the iconoclasm – even such people as the nobles and local
magistrates, who had a legal mandate to act as public officials? Merely citing
the breakdown of political and ecclesiastical authority in the period before the
Troubles does not completely explain this behavior because in France, where
there was a similar breakdown or division of public authority, individuals
showed themselves more than eager to assume these public functions. During
the iconoclastic riots in France it was common for Catholics to murder Protestants in the belief that they were acting in place of the magistrates, who
were unable to protect the States; it was equally common for Protestants to

[127] *Mémoires of Wesembeke*, quoted in E. H. Kossman and A. F. Mellink, *Texts Concerning the Revolt of the Netherlands* (Cambridge, 1974), p. 69.

attack Catholics because, in their view, that was what the magistrates should have done if they had seen the truth.[128] In the Netherlands, Catholics and Calvinists quarreled over the number of sacraments and the significance of communion, and they often attacked one another as heretics, but they did not seem to view each other as ultimate enemies, as deviants who had to be exterminated in order to preserve Society. In France, on the other hand, arguments about the nature of the sacraments could lead to the disembowelment of a pregnant Huguenot woman by a Catholic, to insure that the unborn child should not come into the world a heretic. Why this immense difference in perception and behavior? Why was society in the Netherlands so much less polarized than in France?

In the first place, the divisions in Netherlands society were less acute because of the absence of the king. Philip was viewed by the Calvinists neither as an ally nor as a confirmed enemy. Of course the Reformers were cynical about Margaret's intentions in publishing the Moderation, but no one, not even Margaret herself, was really certain about the policies of the king toward the Protestants and the nobility. Public opinion in 1566 was not directed against Philip, but against the Inquisitors and the 'friends of Granvelle' who lied to the king about the Reformers' activities and incited violence among the people.[129] This absence of a confirmed enemy prevented the Reformed ministers from formulating a political ideology either as adherents to the crown or as revolutionaries; it also prevented the high nobles who were vaguely sympathetic to the Calvinists from taking a stand in support of the Reformers, and the Confederates, as they did a few years later. A second reason for the absence of clear divisions in Netherlands society was simply that there were so many more alternatives; until Alva's Blood Council had defined everyone as either a loyal Catholic citizen or a Protestant traitor, it was possible to be a Catholic who was also hostile to the Inquisition, a Lutheran, a Calvinist, or simply a liberal sceptic.

More important, perhaps, was the Netherlanders' experience with militant Anabaptism. Both Catholics and Protestants considered the Anabaptists to be deviants and anarchists. We know that the Calvinist ministers were continually trying to convince the public authorities, both at home and in Ger-

---

[128] Davis, 'Rites of Violence,' pp. 61–70. Davis cites as reasons for this willingness to assume power, the presence of public officers at the riots, the cues given out by preachers in their sermons, and the conditions of 16th-century society which required that ordinary, private individuals take the law into their own hands.

[129] Kossman and Mellink, p. 68 (Mémoires of Wesembeke). Lagomarsino ('Court Factions') emphasizes Philip's own indecision about dealing with the Netherlands Reformers, and his advisers' conviction that the iconoclasm was not a popular revolution at all, and that the people would welcome Philip's presence in the Netherlands – or at least a statement of his intentions.

many, that they were not to be identified with the Anabaptists who were responsible for the disasters at Münster.[130] And this desire to establish themselves as dedicated to the protection of the constituted authorities was at least as intense as their commitment to advance the cause of the new religion, at least until Philip had finally shown himself to be intractable. The ministers wanted to convince the Catholics (and the Lutherans) that if a circle could be drawn around the members of the social order which would exclude those who were criminals, enemies of that order and that system of values, the circle should be drawn around themselves and the established authorities and it should exclude the Anabaptists. In fact, it seems that even the Anabaptists were eager to disassociate themselves from the Münsterites during this later period. During the Troubles, the Mennonites were by far the most pacifist group; no one accused them of participating in the image-breaking, and they did not join in the 1567 riots at Antwerp as the Lutherans did. In short, the differences between these religious groups were, at this point in their history, no more striking than the things which bound them together; for Catholics, Calvinists, and for the Mennonites as well, the evil to be eradicated was not heresy, but anarchy. This anxiety to believe that society was secure, integrated, and above all normal, did not prevent a relatively small group from committing iconoclasm and taking over a number of cities, but it did prevent these acts of violence from becoming elements of a mass movement.

Thus there is no reason to view the Troubles as a rehearsal for the Dutch Revolt; it seems much more likely that most people would have been satisfied to participate in the hedgepreaching as an alternative to more radical forms of protest. To the average member of the Reformed congregations, Calvinism was probably appealing not as a radical doctrine promising greater personal and political freedom, but as a promise of greater security within the established political hierarchy. But if Calvinism was not widely perceived as a revolutionary ideology in the period of the Troubles, what was the relationship of Calvinism to the Dutch Revolt? Did the ministers help to cause the Revolution? It seems that Calvinism was accepted as a revolutionary, nationalist ideology by members of the high nobility and by moderates within the

130 De Brès got leave from Antwerp to preach at Valenciennes because he said Anabaptists were troubling the churches of Flanders (van Langeraad, Guido de Bray, p. xxxvii). In England, the psalms and literature by Utenhove and à Lasco were replaced by de Brès' Confession and Dathenus' psalms, because they were more unequivocally Calvinist and more hostile to the Anabaptists (Lindeboom, *Austin Friars*, p. 89). Junius' 'Brief Discours,' discussed in Chapter 4, was analyzed by one historian as presenting 'Calvinism as a politically and spiritually safe alternative to Catholicism that it would be wise to tolerate in order to prevent atheism, libertinism and anabaptism from developing further.' (Kossman and Mellink, p. 9). On June 7 Beza wrote to Jean Taffin that the Moderation should exclude Anabaptists (Correspondence of 1566, No. 473, pp. 127–30).

Reformed clergy only when they were forced do to so in order to survive against the Duke of Alva; ironically it was not the preaching of the Reformers but their renewed persecution that led to the popular acceptance of Calvinism as a revolutionary doctrine. For in this latest wave of executions, it was not only the Calvinists who were persecuted; it was the entire society of the Netherlands. The wholesale massacre instigated by the Duke of Alva created a situation of theatrical extremes in which the forces of good and evil could be clearly discerned by everyone, and in which all elements of Netherlands society could feel unified against the malevolent foreigner. For the ministers it must have appeared that a sign from Providence had finally come, and that God intended them to strike down the tyrant.

It was in this situation of extreme pressure that the Netherlands pastors formally adopted the doctrines of Calvin and rejected the possibility of compromise with the Lutherans. The members of the Emden synod (1571) went to considerable trouble to establish solidarity with the Calvinists in France. Dathenus and Taffin, the two most prominent ministers, were commissioned to attend the next national synod in France to announce that they had adopted both the Belgian and the French Confessions of Faith and to suggest that the French accept the Belgian Confession as a reciprocal gesture of solidarity. The Reformers also voted to compose a history of the persecutions in the Netherlands; not a book of martyrs with a universal Christian framework like that of Jean Crespin, but a national history. It was also at this point that the majority of the Netherlands ministers became political revolutionaries.[131] Thus Pieter Carpentier, who had been a moderate during the Troubles, wrote to the London refugee church from Holland during the Revolt: 'I hope that you will pray for all the ministers, and especially for those of this country, not forgetting the Prince of Orange...may the Lord destroy the enemy, so that our people may be more encouraged.'[132] And for Jean Taffin, who had also taken a conciliatory position during the Troubles, the iconoclasm later became part of the nationalist myth:[133]

Those of the Religion wonderfully advanced in Flanders, Brabant, and in several other provinces of the Low Countries; and affairs came to such a pass that...the

---

[131] Ministers who were martyrs: Rudsemelis, de Lesenne, Leseur, Missuens, de Brès, de la Grange, Baerdeloos, Karel le Bron, Cateu. Those in the Reformed movement later on: Boquinus, *Taffin*, *Micheus*, *de Nielles*, Wille, Corro, *Junius*, *Marmier*, *Cappel*, *van der Schuere*, *Pontfort*, Top, *Wingius*, *Carpentier*, *Bacquereel*, *Moded*, de Buzère, *Dathenus*, *Hazard*, Matte, *Lamoot*, *van der Heyden*, *Wybo*, *van Culembourg*, *Lantsochtius*, *Balck*, *Flameng*, *Capito*, *Cubus*, *May*, Garcia, *Bert*, Strobbe, *de Brune*, *Platevoet*, *Mostaert*, Sterkenbrugge, *Habosch*, *Rhetius*. (Those italicized were also active in the Netherlands during the Revolt.)

[132] Hessels, *Ecclesiae*, III, No. 213.

[133] Jean Taffin, *L'Estat de l'église* (Bergen-op-Zoom, 1605), p. 606.

images in the temples of Antwerp were broken...with a swiftness which was unbelievable to the simple people...

If the ministers chose, in 1566, to portray themselves and their doctrine as fundamentally ambiguous, persecution would induce them to become what many have always believed them to be – a band of revolutionary fanatics.

APPENDIX A:
MINISTERS ACTIVE BEFORE THE TROUBLES (1544–65)

Name	Area	Source
Anglus (Angèle)	St Trond	Rahlenbeck, *Liège*, 270
Banc, Arnold	Antwerp	Meyhoffer notes
Brochart, Louis (clers yeux)	Valenciennes	Paillard, *Histoire*, III, pp. 143–4
Broiteur, Hans (Brockeur, Brotsaert)[1]	Nieuwport, Steenwerck, Nieuwkerke	Decavele, *Dageraad*, 401
Cambier, David[2]	Nieuwkerke	*Ibid.*, 407
Capelle, Jean	Fr. Flanders	De Coussemaker, II, 273
Castel, Jean (Catel)	Tourcoing	Crespin, 480
Chevalier, Paul (Millet)	Valenciennes	Moreau, 'Procès'
Claissone, Jan[3]	Eekloo, E. Flanders	Decavele, 'Hendrix,' 24
Clebitius, Guillaume	Antwerp	EA LVIII no fol. nos.
Cleerks	St Trond	Rahlenbeck, *Liège*, 270
Coeman, Jan	Nieuwport	Verheyden, 'Nieuwport', 6
Cole, William	Antwerp	Collinson, 50
Colon, Roland	Antwerp	Wesembeke, 23
Cornu, Guillaume	Valenciennes, Tournai	Moreau, *Histoire*, 190
Cuvelier, Nicolas	Douai	Beuzart, *Hérésies*, 166
Damman, Ghislain (Juliaen van Damme)	W. Flanders	*Ibid.*, 191
Damman, Guillaume	W. Flanders	CT XXI, fol. 473
Dayke, Alexandre (D'Aick, Decque)	Valenciennes	Muret, 'Dayke'
De Bailleul, Gérard	Tournai	Moreau, *Histoire*, 227
De Clerck, Michiel[2]	St Trond	Decavele, *Dageraad*, 364–5
De Hamal, Godfried	Tournai	Moreau, *Histoire*, 120f.
De la Court, Nicolas	Artois	Beuzart, *Hérésies*, 183–4
De la Hay, Philibert[2]	Bruges	Decavele, *Dageraad*, 339–40
De Lannoy, Jean (Jean Tapissier)	Tournai	Moreau, *Histoire*, 151
De Lannoy, Mathieu	Valenciennes, Tournai	Moreau, *Histoire*, 227
De Lo, Jacques	Lille	Reitsma and Lindeboom, 89

[1] Broiteur was in Steenwerck in 1566.
[2] Cambier, de la Hay and de Clerck were cited as holding conventicles and propagandizing; they may not have been preachers.
[3] Claissone was active during the Troubles as a Reformer.

Name	Area	Source
De Pruet, Jan[1]	Eekloo	Decavele, *Dageraad*, 369
De Reyna, Cassiodoro	Antwerp	Hauben, 89
De Sander, Loys	W. Flanders	Decavele, *Dageraad*, 406
Desbarbieux, Symphorien	Lille	Frossard, 32
Desbonnets, Philippe	Lille	Leblanc, Appendix
Desbuyssons, Martin	Tournai, Antwerp Valenciennes	EA 1739/1 old fol. 362; Moreau, *Histoire*, 227
	Steenwerck, Belle	Decavele, *Dageraad*, 393
De Smet, Christophe (Fabri, Marissael, Christophe de Bruges)	Antwerp	De Moreau, *Histoire*, v, 118
Destoubequin, Michel	Tournai	Moreau, *Histoire*, 117, 120
De Zommère, Louis	Bailleul	De Coussemaker, *Troubles*, 1, 14
Dirken, Jean[2]	Antwerp	NNBW, 11, 57
Dufflos, Claude	Valenciennes	Leblanc, 103
Dufour, Robert[3]	Tournai	Moreau, *Histoire*, 222
Erail, Evrard (Herailly-Dumont, Debrard)	Antwerp	Meyhoffer notes
Fabri, Louis (Loys de Leeraere) Savary, Sabry[4]	Oudenberg, Ostend, W. Flanders	Decavele, *Dageraad*, 363–4, 402
Faveau, Simon	Valenciennes	Rahlenbeck, 'Chanteries'
Ferlitto, Geronimo[5]	Antwerp	Van Roosbroeck, *Antwerpen*, 182
Froidure, Jean[6]	Lille	Du Plessis, 617
Gabriel, Pieter	Bruges, Antwerp	BWK Prot. III, 159
Gay, Laurens[6]	Lille	Du Plessis, 617
Godin, Jehan	Mons	Meyhoffer notes
Goris, Adrien (André van Gorin)	Antwerp	Beza, *Correspondance*, no. 448
Guérart, Pierre (Evrard)	Nieuwport	De Moreau, v, 119
Guy, Martin	Tournai, Antwerp	EA, CCLXI fol. 51r
Heckelers, Wilhem	Hasselt	Hansay, 'Le sac,' 4
Hendrix, Jan	W. Flanders	Decavele, 'Hendrix'
Hubert	Antwerp	Paquot, x, 25
Huisman, Alardin	Tournai	Moreau, *Histoire*, 321
Jan	Valenciennes	Paillard, 11, 447
Konink, Charles (Karel de Coninck, Carolus Regius)	Antwerp, Ghent, Bruges	Decavele, *Dageraad*, 325–6
Lap	St Trond	Rahlenbeck, *Liège*, 270
Lemaistre (le beau moine)	Valenciennes	Leblanc, 103

[1] A member of de Pruet's family, maybe himself, committed iconoclasm at Ghent in 1566.

[2] A Jan Dierickxz (Dyrkinus), from Ghent, was a preacher at Emden in 1557 (Decavele, *Dageraad*, 11, pp. 102–3).

[3] Dufour was an elder at Antwerp in 1566.

[4] Fabri killed himself in prison in 1562. A Loys Savary was active as a preacher in Eekloo in 1566.

[5] Ferlitto passed through Antwerp in 1566.

[6] Froidure held a secret conventicle at the beginning of 1566, as did Gay.

Name	Area	Source
Le Roux, Pierre[1]	Bruges	Decavele, *Dageraad,* 339–40
Mallard, Philippe	Valenciennes	Muret, 23
Merula, Ange	Mons	Mahieu, 166–7
Mostaert, Chretien (Sinapius, Leenaertsz)	Bois-le-Duc	NNBW III, 1179
Nigri	St Trond	Rahlenbeck, *Liège,* 270
Obry, Adriaan (Haubry)	Nieuwport	Decavele, *Dageraad,* II, 154–5
Orphanus, Jacques	Dam (Flanders)	De Coussemaker, 202
Pollon, Jean	Tournai	Moreau, *Histoire,* 341
Poullain	Valenciennes	Clark, 172
Quaret, Jacques	Valenciennes	Paillard, IV, 202
Robillart, Michel	Valenciennes, Tournai	Moreau, *Histoire,* 233
Saravia, Adrien	Brussels, Antwerp	Hauben
Van Brugge, Hansken	Ypres	Diegerick, II, 179
Van den Wyer, Hans (Wijer)	Antwerp	Meyhoffer notes
Van Haemstede, Adrien	Antwerp	Gilmont, 'Les martyrologes'
Van Hardenberg, Albert (Rizeus, Durimontanus)	W. Flanders	BWK Prot. III, 504
Van Ostend, Jan	Antwerp	BN XVI, 219
Van Wingen, Jan[2]	Audenarde	Jubilee, 1217
Varlut, François	Valenciennes, Tournai	Muret, 20
Verdickt, Gilles	Antwerp	Decavele, *Dageraad,* 365–6
Vrambout, Georges (Joris Vramman)	Steenvoorde, W. Flanders	De Coussemaker, II, 44–5
Wallet, Jean	Lille, Quesnoy	Te Water, *Gent,* 69
Watelet, Thomas	Liège	Crespin, III, 261
Wyart, Jacques	Valenciennes	Paillard, IV, 177
Zoete, François	Hulst	Decavele, 'Axel,' 2–4

[1] Le Roux was cited as a 'propagandist.'

[2] In June, 1566, van Wingen escorted people from Audenarde and Ghent to Moded's first *prêche* (J. de Jong, *De voorbereiding en constitueering van het kerkverband der Nederlandsche Gereformeerde kerken in de zestiende eeuw* (Groningen, 1911), p. 176.

APPENDIX B:
MINISTERS ACTIVE DURING THE TROUBLES

Name	Status	Area	Violence	Source
Bacquereel, Hermes	'not without means'	Renaix		Raepsaet, 200; NNBW, II, 57
Baerdeloos, Adrien (Bertelot)	student, bourgeois	Hondschoote, Ghent	brother accused of sedition	Closset, 'Andreas' Verheyden, 'Nieuwport,' 6–7
Balck, Isbrand (Trabius)	priest, law degree	Antwerp	accused of seditious writings	BWK Prot. I, 301
Bécourt, Octavien	Dominican	Fr. Flanders	Wattrelos, lodged with iconoclast	De Coussemaker, II, 212, etc.
Bert, Pieter (Bardt)	hatmaker	W. Flanders	accused of iconoclasm, military campaigns	BWK Prot, I, 434–435; BM, Galba CIII. fol. 309
Boquinus, Petrus (Bogainus)	Carmelite theologian	Antwerp		Haag, 1st ed. II, 400
Capito, Jean[1]		Breda		NNBW VII, 277
Cappel, Louis[2]	noble, law student	Antwerp		Haag, 1st ed. III, 206
Carpentier, Pierre (Jacques)*	poor, spoke Latin	Antwerp, E. Flanders	opposed iconoclasm	CC 18, 693, fol. 30v CT 55, fol. 15r
Cateu, Jean	Franciscan	St Amand		Desilve, 74
Corro, Antonio[3]	monk	Antwerp		Hauben
Cubus, Jehan	taught Latin 1569	Bergen-op-Zoom	supported iconoclasm	WMV, I, I, 295, 297
Dathenus, Pieter*	Carmelite, relative échevin	Flanders, Antwerp	raised troops	Ruys
De Brès, Guy*	glass-painter	Lille, Tournai Valenciennes	siege	Braekman
De Brune, Jehan (Camphen)		Bailleul		De Coussemaker, I, 256; Galba, CIII, fol. 307

[1] Arrived in 1568.
[2] Arrived in 1569.
[3] Arrived November 1566.

Name	Status	Area	Violence	Source
De Buzère, Jacobus (Bucer)	Augustin	W. Flanders	iconoclasm, raised troops	De Coussemaker, II, 41, etc.
De la Grange, Peregrine*	noble	Valenciennes	siege	Paillard, 'Prêches'
De Lesenne Cornille	shoemaker	Antwerp, Fr. Flanders, Tournai	Wattrelos	EA, CCLXXXII, fol. 203
De Nielles, Charles*	bourgeois, theologian	Antwerp, Tournai		NNBW I, 1372
De Quekère, Gilles*	no goods	Hondschoote, Bergues	iconoclasm, siege	De Coussemaker, IV, 40
De Schildere, Willem (Claes, Nicolaus Pictor)	bourgeois, goods	W. Flanders		Kerk. Prot. 49, 214; Decavele, *Dageraad*, 393
De Voghele, Lodewijck*	Carmelite; father had property	Eekloo		Beenakker, 41; CT LV fol. 68v
Flameng, Robert	Latin teacher	Ypres	accused of bad acts	CT XXI fol. 473
Garcia, Philippe	Franciscan	W. Flanders, Deinze	supported iconoclasm	Decavele, *Dageraad*, 346. CT LV fol. 15r
Gillain, Jehan[1]	noble, educated	Breda		Beenakker, 119
Hazard, Pieter*	monk or hatmaker	Antwerp, Flanders	iconoclasm, siege	BWK Prot. III, 593–6; CT LV fol. 15r
Junius, François (du Jon)*	noble, law student	Antwerp, Limbourg, Ghent	opposed iconoclasm	Cuno
Lamoot, Jan	weaver	Ypres, W. Flanders	opposed iconoclasm	NNBW III, 733; WMV I, I, 189
Lantsochtius, Christophe	maybe monk	Flanders		BWK IX, 965
Le Bron, Karel	lawyer	Audenarde	Orange's camp	Lenoir, 138
Leseur, Jean	Carmelite, student	Valenciennes	iconoclasm	Desilve, 230, etc.
Lippens, Jan* (Noviportuensis)	burgomaster, surgeon	Breda, Eekloo		Beenakker, 43; CT LV fol. 69r
Marmier, Etienne*	doctor of law	Tournai, Antwerp, Bruges	siege	Meyhoffer, 'Un bourgeois'
Matte, Sebastien*	hatmaker	W. Flanders, Armentières	iconoclasm, siege	De Coussemaker, IV, 22, etc.
May, Jean (Moy)	monk	Enghien, Lessen, Leffinge		Janssen, *Vlaanderen*, 283; Kerk Prot. 264
Micheus, Jan	burgher family	Ghent, Antwerp		Meylan, 'Lettres'

[1] Arrived November 1566.

Ministers active during the troubles

Name	Status	Area	Violence	Source
Michiels, Jan		Bruges, W. Flanders	iconoclasm murder	Backhouse; Galba CIII, fol. 307
Missuens, Jan* (Cornelissen van Diest)	priest	Antwerp, Brussels, Bruges, Thielt		Broer Cornelis, 47; CC XIII, 66
Moded, Herman*	Carmelite, professor	Antwerp, Flanders, Hasselt	iconoclasm, siege	Brutel de la Rivière
Mostaert, Chrétien*[1]	Benedictine	Bois-le-Duc		Kleijntjens, 31
Pieters, Balthasar (Annozius, le rat d'eau)	Dominican	Ghent, Axel	took over church	Janssen, Vlaanderen, 248
Platevoet, Mahieu		Boeschepe		Kerk Prot. 214; Galba CIII, fol. 302; Backhouse, 74
Pontfort, Jacob	relative with property	Ypres, Lo	prevented riot	Diegerick, 226; CT XXI, fol. 473; CC 18.803, fol. 35v
Rhetius, Cornille	lawyer	Antwerp		van Roosbroeck, Emigranten, 65, 82; CC 18.312 fol. 10r
Rudsemelis, Jan	burgher family	Ghent	relatives were iconoclasts	Delmotte, 160; Campene 33
Ryckwaert, Charles (Theofilus)	'man of property'	Ypres	accused of iconoclasm	Diegerick, 254; Decavele, Dageraad, 410
Sterkenbrugge, Jakob van		Ypres		Roosbroeck, Emigranten, p. 94
Strobbe, Jehan (Cromhals)		Steenvoorde, Hondschoote		De Coussemaker, IV, 236; Galba CIII, fol. 301
Taffin, Jean*	bourgeois, magistrate family	Antwerp	opposed iconoclasm	Boer
Top, Erasmus (Dr Spoel, de Weever)*	weaver	Antwerp, Bergen-op-Zoom, Turnhout		CC 18.693; CT XVIII fol. 1
Valencijn[2]		Antwerp		Jubilee
Van Culembourg, Jacobus	priest, U. of Cologne	Bois-le-Duc, Eindhoven	preached after iconoclasm	van der Laar; CT XXI fol. 9r
Van der Heyden, Gaspar*	burgher family	Antwerp, E. Flanders	iconoclasm, military	van Lennep
Van der Schuere, Nicaise	merchant family	Ghent, Audenarde, Turnhout	iconoclasm	CT XXI fol. 492; CT XVIII fol. 1

[1] Mostaert preached in 1561–6; he may have left before the Troubles.
[2] He preached once in March 1566; a Pierre Valentin was pastor at Emden in1554–61.

Name	Status	Area	Violence	Source
Van Vyve, Jan	butcher, nephew of bailiff	Bruges		Campene, 41; Decavele, *Dageraad*, 343
Wille, Ambroise* (Vuille)	shoemaker	Tournai, Antwerp	iconoclasm, siege	Hocquet, 144, etc.
Wingius, Godfried*	knew Hebrew, tutor	Antwerp, Flanders	opposed iconoclasm	NNBW, III, 1433
Wybo, Joris*	son of bailiff, schoolmaster	Antwerp, Flanders, Bois-le-Duc	supported iconoclasm, violence	NNBW III, 1494; CT LV fol. 68v

APPENDIX C:
LAY PREACHERS ACTIVE DURING THE
TROUBLES (BEFORE 1570)

ORIGINS UNKNOWN

Name	Area	Violence	Connection with Reformers	Source
Aert	Eindhoven	accused of inciting iconoclasm		CT XXI fol. 9r
Anonymous	Ghent		brought from France by Refs.	van Vaernewijck II, 124
Anonymous	Antwerp			AA XIII, 56
Augustus	Antwerp		knew Micheus	Meylan, 'L'église,' 79
Callewaert, Lievyn	Antwerp	bearing arms	wrote to Micheus	NNBW IV, 392; Meylan, 77
Carbon, Pierre*	Antwerp[1]			Meyhoffer notes
Carlus, Tousain*	Douai			Beuzart, Hérésies, 275
Coeman, Louis[2]	Nieuwport			Verheyden, 'Nieuwport,' 6
Crapandiau	Armentières		brought from France by Refs.	De Coussemaker, II, 213
Damiseau, Remy	Nivelles			CC III fol. 65r
Daniel, Jean	Bailleul, Antwerp	present at collection of funds	lodged with Refs.	de Coussemaker, I, 55
De Buire, Jehan	Richebourg		fixed preacher after iconoclasm	de Coussemaker, I, 256
De Hase, Pieter	Commines	accused of sedition		BWK VIII, 251–2
De Meen, Cornelis (de Nieen)	Brussels			van Haemstede, 446
De Meester, Adrien	Antwerp			BWK IV, 118
De Meghem, Guillaume	Antwerp		maybe elder	CC CXI fol. 33r

[1] Carbon was in Hainaut before 1566, and a prisoner in Antwerp (for preaching) in 1570.
[2] A Jean Coeman preached in Nieuwport around 1561.

Appendix C

Name	Area	Violence	Connection with Reformers	Source
De Messere, Michiel (Ingels, de Walem)	Ypres, Commines, itinerant			van Haemstede, 437
De Monnier, Meus	Renaix			Raepsaet, 202
De Pourcq, Arnold	Renaix			Raepsaet, 200
De Vlameng, Jan	Hasselt	iconoclasm	icon. with Moded	Daris, 402
Dheutkin, Joos	Beveren			Meyhoffer notes
Du Bois, Josse	Merxem, Eeckeren			CT III, fol. 46v
Dumont, Gilles	Armentières, Poperinge, Furnes	iconoclasm, siege of Furnes	lodged with Refs., wrote to Hond-schoote church	de Coussemaker, IV, 16–17
Du Rieu, Adrien (Olieux, Ol)	Armentières			Sepp Predikanten, 42
Erasme*[1]	Outremeuse	army with Orange	lodged with Refs.	Boehmer, 92–3; Rahlenbeck, Outremeuse, 149
Frizon, Henri (Trizon)	Bergen-op-Zoom			Kleinjtens, 206
Gérard	Antwerp		Walloon church	Leblanc, Appendix
Gheetius, Herman	Audenarde		lodged with Refs., fixed preacher	van den Meersch, 184
Grincourt, Jean	La Gorgue	son carried arms	fixed preacher	de Coussemaker, II, 195, 368
Halewijn, Conrad	Bruges			de Schrevel, 92
Herman	Breda			CC Cart. 129, li. 43
Jodocus	Bruges, Audenarde			Broer Cornelis, 47
Julien	Fr. Flanders	iconoclasm, Wattrelos	fought with Bécourt, Ghent synod, fixed preacher	van Vloten, 86; de Coussemaker, II, 212
Labruicken, Jehan (Laboutgen)	Eupen		fixed preacher	Bax, 84
Loysier, Mahieu	Ypres, Poperinge		tried to replace Ryck-waert at Ypres	CT XXI, fol. 463r
Mariette	Ypres			van Vaernewijck, II, 324
Martenus	Audenarde, Zynghem	iconoclasm	brought by Refs.	v. d. Meersch, 172–3
Nicolas (Jean Clinquemeure)	Warneton, Artois	raised troops	Ghent synod; fixed preacher	de Coussemaker, IV, 81

[1] Family local Reformers.

Lay preachers active during the troubles

Name	Area	Violence	Connection with Reformers	Source
Oude, Jehan (Houde)	Antwerp, Lille			CC III, fol. 95r
Outreleauwe, Jehan	Sailly, La Gorgue, Estaires		preached with Bécourt for weeks at Sailly	de Coussemaker, II, 197; CT XXI, fol. 496
Paneel, Michel	W. Flanders			Meyhoffer notes
Pierre	Quesnoy-sur-Deule			Beuzart, BSHPF, p. 47
Pierre	Hasselt	iconoclasm	icon. with Moded	Daris, p. 402
Pinchart*	Prémont, Honécies	wounded vicar	knew Leseur	Desilve, 59
Pluquet, Nicolas	itinerant Lille area	carried letters for Louis of Nassau	letters for Antwerp consistory	Frossard, 107
Puthuys, Paulus or Frederick	Antwerp			Meyhoffer notes
Pyllian, François	Ypres			Meyhoffer notes
Rattevangerken[1]	Bois-le-Duc, Eindhoven	son did iconoclasm	lodged with Refs.	Cuypers van Velthoven, 359
Ruvart	Antwerp			Meyhoffer notes
Schoemaker, Pierre[2]	W. Flanders	Wattrelos, accused of murder	came with Refs. from England	de Coussemaker, I, 206, III, 254–5
Schoonhove, Gilles	Wormhoudt		fixed preacher	Ibid., III, 57–8
Stoffijn	Antwerp			Meyhoffer notes
Tardif, Jacob	Audenarde			Meyhoffer notes
Theodore	Commines			Messiaen, 20
Thevelin, Walerand	Tourcoing	relative an iconoclast[3]	Ghent synod, fixed preacher	Diegerick, III, 255
Tomas, Laurins	Louvain			Groen van Prinstrer, II, 283
Tuny	Antwerp			BCHEW II, 140
Van Baecx, Lambert	Wessem (Liège)		brought by Refs.	van Hasselt, II, 37
Van der Thomme, Mathijs (Tombe)	Steenwerck		with Refs. in London	Verheyden, Liste No. 10.705
Van Diest, Jan	Bruges		supported by Refs.	de Schrevel, 334; v. Haemstede, 443
Van Hatthem, Melchior	Rexpoede	'dissolute behavior'[4]		Decavele, Dageraad, 410–11
Van Hernen, Gilles	Antwerp			CC III, fol. 97v

[1] This could be the same as Jacobus or Yshondekin – the witnesses are confused on this point.
[2] A Pieter de Schoemakere, born in Flanders, was in London as a Reformer in 1561.
[3] A Jacques Thevelin from Armentières (Beuzart, BSHPF, p. 54).
[4] He was arrested in 1564 for violence to the clergy.

Name	Area	Violence	Connection with Reformers	Source
Van Thorn, Lem (Renttenisse)	Wessem		brought by Refs., lodged	van Hasselt, II, 37
Verrier, Gerardus Loyen[1]	Eindhoven			CT XXI, fol. 9r
Vriese	Audenarde		knew ministers, Ref. meetings	v. d. Meersch, 184
Woudanus, Johannes	Antwerp		signed at Wesel	CC III fol. 97v

ARTISANS OR LABORERS

Name	Area	Violence	Connection with Reformers	Source
Beyers, Hermes, miller	Renaix			Raepsaet, 200–2
Chemin, Denis, blacksmith	Lannoy			Meyhoffer notes
Coomans, Joris, shoemaker	Antwerp			AA XII, 300
De Hasque, Denis rope-maker	Liège			Daris, 399–400
De Hongère, Mailgaert, weaver	Elverdinge, Messine	invasion of Ypres	consecrated by Hazard; fixed preacher	Diegerick, I, 107
De Wilde, Nicasius, fuller	Ypres			Heinderycx, 363
Escaille, Antoine, shoemaker's son	Lestrem, La Gorgue, Estaires	Wattrelos	fought with Bécourt; fixed preacher	de Coussemaker, II. 212–13, 299. Beuzart, *Hérésies*, 294–5
Geerking, Joost, market gardener	Deinze			CT LV fol. 15r
Happaert, Gabriel, cabinet-maker[2]	Deinze			van Vloten, 139
Hector, laborer	Turnhout, Arendonk	iconoclasm		CC III fol. 26v
Hessels, François, fuller	Ypres, Nieuwkerke		accord Ypres	CT VI fol. 176 Janssen, *Ypres*, 250
Houvenagle, Gilles, brewer[3]	Hazebrouck	iconoclasm	org. church	de Coussemaker, II, 43
Laerle, Jan, mason	Bruges		consistory, dealt with Junius	de Schrevel, 791–2
Loonis, Jan, laborer	Renty (Artois)	set dog on soldier		Diegerick, III, 153–4
Louchard, Jean, 'mosnier'	La Gorgue	met troops at Tournai	elder, La Gorgue	de Coussemaker, II, 260

[1] Also called Loyen – perhaps 'verrier' = glassmaker.
[2] Father fled to Sandwich in 1563.
[3] A Willem Hoevenaghel was in the Sandwich church in 1563 (Galba CIII, fol. 308v)

Lay preachers active during the troubles

Name	Area	Violence	Connection with Reformers	Source
Schelins, Josse, upholsterer[1]	Renaix			Raepsaet, 200
Schuddematte, Adriaan, laborer[2]	Renaix			Ibid., 200; Decavele, Dageraad, II, 174–5
Soret, Jean, silk-dresser	Bruges	attacked guard	consistory	de Schrevel, 798; Campene, 41
Van Aken, Goert (heer Gielis), cobbler	Maastricht, Reckheim	iconoclasm	preached with Moded	Bax, 131, 144
Van Joncx, Nemaer, baker	Deinze			CT LV, fol. 15r
Vercoye, Jan, 'legwerker'	Deinze			CT LV, fol. 15r
Watelet, Maurice Baudewin son of weaver	Dolhain			Bax, 88

LAY PREACHERS: MIDDLE CLASS OR PROFESSIONAL

Name	Area	Violence	Connection with Reformers	Source
Bourlette, Adrien, burgomaster	Limbourg	army with Orange	local church	Boehmer, 92–3
Claissone, Jan* merchant[2]	E. Flanders			Decavele, 'Hendrix' 24
Claeysson, Lucas, later prof. of Greek	Ghent			WMV I, I, 123
De Joing, Jehan, schoolmaster	Limbourg			Leblanc, Appendix
De Pourck, Jan, apothecary or grocer	Deinze, Audenarde	iconoclasm,	fixed preacher	van der Meersch, 184
Lems, Gilles, property	Bruges		consistory	de Schrevel, 791–2
Lenaerts, Pieter, merchant	Bois-le-Duc	iconoclasm	treasurer of consistory	Cuypers van Velthoven, 299
Lopez, Martin, merchant, jurist	Antwerp	recruiting troops	consistory, 3 million	Goris, 202
Moyessone Jehan,* clerk	Brussels		Geneva, Emden	CC, III, fol. 53v
Pierre, schoolmaster	Breda	paid iconoclasts	elder, 3 million	Beenakker, 167
Slabbaert, Godfried, owned store	Bruges		consistory	CC 18.803, fol. 27v–29; de Schrevel, 229
Traisnel, Antoine, son of échevin	Sailly	father led icon. Wattrelos	father local Ref.	de Coussemaker, II, 362, etc.

[1] Cited as Protestant in 1564 (Decavele, Dageraad, II, 174–5).
[2] Preached E. Flanders 1562–6; in Antwerp until 1571, maybe as preacher.

Name	Area	Violence	Connection with Reformers	Source
Traisnel, Christophe, échevin	Sailly	iconoclasm, distributed weapons	delegate to Antwerp for 3 million	Ibid., II, 290
Van den Driessche Clement, linen merchant[1]	Audenarde		consistory	Verheyden, 'Audenarde,' 13
Vrancq, Jerome, lawyer with property	Deinze, Antwerp area			CC 18.312, fol. 21v. CC, III, fol. 96v
Waghe, Hendrick, wine merchant	Bruges		consistory	CT VI fol. 267–267v

LAY PREACHERS: CATHOLIC CLERGY

Name	Area	Violence	Connection with Reformers	Source
Adrien	Oostwinkel	iconoclasm		Ryckaert, 109
Algoet, Antoine de Zwarte)	W. Flanders, itinerant	iconoclasm planned siege Ypres	preached with Buzère, Hazard; Wesel in 1568	Janssen, Vlaanderen, 363; BN, I, 221
Anonymous	Ghent			van Vaernewijck, I, 576
Anonymous*	Hedel		lodged Walraeven	Acqouy, 13–14
Anonymous	Outremeuse			Rahlenbeck, Outremeuse, 149
Anonymous	Orques, Bailleul Remegies			Pasquier de la Barre, I, 72; II, 281, 285n.
Bonniel, Jehan* (Ganin l'abbé)	Quesnoy area			Frossard, 99
Cools, Martin	Ghent	brother an iconoclast	preached with van der Schuere	van Vaernewijck, I, 284; II, 103
Corbeel, A.	Bergues area	iconoclasm		de Coussemaker, III, 61–2
Daneel, Carolus	W. Flanders itinerant			Janssen, Ypres, 276–7
De Bestère, Noel	Estaires, La Gorgues	Wattrelos	fought with Bécourt, Ghent synod; fixed preacher	de Coussemaker, II, 212
De Bruninck, Laurent (de Brueseler)	Turnhout		maybe Emden '71	de Jong, De voorbereiding, 197
De Hollandère, Guillaume, (Cromhals)	W. Flanders, itinerant		fixed preacher	CT LV, fol. 121–121v

[1] Had property and a long list of business debts (Enno van Gelder, Gegevens, No. 135).

Lay preachers active during the troubles

Name	Area	Violence	Connection with Reformers	Source
De Lontzen, Dionysius Florin (Heer Nyse Dionysius Vlach)	Liège			Bax, 84
De Lontzen, Jehan (Jean Vlach)	Liège		followed Junius to Germany '67	Bax, 84; Lenoir 108
De Meyere, Gilles	Ghent			Van Nuffel
De Roubaix, Royer	Ypres		knew Ryckwaert	van den Bussch, 363
De Royere, Michiel (d'Oudenburg)	Bruges		married by Dathenus	Broer Cornelis, 63
De Smet, Martin	Mechelen		sent by Antwerp church Wesel '68[1]	van Vaernewijck, I, 321
Habosch, Simon	Ghent area			Janssen, Vlaanderen, 98
Jan	Tournai			Meyhoffer notes
Joost (Josse)	Eekloo			CT LV fol. 68v
Kackhoes* (Jan van Gutekoven, Scheitzhabener, Jan v. Rumunde)	Maastricht Reckheim, itinerant	iconoclasm, barricaded market	preached with Moded, Dathenus; synod Antwerp '66; fixed preacher	Bax, 113, etc.
Kok, Jehan[2] (Cocus)	Antwerp			CT, XXI, fol. 516, Wagener, 124
LeFebvre, Loys	Renaix			CC 18.942, fol. 5v
Lievyn	Commines			Messiaen, 20
Lupis, Martin	St Trond,			Rahlenbeck, Liège, p. 270
Malpau, Jehan	Bergues			CT LXIV, fol. 113
Martin*	Antwerp			Rahlenbeck, Liège, 12
Moermanszone, Heyndrick (v. Beerse)	Turnhout			CC 18.693, fol. 21–21v. CC, 608, fol. 10v
Munt, Jehan (Montanus, Hove, Bergensis, Minet)	Bruges, Zevecote		recruited Junius for church	Janssen, Bruges, 60
Panquert, Nicolas	Kettenis, Eupen, Lontzen			CC III, fol. 68v CC, 18.700, fol. 175r
Robrecht, Martin	Ypres			Diegerick, 226
Savary, Loys	Eekloo		preached with Carpentier. Salaried	Janssen, Vlaanderen, 88; CT, LV fol. 68v

[1] Expelled from Emden in 1571 (de Jong, De voorbereiding, 166).
[2] Jean Cocus at Emden synod '71 – minister from Flanders; a Jehan le Cocq ex-vicar Ypres; a Kok preached at Antwerp.

Name	Area	Violence	Connection with Reformers	Source
Tuerlinck, Jan	Oostwinkel	iconoclasm		van Nuffel, 443
Van Houte, Jan	Turnhout	iconoclasm	brought by Refs.	CC 18.693, fol. 30
Van Kerpen, Willem	Montfort			Marcus, 204
van Lommersen, Willem, Florin	Eupen, Baelen, Lontzen			Bax, 84
Van Maeldegem, Adrien	Sotteghem	accused of sedition	sent by London church	van Nuffel, 441; CC 18.774, fol. 7v
Van Mechelen, Jaspar	Antwerp, Weerdt			van Hasselt, II, 37
Van Til, Thomas	Antwerp	refused to hinder icon.	knew Taffin, Balck	Steenackers
Van Woensel, Goert (also sold flax)	Bois-le-Duc	iconoclasm	consistory	Cuypers van Velthoven, 390
Walraeven, Cornelis (van Diest, Graspape)	Bois-le-Duc	iconoclasm	consistory; fixed preacher; Wesel, 1568	van der Laar
Xhoka, Lenaert (l'Aisnez, Phoca)	Limbourg, Eupen		fixed preacher	Bax, 77

* Active as a preacher in the Netherlands before 1566.

BIBLIOGRAPHY

MANUSCRIPT SOURCES

AGR Chambre des comptes, comptes des confiscations: Vols. 3, 13, 18, 111, 129, 282, 608, 18.312, 18.693, 18.700, 18.774, 18.803, 18.942.

AGR Conseil des troubles: 1567–1573. Vols. 3, 6, 17 (Axel), 18, 21, 38 (Bois-le-Duc, Bergen-op-Zoom), 39–40 (Antwerp), 42 (Armentières, Audenarde), 53 (Maastricht), 55 (Ghent), 64 (Bruges), 65 (Deinze, Ypres), 88, 103–4 (Valenciennes), 91–2 (Alleu, Béthune), 94 (Laventhie), 105 (Tournai).

AGR Papiers des états et audiences: Vols. 58, 261, 282 (Correspondance de Flandre, Artois, Lille et Tournay, 1565–7); 502 (Papiers des troubles); 530, 1175/1 (Troubles religieux, correspondance et placcards, 1566); 1175/7 (réunions secrets des hérétiques); 1739/1 (correspondance de Margaret de Parme, 1566).

Rijksarchief Antwerpen, Priviligiekamer 272: Briefwisseling van het magistraat, II, 1555–68.

Bibliotheque Royale, Brussels:

Mss. HS 17.510–525: Brief discours envoyé au roy Philippe nostre sire et souverain seigneur, pour le bien et profit de sa maiesté, et singulierement de ses pais Bas: Auquel est monstré le moyen qu'il faudroit tenir pour obvier aux troubles et émotions pour le fait de la religion, et extirper les sectes et hérésies pululantes en ses dits pais. 1565.

16591–16592 No. 3892: Thomas van Til. Seyndbrieff aen N.N. signen goeden heeren en vrienden, waerinne die oorsaecken en waeromme hij uuyt den pausdom vertrocken, ende d'abdije van Sint Bernaerts, buyten Antwerpen, verlate heeft, verhaelt worden, ende sijner en der waerheyt vianden valschen achterclap bantwoort wordt. 1568.

Adrianum Zaraphya. Een hertgrondighe beheerte, vanden edelen, lanckmoedighen, hoochgheboren prince van Orangien, mitsgaders alle syne Christelijcke edele, vrome bontghenooten, op alle menschen begheert... welcke landen ny soeckt te bederven ende heef te ruineeren, onder tchijn van beschermingge, eenen ghenaemt Duca de Alba.

Bibliotheque municipale, Valenciennes:

Mss. 689, fol. 9–10 (Iconoclasm).

British Museum, London:

Mss. Galba 103, fols. 301–9: records of the Dutch Reformed consistory at Sandwich, 1563.

Bibliography

WORKS PUBLISHED BEFORE 1650

Alardus, Franciscus. *Een cort vervat van alle menschelycke insettinghen der Roomscher kercke...ghenomen meer dan uut XXII authoren.* Antwerp, 1566.

Anon. *Recueil des choses advenues en Anvers, touchant la fait de la religion, en l'an 1566.* n.p., n.d.

Sommaire de la confession de foy, que doivent faire ceux qui désirent estre tenus pour membres de l'église de Iesus Christ: leu après la prédication publique, faite près d'Anvers, le 28 de Iulet 1566. n.p., n.d.

Cornelis Adriansz, Broer. *Historie van Br. Lornelis Adriansz van Dordrecht, Minnebroeder tot Brugge. Inde welke verhaalt wert...sijne wonderlijke, vuyle, grouwelijke, ia bloetdorstige en lasterlijke sermoonen, die hij binnen Brugge gepredikt heeft.* n.p., 1628.

Corrano, Antonio. *Epistre et amiable remonstrance d'un ministre de l'évangile de nostre rédempteur Iesus Christ, envoyée aux pasteurs de l'église Flamengue d'Anvers, lesquelz se nomment de la confession d'Augsbourg, les exhortant à concorde et amitié avec les autres ministres de l'évangile.* n.p., 1567.

Dathenus, Pieter. *Een Christelijcke verantwoordinghe op die disputacie, ghehouden binnen Audenarde, tusschen M. Adriaen Hamstadt, ende Jan Daelman beschreven met onwaerheyt, ende wtghegheven door Dan Daelman voorseyt.* Antwerpen: By Jasper Troyens woonende op die carte velte in den Tennen Pot, 1582.

De Brès, Guy, ed., *Histoire notable de la trahison et emprisonnement de deux bons et fidèles personnages en la ville d'Anvers: c'est assavoir, de Christophle Fabri ministre de la parole de Dieu en ladite ville, et d'Olivier Bouck professeur...desquels l'un estant grievement malade a esté delivré...et l'autre a esté cruellement meurtri, et offert en sacrifice à Dieu par le feu.* Antwerp, 1565.

La racine, source et fondement des Anabaptistes ou rebaptisez de nostre temps. Avec trèsample réfutation des arguments principaux, par lesquels ils ont accoutumé de troubler l'église de nostre Seigneur Iesus Christ, et séduire les simples. n.p.: Chez Abel Clemence, 1565.

Frarin, Peter. *An Oration against the Unlawfull Insurrections of the Protestantes of our Time, under Pretence to Refourme Religion. Made and Pronounced in Latin, in the Schole of Artes at Louvaine, the XIIII of December Anno 1565.* Antwerp: Ex Officina Ioannis Fouleri, 1566.

Marnix de St Aldegonde, Philippe. *Vraye narration et apologie des choses passées au Pays-Bas, touchant le fait de la religion en l'an 1566 par ceus qui font profession de la religion Réformée audit pays.* n.p., 1567.

Remonstrance et supplication de ceus de l'église Réformée de la ville de Valencenes sur le mandement de Son Altesse, fait contre eus le 14 jour de Decembre 1566. n.p., 1567. [Preface published in BSHPF, cviii (1962), pp. 22–4.]

Richardot, François. *Epistre d'un evesque, aux ministres des églises nouvelles.* Paris: Chez la veufve de Guillaume Morel, 1566.

Sermon des images faict à Armentiers par messire Francoys Richardot, evesque d'Arras. Louvain: De l'imprimerie de Jean Bogard, à la Bible d'Or, 1567.

Bibliography

Stapletonus, Thomas. *A Returne of Untruthes upon M. Jewelle's Replie*. Antwerp, 1566.

Taffin, Jean. *L'Estat de l'église, avec le discours des temps depuis les apostres iusques au present*. Bergen-op-Zoom: Jaques Canin, 1605.

Verlinde, Willem (Lindanus). *Een clair betooch vanden oorspronck der Lutherie, van die menichvuldicheyt der secten...Van die schade ende bloetstortinghe die ter cause der secten is gheschiet int Christendom vanden jare duust 1517 tot den jare duust 1566*. tr. B. Jacop vande Weede. Bruges: inde Peerde Strate bij mij Pieter de Clerck, 1567.

MODERN EDITIONS OF CONTEMPORARY DOCUMENTS

Alard, Franciscus. 'Die catechismus op vrage ende andtwoorde gestelt door Franciscum Alardum pastoor tho Wilster eertijt predicant thantwerpen in de schuere.' 1568. Rpt. *Jaarboek der vereeniging van Nederlanden-Luthersche kerkgeschiedenis*. Ed. J. W. Pont. Amsterdam: Ten Brink en De Vries, 1909.

Balck, Isbrand. *Leerrede over Marcus 4. Vs. 30-33. Door Isbrandus Balckius of Trabius, uitgesproken te Antwerpen, op den April 1567, daags voordat de predikanten uit die stad verdreven werden en twee dagen, voordat Prins Willem I uit haar en uit Nederland naar zijne Duitsche staten week*. Ed. B. Glasius. Dordrecht: H. Lagerweij, 1858.

Baum and Cunitz, eds., *Histoire écclésiastique des églises Réformées au royaume de France*. Vols. 1–3. Paris: Librairie Fischbacher, 1883–4.

Bertrijn, Geeraard. *Chronyck der stadt Antwerpen*. Ed. Geest. van Havre, Antwerp, 1879.

Beza, Theodore. *Correspondance de Theodore de Bèze, recueillié par Hippolyte Aubert, publiée par Fernand Aubert et Henri Meylan. Vol. VI: 1566*. Geneva: Droz, 1960–.

Burgon, J. W. *The Life and Times of Sir Thomas Gresham*. Vol. 2. London: Robert Jennings, 1839.

Calvin, John. *Institutes of the Christian Religion*. 1559. Trans. John Allen, Rpt. Philadelphia: Presbyterian Board of Christian Education, 1936.

Ioannis Calvini Opera (59 vols), Ed. J. Baum, E. Cunitz and E. Reuss. Brunswick, 1863–1900.

Cramer, S. and Pijper, F. eds. *Procedures tenues à l'endroit de ceux de la religion du Pais Bas. Auquelles est amplement déduit comme Guy de Brès et Peregrin de la Grange ont signé par leur sang la doctrine de l'évangile*. Biblioteca Reformatoria Neerlandica. Vol. 8. The Hague: Martinus Nijhoff, 1911.

Crespin, Jean. *Histoire des martyrs, persecutez et mis à mort pour la vérité de l'évangile, depuis le temps des apostres iusques à present*. 1619. Ed. D. Benoit. Rpt. Toulouse: Société des livres religieux, 1889.

De Brès, Guy. *Le baton de la foi*. 1555. Rpt. *Guy de Brès: Pages choisies*. Ed. E. Braekman: Brussels: Société Calviniste de Belgique, 1967.

Epitres. Rpt. *Guy de Brès: Pages choisies*.

De Coussemaker, Ed. *Troubles religieux du XVI⁰ siècle dans la Flandre maritime*,

1560–1570. 4 vols. Bruges: Aimé de Zuttère, successeur de van de Casteele-Werbrouck, 1876.

De Mendoça, B. *Commentaires de Bernardino de Mendoca sur les événements de la guerre des Pays-Bas, 1567–1577*. Trans. Loumier. Vol. 1 Brussels: Société de l'histoire de Belgique, 1860.

De Sainctes, F. C. *Discours sur le saccagement des églises Catholiques par les hérétiques anciens, et nouveaux Calvinistes, en l'an 1562*. Paris, 1563. Rpt. *Archives curieuses de l'histoire de France, depuis Louis XI jusqu 'à Louis XVII*. Ed. L. Climber and F. Danjou. 1 ser. Vol. 4. Paris: Beauvais, membre de l'institut historique, 1835.

De Schrevel, A. C., ed. *Troubles religieux du XVIᵉ siècle au quartier de Bruges, 1566–1568*. Bruges: Imprimerie de Louis de Plancke, 1894.

Des Marez, G. 'Documents relatifs aux excès commis à Ypres par les iconoclastes (le 15 et le 16 Août 1566).' BCRH 5 ser. Vol. 7 (1897), pp. 547–82; Vol. 89 (1925), pp. 95–127.

De Vries, H. ed. *Geneve pépinière du Calvinisme Hollandais*. Vol. 1: *Les étudiants des Pays-Bas à Genève au temps de Theodore de Bèze*. Fribourg (Suisse): Fragnière frères, éditeurs, 1918. Vol. 11: *Correspondance des élèves de Theodore de Bèze après leur départ de Genève*. Ed. H. de Vries de Heekelingen. The Hague: Martinus Nijhoff, 1924.

De Wesembeke, J. *Mémoires de Jacques de Wesembeke*. Ed. C. Rahlenbeck. Brussels: Chez M. Weissenbruch, imprimeur du roi, 1859.

Diegerick, I. L. A., ed. *Documents du XVIᵉ siècle, Archives d'Ypres (Documents concernant les troubles religieux)*. Vol. 1: *Mémoire justificatif du magistrat d'Ypre sur les troubles religieux arrivés en cette ville, en 1566 et 1567*. Bruges: Imprimé chez Aimé de Zuttère, 1874.

Enno van Gelder, H. A., *Gegevens betreffende roerend en unroerend bezit in de Nederlanden in de 16ᵉ eeuw*. The Hague: Martinus Nijhoff, 1972.

Fery de Guyon. *Mémoires de Fery de Guyon, écuyer, bailly general d'Anchin et de Pesquencourt*. Ed. De Robaulx de Soumoy. Brussels: Société de l'histoire de Belgique, 1858.

Fris, V., ed. *Notes pour servir à l'histoire des iconoclastes et des Calvinistes à Gand de 1566 à 1568*. Ghent: Société de l'histoire et d'archéologie de Gand, 1909.

Gachard, M., ed. *Correspondance de Philippe II sur les affaires des Pays-Bas*. Vol. 1. Brussels: Librairie ancienne et moderne, 1848.

'La chainture des gheustz du jour Saint-Andrieu 1566, de laquelle chainture lesdicts gheustz se vantoient de chaindre la ville de ville,' *La bibliotheque nationale à Paris*, Vol. 1, pp. 388–93.

Gaillard, V., ed. *Archives du conseil de Flandres*. Ghent: Imprimerie et lithographie de De Busscher frères, 1856.

Geisendorf, P. -F., ed. *Livre des habitants de Genève*. Vol. 1: *1549–1560*. Vol. 2: *1572–1574, 1585–1587*. Geneva: Librairie Droz, 1963, 1957.

Le livre du recteur de l'académie de Genève, 1559–1878. Travaux d'humanisme et Renaissance. Vol. 33. Geneva, 1959.

Génard, P., ed. *Personen te Antwerpen in de XVIᵉ eeuwe voor het feit van religie gerechtelyk vervolgd. List en ambtelyke bijhoorige stukken*. AA. Vols. 7–14, 1926, etc.

Bibliography

Goeters, W. G., ed. 'Dokumenten van Adriaan van Haemstede, waaronder eene Gereformeerde geloofsbelijdenis van 1559.' NAvKG Vol. 5 afl. 1 (1907), pp. 1–64.

Groen van Prinstrer, J. G., ed. *Archives ou correspondance inédite de la maison d'Orange-Nassau.* 1 ser. Vol. 2: 1566. Leiden: S. and J. Luchtmans, 1835.

Halkin, L. -E. and Moreau, G. 'Le procès de Paul Chevalier à Lille et Tournai en 1564.' BCRH Vol. 131 (1965), pp. 1–74.

Haton, C. *Mémoires de Claude Haton contenant le récit des événements accomplis de 1553 à 1592, principalement dans la Champagne et la Brie.* Ed. F. Bourquelot (Collection de documents inédits sur l'histoire de France) Paris, 1857.

Heinderycx, P. *Jaerboeken van Veurne en Veurnambacht.* Ed. E. Ronse. Vol. 2. Veurne: J. Bonhomme, boekdrukker, 1855.

Hessels, J. H., ed. *Ecclesiae Londino-Batavae Archivum.* Vol. 2: *Epistolae et Tractatus cum Reformationis tum Ecclesiae Londino-Batavae Historiam Illustrantes 1544–1622.* Cambridge: Tupis Academicis Excudebant C. J. Clay A. M. et Fil., 1889.

Janssen, H. Q. and van Dale, J. H. 'De Hervormde vlugtelingen van Yperen in Engeland. Geschetst naar hunne brieven. Een bijdrage tot de Hervormings geschiedenis van Yperen en Norwich.' *Bijdragen tot de oudheidkunde en geschiedenis, inzonderheid van Zeeuwsch-Vlaanderen.* 1857 2: 211–306.

Janssen H. Q. and van Toorenenbergen, J. J. *Brieven uit onderscheidene kerkelijke archieven.* WMV 3 ser. Vol. 3.

Johnston, E., ed. *Actes du consistoire de l'église Française de Threadneedle Street, Londres.* 1: 1560–1565. *Publications of the Huguenot Society of London.* Vol. 38.

Junius, Franciscus. *Francisci Junii Theologileidensis Vita. Scrinium Antiquarium Sive Miscellanea Groningana Nova ad Historiam Reformationis Ecclesiasticam Praecipue Spectantia. Inseruntur Tractatus Varii Generis. Epistolae. Orationes. Bibliographiae.* Vol. 1). Groningen 1749.

Kist, N. C., ed. 'De synoden der Nederlandsche Hervormde kerken onder het kruis, gedurende de jaren 1563–1577, gehouden in Braband, Vlaanderen, etc.' NAvKG Vol. 9 (AvKG, Vol. 20) 1849, pp. 113–210.

Kluckholn, A., ed. *Briefe Friedrich des frommen, Kurfürsten von der Pfalz, mit verwandten Schriftstücken.* 2 Vols. Braunschweig: C. U. Schwetschte und Sohn, 1868.

Kossman, E. H. and Mellink, A. F., *Texts Concerning the Revolt of the Netherlands.* Cambridge: Cambridge University Press, 1974.

Kuyper, A., ed. *Kerkeraads-protocollen der Hollandsche gemeente te Londen 1569–1571.* WMV ser. 1, Vol. 1.

'Liste de 121 pasteurs envoyés par l'église de Genève aux églises de France de 1555 à 1566.' BSHPF Vol. 8 (1859).

Marcus, J., ed. *Sententien en indagingen van den hertog van Alba. Uitgesproken en geslagen in zynen bloedtraedt: Mitsgaders die van byzonder steden. . .van Hollandt, Zeelandt en andere provincien, van den jaere 1567 tot 1572.* Amsterdam: Hendrik Viervot, 1735.

Meylan, H. 'L'Eglise d'Anvers sous la terreur. Lettres inédites de Johannes

Bibliography

Helmichius (1567).' *Mélanges historiques offerts à Monsieur Jean Meyhoffer, docteur en théologie.* Lausanne: Faculté de théologie de l'église évangelique libre du canton de Vaud, 1952. pp. 73–85.

Oultreman, Fr. *Histoire de la ville et comté de Valenciennes.* 1639. *Bibliotheca Belgica,* Vol. 1 (1964).

Paillard, Ch., ed. 'Interrogatoires politiques de Guy de Brès.' BSHPF ser. 2, Vol. 28 (1879), pp. 59–67.

'Interrogatoires politiques de Peregrine de la Grange.' BSHPF ser. 2, Vol. 28 (1879), pp. 224–33.

'Papiers d'état et documents inédits pour servir à l'histoire de Valenciennes pendant les années 1566 et 1567.' *Mémoires historiques sur l'arrondissement de Valenciennes. Société d'agriculture, sciences et arts.* Vol. 5–6. 1878.

Pasquier de la Barre. *Mémoires de Pasquier de la Barre et de Nicolas Soldoyer pour servir à l'histoire de Tournai 1565–1570.* Ed. A. Pinchart. 2 vols. Brussels: Société de l'histoire de Belgique, 1859, 1865.

Petit, J. F. *A General History of the Netherlands.* Ed. Grimeston. London: A. Islip and G. Eld, 1609.

Poullet, M. E., ed. *Correspondance du Cardinal de Granvelle, 1565–1586.* Brussels: F. Hayez, imprimeur de l'académie royale de Belgique, 1877.

Prosper Cuypers van Velthoven, ed. *Documents pour servir à l'histoire des troubles religieux du XVIme siècle dans le Brabant septentrional Bois-le-Duc (1566–1570).* Vol. 1. Brussels: Henri Samuel, imprimeur-éditeur, 1858.

Raepsaet, H., ed. 'Mémoire justificatif du magistrat de Renaix 1566–1567. Information tenue le Ve jour d'Octobre 1567, en la ville de Renaix, par nous Franchois de Cortewille et Jehan van der Burcht, conseillers au conseil de Flandres, sur les troubles et désordres commiz par les sectaires en la dicte ville de Renaix.' *Messager des sciences historiques des arts et de la bibliographie de Belgique.* Ghent: Imprimerie et lithographie de L. Hebbelynck, 1853.

'Request der Doopschgezinden te Antwerpen aan prins Willem I in 1566.' *De Navorscher.* Vol. 12 (1862), p. 366.

Ruytinck, Sm. *Geschiedenissen ende handelingen die voornemelick aengaen de Nederduytsche natie ende gemeynten, wonende in Engelant bysonder tot Londen.* Ed. J. J. van Toorenenbergen. WMV ser. 3 Vol. 2.

Strada, F. *Histoire de la guerre de Flandre.* Trans. P. Du-nier.

Ullens, F. G. *Antwerpsch chronykje, in het welk zeer veele en elderste te vergeefsch gezogte geschiedenissen, sedert den jare 1500 tot het jaar 1574...en wel byzonderlyk op het stuk der geloofshervorminge voorgevallen, omstandig zyn beschreeven.* Leyden: Pieter van der Eyk, 1743.

Van Braght, T. J. *The Bloody Theater or Martyrs Mirror of the Defenseless Christians. Who Baptized only upon Confession of Faith, and Who Suffered and Died for the Testimony of Jesus, their Saviour, from the Time of Christ to the Year A.D. 1660.* Trans. J. F. Sohm. 1660. Rpt. Scottsdale, Pa: Mennonite Publishing House, 1951.

Van Campene, C. and P. *Dagboek van Cornelis en Philip van Campene, behelzende het verhaal der merkwaardigste gebeurtenissen, voorgevallen te Gent sedert het begin der godsdienstberoerten tot den 5^en April 1571.* Ed. F. de Potter. Ghent: Drukkerij C. Annoot-Braeckman, 1870.

Bibliography

Van der Essen, L., ed. 'Rapport sécret de Geronimo de Curiel, facteur du roi d'Espagne à Anvers, sur les marchands hérétiques ou suspects de cette ville, 1566.' BCRH Vol. 80 (1911).

Van Haecht, G. *De kroniek van Godevaert van Haecht over de Troebelen van 1565 tot 1574 te Antwerpen en elders.* Ed. R. van Roosbroeck. (Uitgaven van het genootschap voor Antwerpsche geschiedenis. Vol. 2). Antwerp: 'De Sikkel', 1929.

Van Haemstede, A. *Historien der vromer martelaren, die om het getuygenisse der evangelischer waerheydt haer bloet gestort hebben, van de tijden Christi onses salighmaeckers af tot den jare sesthien hondert vijf-en-fiftigh toe.* Dordrecht: Iacobus Savry, woonende in't kasteel van Gendt, n.d.

Van Hasselt, G., ed. *Stukken voor de vaderlandsche histoire.* 4 Vols. Arnhem en Amsterdam: W. Troost en zoon en J. Allart, 1792.

Van Schelven, A. A., ed. 'Een brief van Pieter Hazaert.' NAvKG n.s. Vol. 8 (1911), pp. 202–4.

'Het "Scriptum de Fide" van Franciscus Junius (Juli 1566).' BMHGU Vol. 51 (1930), pp. 104–14.

Kerkeraads-protocollen der Nederduitsche vluchtelingenkerk te Londen 1560–1563. Amsterdam: Johannes Muller, 1921.

Van Vaernewijck, M. *Troubles religieux en Flandre et dans les Pays-Bas au XVIe siècle. Mémoires d'un patricien Gantois du XVIe siècle.* Trans. H. van Duyse. 2 vols. Ghent: Maison d'éditions d'art, N. Heins, 1905.

Verheyden, A. L. E. *Le conseil des troubles. Liste des condamnés, 1567–1573.* Brussels, 1961.

SECONDARY WORKS

Acquoy, J. G. R. *Jan van Venray (Johannes Ceporinus) en de wording en vestiging der hervormde gemeente te Zaltbommel,* Bois-le-Duc: G. H. van der Schuyt, 1873.

Ainslee, J. L. *The Doctrines of Ministerial Order in the Reformed Churches of the Sixteenth and Seventeenth Centuries.* Edinburgh, 1940.

Altmeyer, J. J. *Les précurseurs de la Réforme aux Pays-Bas.* Vol. 1. Brussels: Librairie Européenne C. Muquardt, 1886.

Backhouse. M. 'Beeldenstorm en bosgeuzen in het Westkwartier (1566–1568),' *Handelingen van de koninklijke geschied-en oudheidkundige kring van Kortrijk.* n.s. Vol. 38 (1971), p. 78.

Bax, W. *Het Protestantisme in het bisdom Luik en vooral te Maastricht 1557–1612.* The Hague: Martinus Nijhoff, 1941.

Beenakker, A. J. M. *Breda in de eerste storm van de opstand 1545–1569. Tilburg:* Stichting zuidelijk historisch contact, 1971.

Berkhofer, R. F. *A Behavioral Approach to Historical Analysis.* New York: The Free Press, 1969.

Beuzart, P. 'La culte des images et la Réforme dans les Pays-Bas.' BSHPB Vol. 10 (1913), pp. 7–28.

'La Réforme dans les environs de Lille, specialement à Armentières en 1566.' BHSPF Vol. 78 (1929), pp. 42–62.

Bibliography

Les hérésies pendant le Moyen Age et la Réforme jusqu'à la mort de Philippe II, 1598. Dans la région de Douai, d'Arras et au pays de l'Alleu. Paris: Librairie ancienne, Honoré Champion, éditeur, 1912.

Biographie nationale publiée par l'académie royale des sciences, des lettres et des beaux-arts de Belgique. Brussels: Bruylant-Christophe et Cⁱᵉ Imprimeurs-éditeurs, successeur Emile Bruylant, 1866–1969.

Blenk, C. 'Hagepreek en beeldenstorm in 1566. Een historische analyse.' *Hagepreek en beeldenstorm. Een uitgave bij het derde lustrum van de C.S.F.R. met opstellen over wetenschap, maatschappij en kerk.* 1966. pp. 16–36.

Boehmer, J. *Evangelium und Evangelisch in Eupen-Malmedi.* Aachen: Aachener verlags- und druckerei Gesellschaft, 1937.

Boer, C. *Hofpredikers van prins Willem van Oranje. Jean Taffin en Pierre Loyseleur de Villiers* (Kerkhistorische studien, Nederlands archief voor kerkgeschiedenis, Vol. 5). The Hague: Martinus Nijhoff, 1952.

Braekman, E. M. *Guy de Brès: sa vie (premier partie)* (Histoire du Protestantisme en Belgique et au Congo Belge, Vol. 6). Brussels: Editions de la librairie des éclaireurs unionistes, 1960.

'La pensée politique de Guy de Brès.' BSHPF Vol. 111 (Jan.–Mar. 1969), pp. 1–28.

Brulez, W. 'De opstand van het industrie-gebied in 1566.' *Standen en landen* Vol. 4 (1954), pp. 79–101.

Brutel de la Rivière, G. J. *Het leven van Hermannus Moded, een der eerste Calvinistische predikers in ons vaderland.* Haarlem: De Erven F. Bohn, 1879.

Burn, J. S. *The History of the French, Walloon, Dutch and other Foreign Protestant Refugees Settled in England, from the Reign of Henry VIII to the Revocation of the Edict of Nantes.* London: Longman, Brown, Green, and Longmans, 1846.

'Calvin et les briseurs d'images. Note rectificative d'une assertion de M. Rosseeuw Saint-Hilaire.' BSHPF Vol. 14 (1865), pp. 127–31.

Christensen, C. 'Iconoclasm and the Preservation of Ecclesiastical Art in Reformation Nuernberg.' AGR Vol. 61 (1970), pp. 205–21.

Clark, G. W. 'An Urban Study During the Revolt of the Netherlands: Valenciennes 1540–1570.' Diss. Columbia University, 1972.

Clasen, C-P. *Anabaptism. A Social History, 1525–1618. Switzerland, Austria, Moravia, South and Central Germany.* Ithaca and London: Cornell University Press, 1972.

Closset, C. 'Andreas Baerdeloos. Martyr à Alost en 1566.' BSHPB Vol. 3 (1954), pp. 175–82.

Cochrane, A. *Reformed Confessions of the Sixteenth Century.* Philadelphia, 1966.

Cohn, N. *The Pursuit of the Millenium: Revolutionary Messianism in Medieval and Reformation Europe and its Bearings on Modern Totalitarian Movements.* New York: Harper and Row, 1961.

Collinson, P. *The Elizabethan Puritans and the Foreign Reformed Churches in London.* London: Publication of the Huguenot Society, Vol. 20.

Coornaert, E. *Un centre industriel d'autrefois: la draperie-sayetterie d'Hondschoote: XIVᵉ siècles.* Paris, 1930.

Bibliography

Cordeweiner, A. 'Prêche Calviniste à Boeschepe 12 Juillet 1562.' BSHPF Vol. 112 (1966), pp. 105–20.

Coulton, G. G. *Art and the Reformation*. Cambridge: Cambridge University Press, 1953.

Cuno, F. W. *Franciscus Junius der ältere, Professor der Theologie und Pastor (1545–1602). Sein Leben und Werken, seine Schriften und Briefe*. Amsterdam Verlag von Scheffer und Co., 1891.

Daris, J. *Histoire du diocèse et de la principauté de Liège pendant le XVIᵉ siècle*. Liège: Librairie Catholique Louis Demarteau, 1884.

Davis, N. Z. 'The Rites of Violence: Religious Riot in Sixteenth Century France.' *Society and Culture in Early Modern France*. Stanford, Calif.: Stanford University Press, 1975. pp. 152–88.

De Bie, J. P. and Loosjes, J., eds. *Biographisch woordenboek van Protestantsche godgeleerden in Nederlanden*. The Hague: Martinus Nijhoff, 1943.

Decavele, J. 'De correlatie tussen de sociale en professionele struktuur en de godsdienstkeuze op het Vlaamse platteland (1560–1567). Samenvatting.' SHRB pp. 280–5.

De dageraad van de reformatie in Vlaanderen (1520–1565). (Verhandelingen van de koniklijke academie voor wetenschappen, letteren en schone kunsten van Belgie. Klasse des letteren, Vol. 37, Nr. 76). Brussels: Paleis der academien, 1975.

'De Reformatorische beweging te Axel en Hulst, 1556–1566.' BvGN Vol. 22 (1968–9), pp. 1–42.

'Jan Hendrickx en het Calvinisme in Vlaanderen (1560–1564).' *Handelingen van het genootschap te Brugge*. Vol. 16 (1969), pp. 17–32.

De Clercq, C. 'Jean et Jacques Taffin, Jean d'Arras et Christophe Plantin.' *De Gulden Passer*. Vol. 36 (1958), pp. 125–36.

De Jong, J. *De voorbereiding en constitueering van het kerkverband der Nederlandsche Gereformeerde kerken in de zestiende eeuw. Historische studien over het convent te Wezel (1568) en de synode te Emden (1571)*. Groningen: Firma Jan Haan, 1911.

De Jong, O. J. *De Reformatie in Culembourg*. Van Gorcum en comp. n.v. G. A. Hak en Dr H. J. Prakke.

Delmotte, M. 'Het Calvinisme in de verschillende bevolkingslagen te Gent (1566–1567),' TvG Vol. 76 (1963), pp. 145–76.

De Moreau, E. 'Le clergé des Pays-Bas méridionaux à l'époque des troubles.' BCRH 5 ser. Vol. 33 (1947), pp. 195–214.

De Schickler, F. *Les églises du refuge en Angleterre*. 3 vols. Paris: Librairie Fischbacher, 1892.

De Schrevel, A. C. *Histoire du séminaire de Bruges*. Vol. 1. Bruges: Imprimerie de Louis de Plancke, 1895.

Desilve, J. *Le Protestantisme dans la seigneurie de Saint-Amand de 1562 à 1584*. Valenciennes: Imprimerie Georges Hollande, 1910.

De Troeyer, B. *Bio-Bibliographia Franciscana Neerlandica Saeculi XVI*. Vol. 1: *Pars Biographica*. Nieuwkoop: B. de Graaf, 1969.

Dierickx, M. 'Beeldenstorm in de Nederlanden in 1566.' *Streven*. Vol. 19. (1966), pp. 1040–8.

Duke, A. C. and Kolff, D. H. A. 'The Time of Troubles in the County of Holland, 1566–1567.' TvG Vol. 82 (1969), pp. 316–37.

Dumont, G. H. *La vie aventureuse d'Antoine van Bomberghen, compagnon de lutte de Guillaume le taciturne.* Antwerp: Le Papegay, Publiservice, 1952.

Du Plessis, R. 'Urban Stability in the Netherlands Revolution. A Comparative Study of Lille and Douai.' Diss. Columbia University, 1974.

Enno van Gelder, H. A. 'Erasmus, schilders en rederijkers.' TVG Vol. 71 (1958), pp. 1–16, 206–41, 289–331.

Frederichs, J. 'Un Lutherien Français devenu Libertin spirituel: Christophe Hérault et les Loïstes d'Anvers, 1490–1544:' BSHPF Vol. 41 (1892), pp. 250–269.

Frossard, C.-L. *L'Eglise sous la croix, pendant la domination Espagnole. Chronique de l'église Reformée de Lille.* Lille: Imprimerie de Leleux, 1867.

Garside, C. *Zwingli and the Arts.* New Haven, Conn.: Yale U. Press, 1966.

Gerth, H. H. and C. Wright Mills, ed., *From Max Weber; Essays in Sociology.* New York, 1971.

Geertz, C. *The Interpretation of Cultures.* New York: Basic Books. 1973.

Geyl, Pieter. *The Revolt of the Netherlands.* London: Ernest Benn, Ltd., 1966.

Gilmont, J.-F. 'La genèse du martyrologe d'Adrien van Haemstede, 1559.' RHE Vol. 63 (1968), pp. 379–414.

'Les martyrologes Protestantes du XVIᵉ siècle.' Diss. University of Louvain, 1966.

Glasius, B. ed. *Godgeleert Nederland. Biographisch woordenboek van Nederlandsche godgeleerden.* Bois-le-Duc, 1852–6.

Goris, J. A. *Etude sur les colonies marchandes méridionales (Portugais, Espagnols, Italiens) à Anvers de 1488 à 1567. Contribution à l'histoire des débuts du capitalisme moderne.* (Recueil de travaux publiés par les membres des conferences d'histoire et de philologie. 2 ser. 4 fasc.). Louvain: Librairie Universitaire, 1925.

Haag, M. M. *La France Protestante.* Ed. H. Bordier. 6 vols. 2nd ed. Paris: Librairie Sandoz et Fischbacher, 1877–78.

Halkin, L.-E. 'Hagiographie Protestante.' *Mélanges Paul Pieters.* Vol. 2. (*Analecta Bollandiana.* Vol. 68). 1950, pp. 453–63.

Haller, W. *Foxe's Book of Martyrs and the Elect Nation.* London: Jonathan Cape, 1967.

Hansay, A. *La dame de Vogelzang et les Calvinistes en 1566–7.* Hasselt, 1932.

Le sac de l'église de Saint-Quentin à Hasselt, le Janvier 1567. Hasselt: Drukkerij Leon Crollen, 1932.

Hauben, P. *Three Spanish Heretics and the Reformation.* Geneva: Librairie Droz, 1967.

Hocquet, A. *Tournai et le Tournaisis au XVIᵉ siècle au point de vue politique et social.* (Mémoires. Académie royale de Belgique classe des lettres et des sciences morales et politiques et classe des beaux-arts. 2 ser. Vol. 1). Brussels: Hayez, imprimeur des academies, 1906.

Hoffer, E. *The True Believer: Thoughts on the Nature of Mass Movements.* New York: Harper, 1951.

Bibliography

Hoffman, G. J. 'French Calvinism: A "Subversive" Movement in the Spanish Netherlands.' *The Dawn of Modern Civilization.* Ed. K. A. Strand. 2nd ed. Ann Arbor Publishers, 1964, pp. 197–224.

Janssen, H.-Q. *De Kerkhervorming te Brugge. Een historisch tafereel voor Christenen, die voedsel zoeken van den geest en op Gods wegen letten.* 2 vols. Rotterdam: Van der Meer en Verbruggen, 1856.

De Kerkhervorming in Vlaanderen. Historisch geschetst meest naar onuitgegeven bescheiden. 2 vols. Te Arnhem: J. W. en C. F. Swan, 1868.

Keeney, W. *The Development of Dutch Anabaptist Thought and Practice from 1539–1564.* Nieuwkoop: B. de Graaf, 1968.

Kervyn de Lettenhove, M. *Les Huguenots et les Gueux: Etude histoire sur vingt-cinq années du XVI⁰ siècle (1560–1585).* Bruges: Beyaert-Storie, 1883.

Kingdon, R. *Geneva and the Coming of the Wars of Religion in France 1555–1563.* Geneva: Librairie E. Droz, 1956.

Geneva and the Consolidation of the French Protestant Movement 1564–1572. A Contribution to the History of Congregationalism, Presbyterianism, and Calvinist Resistance Theory. Geneva: Librairie E. Droz, 1967.

'The Political Resistance of the Calvinists in France and the Low Countries.' *Church History,* Vol. 27 (1958).

Kleijntjens, J. 'Bijdrage tot den beeldenstorm. Beeldenstorm te Wessem.' *De Navorscher.* Vol. 83 (1935), pp. 145–54.

Koenigsberger, H. G. 'The Origin of Revolutionary Parties in France and the Netherlands during the Sixteenth Century.' *Journal of Modern History,* Vol. 27 (1955), pp. 335–51.

Krahn, C. *Dutch Anabaptism. Origin, Spread, Life and Thought (1450–1600).* The Hague: Martinus Nijhoff, 1968.

Kuttner, E. *Het hongerjaar, 1566.* Amsterdam, 1949.

Lagomarsino, P. D. 'Court Factions and the Formulation of Spanish Court Policy towards the Netherlands (1559–1567). Diss. University of Cambridge, 1973.

Leblanc, M. 'Les prédicants Calvinistes et leur rôle dans les Pays-Bas de 1559 à 1567. Contribution à l'étude du Calvinisme primitif dans les dix-sept provinces.' Diss. University of Brussels, 1949–1951.

Lecler, J. *Toleration and the Reformation.* Trans. T. L. Westow. Vol. 2. London: Longmans, 1960.

Lenoir, D. *Histoire de la Réformation dans l'ancien pays de Liège.* Brussels: Librairie Chrétienne Evangelique, 1861.

Léonard, E. G. *A History of Protestantism.* Vol. 2: *The Establishment.* Trans. R. M. Bethell. London: Thomas Nelson and Sons, Ltd., 1967.

Lévi-Strauss, C. *Tristes Tropiques.* Trans. J. Russell. New York: Atheneum, 1971.

Liebrecht, H. *Les chambres de rhétorique des Pays-Bas.* Brussels: La Renaissance du Livre, 1948.

Lindeboom, J. *Austin Frairs. History of the Dutch Reformed Church in London 1550–1950.* Trans. D. de Iongh. The Hague: Martinus Nijhoff, 1950.

Mahieu, E. 'La Réforme à Mons des origines à 1575.' Diss. University of Liège, 1961.

Bibliography

Meindersma, W. 'De Reformatorische beweging der XVI° eeuw te 'S-Hertogenbosch.' NAvKG n.s. Vol. 7 (1910), pp. 262–76, 380–92. Vol. 8 (1911),
pp. 62–73.
'Over het Protestantisme in Westelijk Brabant.' NAvKG n.s. Vol. 8 (1911),
pp. 297–321.
Meiners, E. *Oostvrieschlandts kerkelyke geschiedenisse of een historisch en oordeel-
kundig verhaal van het gene nopens het kerkelyke in Oostvrieschlandt, en
byzonder te Emden, is voorgevallen, zedert den tydt der Hervorminge, of de
jaren 1519 en 1520, tot op den huidigen dag. Vol. 1.* Groningen: Laurens
Groenewout en Hermannus Spoormaker, boekverkopers, 1738.
Messiaen, L-J. *Histoire chronologique, politique et religieuse des seigneurs et de
la ville de Comines.* 3 vols. Courtrai: Typographie de Veuve Nys et Fils, 1892.
Meyhoffer, J. *Le martyrologe Protestant des Pays-Bas 1523–1597. Etude critique.*
Brussels: Imprimerie de Nessonvaux, 1907.
Meylan, H. 'Le récrutement et la formation des pasteurs dans les églises Réform-
ées du XVI° siècle.' *Miscellanea historiae ecclesiasticae. Colloque de Cambridge 24–28 Sept. 1968.* Ed. Derek Baker. Vol. 3. (Bibliothèque de la revue
d'histoire écclésiastique. fasc. 50), pp. 127–50.
Moens, W. J. C. *The Walloons and their Church at Norwich 1565–1832.* Lymington: Printed for the Huguenot Society of London, 1888.
Molhuysen, P. C. and Blok, P. J. *Nieuw Nederlandsch Biographisch Woorden-
boek.* Leiden: A. W. Sijthoff's uitgevers-maatschappij, 1911.
Moreau, G. *Histoire du Protestantisme à Tournai jusqu'à la veille de la révolution
des Pays-Bas.* (Bibliothèque de la faculté de philosophie et lettres de l'univer-
sité de Liège. fasc. 167). Paris: Société d'édition 'Les belles lettres,' 1962.
'La corrélation entre le milieu social et professionel et le choix de religion à
Tournai.' SHRB, pp. 286–301.
Motley, J. L. *The Rise of the Dutch Republic.* 3 vols. New York: Harper and
Brothers, 1855.
Moxey, K. Pieter Aertzen, Joachim Beuckelaer and the Rise of Secular Painting
in the Context of the Reformation (New York and London: Garland Press),
1977.
Muret, Ph. 'François Varlut et Alexandre Dayke, martyrs Calvinistes à Tournai
en 1562.' BSHPF Vols. 110–11 (1964), pp. 19–53.
Oxley, J. *The Reformation in Essex.* Manchester, 1965.
Paillard, Ch. *Histoire des troubles religieux de Valenciennes. 1560–1565.* 4 vols.
Brussels: C. Muquardt, éditeur, 1876.
*Huit mois de la vie d'un peuple. Les Pays-Bas du premier Janvier au premier
Septembre 1566, d'après les mémoires et les correspondances du temps.*
(Mémoires de l'académie royale de Belgique. Vol. 27). Brussels: F. Hayez,
imprimeur de l'académie royale, 1877.
'Les grands prêches Calvinistes de Valenciennes (Juillet et Août 1566).' BSHPF
Vol. 26 (1877), pp. 33–43, 73–90, 121–33.
'Note sur Jean Crespin. A Monsieur Jules Bonnet.' BSHPF Vol. 27 (1878),
pp. 380–4.
Phillips, J. *The Reformation of Images: Destruction of Art in England, 1535–
1660.* Berkeley: University of California Press, 1973.

Bibliography

Pirenne, H. 'Une crise industrielle au XVIᵉ siècle: La draperie urbaine et la nouvelle draperie de Flandre.' *Histoire économique de l'occident médiéval.* Paris, 1951, pp. 624–41.

Pont, J. W. *Geschiedenis van het Lutheranisme in de Nederlanden tot 1618.* Haarlem: De Erven F. Bohn, 1911.

Prims, Fl. *De Antwerpsche ommeganck op den vooravond van de beeldenstormerij.* Antwerp, 1946.

Het wonderjaar (1566–1567). 2nd ed. Antwerp: Bureel der 'Bijdragen tot de geschiedenis,' 1941.

Rahlenbeck, C. 'Jean Taffin. Un Reformateur Belge du XVIᵉ siècle.' BCHEW Vol. 2 (1887), pp. 117–79.

L'Eglise de Liège et la révolution. 2nd ed. Brussels: Imprimerie de J. B. Schilders, 1864.

'Les chanteries de Valenciennes. Episode de l'histoire du seizième siècle.' BCHEW Vol. 3 (1888), pp. 121–59.

Les pays d'Outre-Meuse. Etudes historiques sur Dalhem, Fauquemont et Rolduc. Brussels: P. Weissenbruch, imprimeur du roi, 1888.

Renaudet, A. *Préréforme et humanisme à Paris.* 2nd ed. n.p., n.d.

Renon de France. *Histoire des troubles des Pays-Bas.* Ed. Ch. Piot. Brussels: F. Hayez, imprimeur de l'académie royale, 1886.

Russe, J. 'Le procès et le martyre de Hans Tuscaens à Audenarde en 1566.' BSHPB (1953), pp. 90–122.

Rutgers, F. L. *Calvijns invloed op de Reformatie in de Nederlanden, voor zooveel die door hemselven is uitgeoefend.* 2nd ed. Leiden: D. Donner, 1901.

Ruys, Th. *Petrus Dathenus.* Utrecht: G. J. A. Ruys, 1919.

Ryckaert, M. 'Een beeldenstorm in de kerk van Oostwinkel op 23 Augustus 1566.' *Appeltjes van het Meetjesland. Jaarboek van het heemkundig genootschap van het Meetjesland.* Vol. 8 (1957), pp. 109–12.

Scheerder, J. 'Eenige nieuwe bijzonderheden betreffende het 3.000.000 goudguldens rekwest (1566).' *Miscellanea Historica in Honorem Leonis van der Essen. Universitatis Catholicae in Oppido Lovaniensi Iam Annos XXXV Professoris.* Vol. 1. Brussels–Paris: Editions universitaires, 1947, pp. 559–66.

Sepp, Ch. *Drie evangeliedienaren uit den tijd der Hervorming.* Leiden: E. J. Brill, 1879.

Geschiedkundige nasporingen. 3 vols. Leiden: De Breuk en Smits, 1872–1875.

Uit het predikanten-leven van vroedere tijden. Leiden: E. J. Brill, 1890.

Smelzer, N. *Theory of Collective Behavior.* London: Routledge and Kegan Paul, 1962.

Sprengler-Ruppenthal, A. *Ausdehnung und Grenzen der Befugnisse der Diakonen, in der Londoner Niederlandischen Gemeinde 1560–1564. Eine Studie zum Amterrecht.* Sonderdruck aus dem Jahrbuch der Gesellschaft fur niedersachsische Kirchengeschichte. 63 bd. 1955.

Steenackers, Em. 'L'abbaye de Saint-Bernard, à Hemixem et Thomas van Thielt, administrateur du dit lieu 1564–1567.' *Bulletin du Cercle archéologique littéraire et artistique de Malines.* Vol. 22 (1912), pp. 31–48.

Bibliography

Surtz, E. L. *The Praise of Wisdom. A Commentary on the Religious and Moral Problems and Backgrounds of St. Thomas More's 'Utopia'*. Chicago: Loyola University Press, 1957.

Te Water, J. W. *Historie der hervormde kerke te Gent, van haeren aenvang tot derzelver einde: mitsgaders een kort verhael der gereformeerde doorluchtige school te Gent. Zedert den jaere 1578 tot het jaer 1784*. Utrecht: Gisbert, Tieme van Paddenburg and Abraham van Paddenburg, boekverkopers, 1756.

Thomas, K. *Religion and the Decline of Magic*. New York: Charles Scribner's Sons, 1971.

Toussaert, J. *Le sentiment religieux en Flandre à la fin du Moyen Age*. Paris: Librairie Plon, 1968.

Trachsel, E. *De Colomban aux Gueux*. Brussels, 1949.

Trexler, R. 'Florentine Religious Experience: The Sacred Image.' *Studies in the Renaissance*. Vol. 19 (1972), pp. 7–41.

Trinterud, L. J. ed. *Elizabethan Puritanism*. New York: Oxford University Press, 1971.

Tukker, C. A. 'The Recruitment and Training of Protestant Ministers in the Netherlands in the Sixteenth Century.' *Miscellanea Historiae Ecclesiasticae. Colloque de Cambridge 24–28 Sept. 1968*. Ed. D. Baker. Vol. 3. (Bureau de la revue d'histoire écclésiastique, bibliothèque de la université. fasc. 50). Louvain, 1970, pp. 198–215.

Turner, V. *The Ritual Process. Structure and Anti-Structure*. Chicago: Aldine Publishing Co., 1969.

Van Autenboer, E. 'Uit de geschiedenis van Turnhout in de 16e eeuw.' *Taxandria*, n.s. Vol. 41 (1969).

Van den Bussche, E. *Historie de la commune de Rousbrugge-Haringhe*. Bruges: Typ-Lith. Edw. Gaillard and Cie, 1867.

Van der Elst, P.-C. *Le Protestantisme Belge avant, pendant et après les troubles du XVIe siècle. Considerations historiques*. Brussels: L. Deltenre-Walker, éditeur. Amsterdam: R. C. Meijer, Librairie étrangère, 1856.

Van der Essen. L. 'Les progrès du Lutheranisme et du Calvinisme dans le monde commercial d'Anvers et l'espionage politique du marchand Philippe Dauxy, agent secrèt de Marguerite de Parme, en 1566–1567.' *Vierteljahrschrift fur Sozial- und Wirtschaftsgeschichte*. Vol. 12 (1914), pp. 152–234.

Van der Haeghen, F. ed. 'Martyrologes Protestants Néerlandais. Notes pour servir d'introduction à la bibliographie des martyrologes.' Re-éd. M.-T. Lenger. *Bibliotheca Belgica. Bibliographie générale des Pays-Bas*. Vol. 4. Brussels: Culture and Civilization, 1964, pp. 223–309.

Van der Laar, L. J. A. 'Wie waren Cornelius Walraeven en Jacobus Michaelis?' *NAvKG* n.s. Vol. 49 (1969), pp. 169–82.

Van der Meersch, P. C., ed. *Memorie boek der stad Ghendt, 1301–1793*. Vol. 2. Ghent, 1854.

Van der Wee, H. 'La Réforme Protestante dans l'optique de la conjoncture économique et sociale des Pays-Bas Méridionaux au XVIe siècle.' SHRB pp. 303–15.

The Growth of the Antwerp Market and the European Economy (Fourteenth to Sixteenth Centuries). Vol. 2. The Hague: Martinus Nijhoff, 1963.

Van Deventer, M. L. *Het jaar 1566. Een historische proeve uit den Nederlandschen vrijheidsoorlog.* The Hague, 1856.

Van Langeraad, L. *Guido de Bray, zijn leven en werken. Bijdrage tot de geschiedenis van het Zuid-Nederlandsche Protestantisme.* Zierikzee: S. Ochtman en Zoon, 1884.

Van Lennep. *Maximiliaan Frederick. Gaspar van der Heyden 1530–1586.* Amsterdam: C. A. Spin en zoon, 1884.

Van Nuffel, H. 'Gillis de Meyere, pastoor van Vinderhoute en martelaar voor de Hervorming.' BSHPB 4 ser. Vol. 10 (1967), pp. 440–50.

Van Oppenraaij, Theodore. *La doctrine de la prédestination dans l'église réformée des Pays-Bas depuis l'origine jusqu'au synode national de Dordrecht en 1618 et 1619.* (Université Catholique de Louvain. Dissertations doctorales de la faculté de théologie. 2 ser.). Louvain: Typ. et lith. Joseph van Linthout, 1906.

Van Roosbroeck, R. *Emigranten. Nederlandse vluchtelingen in duitsland (1550–1600).* Louvain: Davidsfonds, 1968.

Het wonderjaar te Antwerpen. 1566–1567. Inleiding tot de studie der godsdienstonluston te Antwerpen van 1566 tot 1567. Antwerp: 'De Sikkel,' 1930.

Van Schelven, A. A. *De Nederduitsche vluchtelingen kerken der zestiende eeuw in Engeland en Duitschland in hunne beteekenis voor de Reformatie in de Nederlanden.* The Hague: Martinus Nijhoff, 1908.

'Het begin van het gewapend verzet tegen Spanje in de 16ᵉ eeuwsche Nederlanden.' *Handelingen en mededeelingen van de maatschappij der Nederladsche letterkunde te Leiden over het jaar 1914–1915.* pp. 126–56.

Van Vloten, J. 'Losse aanteekeningen betrekkelijk den vrijheidsoorlog: Axel en Hulst,' *Bijdragen tot de oudheidkunde en geschiedenis inzonderheid van Zeeuwsch-Vlaanderen.* Vol. 2. (1857), pp. 307–14.

'Losse aanteekeningen betrekkelijk den vrijheidsoorlog: Deinze, Eekloo, Petegem.' *Bijdragen tot de oudheidkunde en geschiedenis inzonderheid van Zeeuwsch-Vlaanderen,* Vol. 2 (1857), pp. 178–88, Vol. 3 (1858), pp. 59–65, 138–147.

Nederlands opstand tegen Spanje, in zijn beginselen, aart en strekking geschetst (1564–1567). Haarlem: De Erven F. Bohn, 1856.

Verheyden, A. L. E. *Anabaptism in Flanders 1530–1650. A Century of Struggle.* Scottsdale, Pa.: Herald Press, 1961.

'Le Protestantisme à Audenarde au XVIᵉ siècle.' *Cercle royale historique et archéologique de Courtrai. Mémoires.* n.s. Vol. 22 (1946–8), pp. 3–45.

'Le Protestantisme à Nieuwport au XVIᵉ siècle.' BCRH Vol. 116 (1951), pp. 1–60.

Visscher, H. and van Langeraad. *Het vaderlandsch biographsch woordenboek van Protestantsche godgeleerden in Nederlanden.* Utrecht, 1907.

Wagener, J. H. C. 'Histoire de l'église Protestante évangelique d'Anvers de 1519 jusqu'en 1815.' and 'Notice historique sur l'église évangelique de Maria-Hoorebeke.' *Jubilé cinquantenaire. Célébration du cinquantenaire du synode de l'union des églises Protestantes évangeliques de Belgique.* (25, 26 and 27 June 1889). Brussels: Imprimerie L. Verhavert, 1890. pp. 111–41, 215–25.

Bibliography

Walzer, M. *The Revolution of the Saints. A Study in the Origins of Radical Politics.* Cambridge, Mass.: Harvard University Press, 1965.

Weber, M. *The Sociology of Religion.* Trans. E. Fischoff. Boston: Beacon Press, 1963.

Williams, G. H. *The Radical Reformation.* Philadelphia: The Westminster Press, 1962.

Worsley, P. *The Trumpet Shall Sound. A Study of 'Cargo' Cults in Melanesia.* London: MacGibbon and Kee, 1957.

Yates, F. *Giordano Bruno and the Hermetic Tradition.* Chicago: The University Press, 1964.

INDEX

N.B. Names with the prefixes De, Van, Van den, Van der are listed here under 'D' or 'V' and not under the first letter of the surname proper.

Adrien, vicar of Oostwinkel, lay preacher, 166–7 & n, 195
Aert, lay preacher, 46, 189
Alard, François, Lutheran pastor, 147n
A Lasco, John, Reformed leader at Emden, 97, 102, 179n
Algoet, Antoine, Reformed minister, 7, 8, 124, 162n, 195
Alva, Ferdinand Alvarez de Toledo, Duke of, 1, 20, 106, 117, 132, 134, 142, 178, 180
Anabaptism: in the Netherlands, 6, 56, 58, 72, 137 & n, 138 & n, 145; in Germany, 91, 138, 141; in Switzerland, 138; in relation to Calvinism, 74, 79, 97, 101, 103, 114, 115–16, 118, 119, 126, 130, 133–4, 135, 142, 148 & n. 149, 150, 176, 178–9 & n; theology, 146, 148 & n
Anglus, Reformed minister, 182
Antwerp, Reformer community of, 1, 7, 47, 62, 65 & n, 66, 71, 80, 81, 82n, 83, 84, 85 & n, 95, 103, 104 & n, 119, 121n, 123, 124
Augsburg Confession, 93, 94, 131
Augustus, lay preacher, 189

Bacquereel, Hermes, Reformed minister, 49, 91n, 93, 94, 95, 97n, 98n, 103, 120n, 137n, 180n, 185
Baerdeloos, Andries, Reformed minister, 42n, 45n, 49, 97n, 98, 114, 137n, 144, 175, 180n, 185
Balck, Isbrand (Trabius), Reformed minister, 20, 45, 49, 80n, 95n, 114, 115, 119n, 124, 127, 180n, 185

Banc, Arnold, Reformed minister, 58, 182
Batembourg, Catherine de Bronckhorst de, 160n
Batembourg, Count of, 8
Bécourt, Octavien, Reformed minister, 45n, 49, 97n, 98, 185
Beggars, see Confederates
Berghes, Marquis of, 152–3
Bert, Pieter, Reformed minister, 45, 49, 98n, 100n, 162n, 180n, 185
Beyers, Hermes, lay preacher, 192
Beza, Theodore, 6, 85, 86, 88n, 89, 97, 100, 104, 105, 126n, 127n, 131, 141 & n, 175 & n, 179n
Bloccius, Petrus, Lutheran reformer in Germany, 121n
Bonniel, Jean, lay preacher, 59n, 162n, 193
Boquinus, Pierre, Reformed minister, 49, 88, 91n, 93, 180n, 185
Bourlette, Adrien, lay preacher, 162n, 193
Brederode, Hendrik Count of, 18, 19, 160n
Brethren of the Common Life, 150n
Brochart, Louis, Reformed minister, 60, 182
Broiteur, Hans, Reformed minister, 182 & n
Brully, Pierre, Reformed minister, 57 & n, 58, 74, 75
Bucer, Martin, 57
Bullinger, Heinrich, 102

Callewaert, Lievyn, lay preacher, 162n, 189

Calvin, John: influence on Reformed movement in the Netherlands, 18, 51, 53, 58–9, 63, 70, 82, 83, 102, 163, 180; relations with Netherlands clergy, 45, 84, 85, 92, 94, 100, 103, 105, 116, 121, 124, 125n, 128, 129, 131; and Huguenot clergy, 141; and Geneva, 118; and English refugee church, 97; views on iconoclasm, 28; on the nature of the clergy, 110, 111; on martyrdom, 51, 74, 79; on Spiritual Libertines, 56, 57. *See also* Calvinism

Calvinism: and the sacraments, 48, 104, 107–8, 119–23, 137; and prophecy, 109–17; and church organization, 57–8, 71, 79–81, 117–24; and language, 124–8; and pastoral training, 84–7; and martyrdom, 73–5, 77–8; and iconoclasm, 28–9, 48, 50, 98–9; and politics, 2–3, 13, 106, 113–17, 128–34, 175–80; and preaching, 144–50; and the problem of authority, 135–9, 161

Cambier, David, Reformed minister, 99n, 182 & n

Camerlynck, Jan, lay Reformer, 20

Capelle, Jean, Reformed minister, 182

Capito, Jean, Reformed minister, 180n, 185 & n

Cappel, Louis, Reformed minister, 48n, 85n, 86n, 88, 90, 105, 180n, 185 & n

Carbon, Pierre, lay preacher, 162n, 189 & n

Carlus, Toussain, lay preacher, 162n, 189

Carpentier, Pierre, Reformed minister, 13, 48n, 49, 80n, 98, 120n, 142n, 145 & n, 180 & n, 185

Castel, Jean, Reformed minister, 78, 182

Castelius, Jean, apostate priest, 164n

Cateu, Jean, Reformed minister, 41, 49, 87n, 144, 180n, 185

Catholicism: anti-clericalism, 2, 9–10, 22–3, 25–7, 31, 32–4, 42, 51–2, 56, 69, 111–12, 113, 149–50, 159, 170; bishoprics, 42, 112, 177; popular worship, 10, 24–5, 53–6, 72

Chambers of Rhetoric, 52–3, 54, 63–4 & n, 146, 149, 172

Chanteries, 68–9, 70, 81, 89, 129

Charles V (ruled the Netherlands 1515–55), 76, 152

Chemin, Denis, lay preacher, 192

Chevalier, Paul, Reformed minister, 60–1, 62n, 63, 78, 82, 182

Claeysson, Lucas, lay preacher, 194

Claeyssone, Jan, Reformed minister, 80 & n, 82n, 182 & n, 193 & n

Clebitius, Guillaume, Reformed minister, 182

Cleerks, Reformed minister, 182

Cleves, Duke of, 93 & n

Clough, Richard, English merchant in Antwerp, 5, 9, 12, 32, 34, 147

Coeman, Jan, Reformed minister, 182, 189n

Coeman, Louis, lay preacher, 189

Cole, William, Reformed minister, 58n, 65n, 80n, 182

Coligny, Gaspard de, 21, 76, 87, 89

Colon, Roland, Reformed minister, 182

Condé, Louis, prince of, 21, 87, 88

Confederates, 6, 7, 9 & n, 12, 15, 18, 19, 20, 21, 33–4, 87–8, 94, 104, 105, 107, 153, 154, 158, 171, 172, 173, 175, 178

Consistories, Netherlands churches, 6, 7, 12–3, 16, 18, 21, 30, 37, 48, 60–1, 65–7, 79, 80, 95, 118, 132, 142–3, 162, 174

Cools, Martin, lay preacher, 163n, 193

Coomans, Joris, lay preacher, 162n, 192

Corbeel, A., lay preacher, 193

Cornelis Adriansz, Broer, Catholic friar, 14–15, 27n, 39–40, 145, 171

Cornu, Guillaume, Reformed minister, 59n, 68n, 182

Cornu, Jean, lay Reformer, 63, 82n

Corro, Antonio, Reformed minister, 47, 49, 85n, 86n, 88, 89, 90, 103, 105, 119, 123 & n, 125, 127 & n, 131, 180n, 185 & n

Council of Troubles, 4, 20, 46, 178

Crapandiau, lay preacher, 46n, 88n, 189

Crespin, Jean, martyrologist, 24, 35, 74, 75, 86, 113, 174, 180

Cubus, Jehan, Reformed minister, 42n, 49, 124, 180n, 185

Culembourg, Floris van Pallandt, Count of, 159, 169 & n

Cuvelier, Nicolas, Reformed minister, 61n, 182

Daelman, Jan, debated with minister, 66

D'Albret, Jeanne, 89

Damiseau, Rémy, lay preacher, 162n, 189

Damman, Ghislain, Reformed minister, 67, 182

Damman, Guillaume, Reformed minister, 59n, 61n, 67n, 182

Daneel, Carolus, lay preacher, 7, 36, 162n, 193

Daniel, Jean, lay preacher, 162n, 189

Dathenus, Pieter, 18, 41, 43, 47n, 49, 50 & n, 85n, 91 & n, 92 & n, 93, 94, 96, 98n, 100, 103, 105, 111, 113, 115n, 117, 118, 120–1 & n, 124, 125n, 126 & n, 127, 128, 131, 132, 133n, 134, 137n, 143, 166n, 169, 179n, 180 & n, 185

Dayke, Alexandre, Reformed minister, 58, 59n, 72, 76, 78, 82n, 182

De Bailleul, Gérard, Reformed minister, 69, 182

De Bestère, Noel, lay preacher, 162n, 193

De Bock, Olivier, German Reformer, 63

De Bois, Josse, lay preacher, 162n, 190

De Brès, Guy, Reformed minister, 4, 17, 21n, 24, 40, 46n, 47 & n, 48n, 49, 50 & n, 57n, 59 & n, 61 & n, 62 & n, 63, 64–5 & n, 68–9, 70, 72, 73, 75, 77, 80n, 82, 83, 85n, 86, 87 & n, 88 & n, 89, 90, 98n, 103, 104, 105, 107, 110, 111–12, 113, 114, 115, 116, 118, 119, 122, 124, 127–9, 130, 131, 133, 143, 160, 175, 179n, 180n, 185

De Brune, Jan (Camphen), Reformed minister, 49, 98n, 180n, 185

De Brunink, Laurent, lay preacher, 162n, 163, 193

De Buire, Jehan, lay preacher, 189

De Buzère, Jacques, Reformed minister, 8, 11, 15, 30n, 41, 49, 50, 98, 99, 103, 113, 180n, 186

De Clerck, Michiel, Reformed minister, 182 & n

De Croy, Charles, Netherlands Nobleman, 76

De Guyon, Fery, Netherlands nobleman, 36

De Hamal, Godfried, Reformed minister, 57n, 182

De Hames, Nicolas, Netherlands nobleman, 101n

De Hase, Pieter, lay preacher, 100n, 162n, 189

De Hasque, Denis, lay preacher, 162n, 163n, 192

De Hollandère, Guillaume, lay preacher, 162n, 163n, 164 & n, 194

De Hongère, Mailgaert, lay preacher, 162n, 166, 192

De Joing, Jehan, lay preacher, 194

De la Court, Nicolas, Reformed minister, 182

De la Grange, Peregrine, Reformed minister, 13, 40, 46n, 48n, 49, 50, 80n, 85n, 90, 133, 143, 173, 180n, 186

De la Hay, Philibert, Reformed minister, 182 & n

De Lannoy, Jean, Reformed minister, 59, 61n., 63, 68, 182

De Lannoy, Mathieu, Reformed minister, 68n, 69n, 182

Delenus, Petrus, Reformed minister at Emden, 92

De Lesenne, Cornille, Reformed minister, 18, 21, 37, 41, 43, 46n, 47 & n, 49, 66n, 80n, 91n, 93 & n, 137n, 149n, 180n, 186

De Lo, Jacques, Reformed minister, 182

De Lontzen, Dionysius Floris, lay preacher, 194

De Lontzen, Jehan, lay preacher, 194

De Meen, Cornelis, lay preacher, 162n, 189

De Meester, Adrien, lay preacher, 162n, 189

De Meghem, Guillaume, lay preacher, 189

De Mendoza, Bernardino, Spanish nobleman, 20

De Messere, Michiel, lay preacher, 119n, 162n, 190

De Meyere, Gilles, lay preacher, 162n, 163 & n., 164n, 194

De Monnier, Meus, lay preacher, 162n, 190

De Navarre, Marguerite, 56, 57

De Nielles, Charles, Reformed minister, 46 & n., 47 & n, 48n, 49, 50 & n, 80n, 85n, 101n, 104, 105, 180n, 186

Denys, Jan, lay Reformer, 18, 48n

De Pourcq, Arnold, lay preacher, 190

De Pourck, Jan, lay preacher, 162n, 194

De Pruet, Jan, Reformed minister, 183 & n

De Quekere, Gilles, Reformed minister, 49, 98n, 186

De Rassenghien, Maximilien Vilain, Lord of, 18

De Reina,Cassiodoro, Reformed minister, 58, 103, 123, 183

De Rore, Jacob, Anabaptist minister, 148

De Roubaix, Royer, lay preacher, 194

De Royere, Michiel (d'Oudenburg), lay preacher, 14, 166n, 195

De Salcède, Pierre, French nobleman, 89, 90

De Sander, Loys, Reformed minister, 183

Desbarbieux, Symphorien, Reformed minister, 183

Desbonnets, Philippe, Reformed minister, 183

Desbuyssons, Martin, Reformed minister, 69, 82n, 183

De Schildere, Willem, Reformed minister, 49, 98n, 186

Des Gallars, Nicolas, French Reformed minister, 88n, 97

De Smet, Christophe (Fabri), Reformed minister, 61n, 62n, 63, 70, 73–4, 77, 78, 103, 183

De Smet, Martin, lay preacher, 55, 144, 162n, 163n, 164 & n, 194

Destoubequin, Michel, Reformed minister, 74, 183

De Vlameng, Jan, lay preacher, 166, 190

De Voghele, Loys, Reformed minister, 49, 67n, 80, 95n, 186

De Wilde, Nicaise, lay preacher, 162n, 192

De Zommère, Louis, Reformed minister, 183

Dheutkin, Joos, lay preacher, 190

Dirkens, John, Reformed minister, 92, 183 & n

Du Bois, Josse, lay preacher, 190

Duflos, Claude, Reformed minister, 61n, 183

Dufour, Robert, Reformed minister, 59n, 68, 183 & n.

Dumont, Gilles, lay preacher, 16, 190

Du Rieu, Adrien, lay preacher, 162n, 190

Dutch Revolt, 2, 134, 176, 179–80

Edward VI, king of England, 96, 97, 102

Egmont, Lamoral Count of, 11, 14, 21, 22, 153, 158 & n, 159 & n, 174

Elizabeth I, queen of England, 83, 96, 106

Emden and N. Netherlands, Reformed churches of, 1, 2, 47, 48, 58, 60, 65, 66 & n, 71, 80, 84, 92, 94–6 & n, 97, 100, 103, 104, 118, 119, 124, 136, 141; Synod of 1571, 126n, 180

Engelram, John, Reformer in England, 44, 132

England, Reformed churches of, 1, 47, 48, 60, 81, 83–4, 96–100, 102, 106, 113, 129, 135

Erail, Evrard, Reformed minister, 58, 59n, 183

Erasme, lay preacher, 190 & n

Erasmus, Desiderius: and Netherlands Protestantism, 52–3 & n, 102, 116, 130, 135, 146 & n; and iconoclasm, 28

Escaille, Antoine, lay preacher, 49, 162n, 192

Escoubecque, lord of, 18

Fabri, Louis (Savary), Reformed minister, 183 & n

Family of Love, 57n

Farel, Guillaume, 89

Faveau, Simon, Reformed minister, 59n 68n, 69, 72, 183

Ferlitto, Geronimo, Reformed minister, 183 & n

Flameng, Robert, Reformed minister, 42n, 48n, 49, 98n, 180n, 186

France, Reformed churches of, 1, 47, 48, 59, 82, 85, 87–90, 96, 103–5, 116, 122, 123, 129, 180

Frankenthal, Netherlands refugee church, 91, 93, 95

Frankfurt, Netherlands refugee church, 91–2, 95, 120–1, 122, 126, 131

Frarin, Peter, Netherlands academic, 39, 41, 81, 83, 101, 133–4, 140, 155

Frederick III, prince of the Palatinate, 41, 91, 92, 93, 94, 143, 173n

Frizon, Henri, lay preacher, 190

Gabriel, Pieter, Reformed minister, 80n, 183

Garcia, Philip, Reformed minister, 49, 98n, 132 & n, 180n, 186

Gay, Laurens, Reformed minister, 183 & n

Geerking, Joost, lay preacher, 192

Geneva, Reformed church of, 46, 47, 48, 49, 50, 58, 65, 70, 74–5, 81, 84–7, 88, 96, 100, 101, 104–5, 107, 118, 136

Index

Gérard, lay preacher, 190

Germany, Reformed churches of, 1, 41, 47, 48, 90–5, 98, 100–5, 107, 120, 122, 126, 129, 131

Geyl, Pieter, 31

Gheetius, Herman, lay preacher, 190

Gillain, Jehan, Reformed minister, 42n, 49, 95n, 186 & n

Godin, Jehan, Reformed minister, 183

Goris, Adrien, Reformed minister, 183

Granvelle, Antoine Perrenot, Lord of, 32, 40, 54n, 126, 152, 153, 178

Gresham, Thomas, English merchant, 147

Grincourt, Jean, lay preacher, 88n, 190

Grindall, Edmund, bishop of London, 97, 123

Guelder, Adolph, Duke of, 160n

Guérart, Pierre, Reformed minister, 183

Guy, Martin, Reformed minister, 183

Habosch, Simon, lay preacher, 162n, 163, 180n, 194 & n

Halewijn, Conrad, lay preacher, 190

Happaert, Gabriel, lay preacher, 162n, 192 & n

Hazard, Pieter, Reformed minister, 44, 45, 47n, 49, 61n, 75n, 80 & n, 88 & n, 98n, 99 & n, 118n, 143n, 144, 166, 180n, 186

Heckelers, Wilhem, Reformed minister, 62 & n, 63, 71, 183

Hector, lay preacher, 192

Hedgepreaching, 1, 5–10, 38, 39, 69–70, 111, 140, 144–6, 149, 167–73, 174, 177

Hendrix, Jan, Reformed minister, 75n, 183

Herlin, Michel, lay Reformer, 16

Herman, lay preacher, 190

Hessels, François, lay preacher, 192

Hobé, Lucas, Huguenot minister, 166n

Hornes, Philippe de Montmorency, Count of, 19, 153, 155

Houvenagle, Gilles, lay preacher, 162n, 192 & n

Hubert, Reformed minister, 183

Huberti, Cornelis, Lutheran minister, 6, 140

Huguenots, 2, 3, 21, 87, 88, 89, 90, 106, 116, 129, 138, 141, 156, 178

Huisman, Alardin, Reformed minister, 183

Iconoclasm: in the Netherlands, 1, 5, 10–12, 20–38, 45–6, 50, 64n, 133, 142, 158–61, 173–5, 180–1; in France, 5, 10, 33 & n, 35 & n, 160 & n, 166n, 177–8 & n; in Switzerland, 35; in Germany, 35, 159n; in England, 26n; and Reformed theology, 28–9, 43–5, 47–8, 131–2, 136 & n

Inquisition, 1, 6, 170, 171

Jacobus, *see* Van Culembourg

Jan, lay preacher, Tournai, 194

Jan, lay preacher, Valenciennes, 183

Jodocus, lay preacher, 190

Joost, lay preacher, 194

Julien, lay preacher, 33n, 165, 166, 167, 190

Junius, Franciscus (du Jon) Reformed minister, 6, 14, 27, 39, 40, 43, 48 & n, 49, 80 & n, 85 & n, 86, 90, 101–2, 107, 112, 130, 132, 133 & n, 134, 149n, 163, 165, 172, 175, 179n, 180n, 186

Kackhoes, lay preacher, 6, 60, 146, 165, 194

Kingdon, Robert, 85, 115

Knox, John, 111, 132

Kok, Jehan, lay preacher, 162n, 163n, 195 & n

Konink, Charles, Reformed minister, 183

Labruicken, Jan, lay preacher, 190

Laerle, Jan, lay preacher, 192

Lamoot, Jan, Reformed minister, 48 & n, 49, 98 & n, 99n, 180n, 186

Lantsochtius, Christophe, Reformed minister, 49, 95n, 180n, 186

Lap, Reformed minister, 183

Le Bron, Charles, Reformed minister, 49, 85n, 93n, 98n, 180n, 186

Le Clercq, Gilles, lay Reformer, 17

Le Febvre, Loys, lay preacher, 192

Lemaistre, Reformed minister, 183

Lems, Gilles, lay preacher, 162n, 194

Lenaerts, Pieter, lay preacher, 194

Le Roux, Pierre, Reformed minister, 184 & n

Leseur, Jean, Reformed minister, 36, 49, 85n, 86n, 88, 120, 142n, 143, 144, 159n, 180n, 186

Lévi-Strauss, Claude, 107

Leyden, John of, 167
Libertines, *see* Spiritual Libertines
Lievyn, lay preacher, 163n, 195
Lippens, Jan, Reformed minister, 49, 80, 186
Loïstes, *see* Spiritual Libertines
London, Reformed churches of, 4, 43, 44–5, 47, 48, 65, 66n, 96–100, 103, 121–2, 123, 124 & n, 126n, 132, 136, 162n
Loonis, Jan, lay preacher, 192
Lopez, Martin, lay preacher, 162n, 163, 165–6, 194
Louchard, Jehan, lay preacher, 162n, 163, 192
Loysier, Mahieu, lay preacher, 165n, 190
Lupis, Martin, lay preacher, 195
Luther, Martin: influence in the Netherlands, 52, 53, 57n, 102; and the Spiritual Libertines, 56; and prophecy, 110; and language, 125; *see also* Lutheranism
Lutheranism: in the Netherlands, 6, 7, 17n, 19, 23, 33n, 73n, 79, 116, 119, 123, 140, 143, 145, 147 & n, 148–9, 150, 161, 174, 178; relations of German Lutherans and Netherlands Reformers, 37, 45, 46, 47, 48, 71, 90–4, 95, 100, 104, 105–6, 107, 120, 131, 137, 141, 153, 154n, 179–80; and Anabaptism, 138

Mallard, Philippe, Reformed minister, 59n, 68n, 69, 184
Malpau, Jehan, lay preacher, 195
Mansfeld, Peter Ernst Count of, 21
Marian persecution, 96, 111, 113, 116, 129
Mariette, lay preacher, 190
Marmier, Etienne, Reformed minister, 37, 39, 42n, 46n, 47 & n, 49, 50, 80n, 85n, 86, 123, 144, 175, 180n, 186
Marnix of Thoulouse, Philippe de, Lord of St Aldegonde, 6, 19, 23, 87, 101n, 174
Marot, Clément, 126n
Martenus, lay preacher, 190
Martin, lay preacher, 195
Martyrdom, 1, 51, 58, 63, 70, 73–9, 81–2, 83, 112–13, 180–1
Mary, queen of England, 91, 116

Matte, Sebastien, Reformed minister, 11, 30n, 41, 49, 50, 98 & n, 99n, 158, 180n, 186
May, John, Reformed minister, 49, 98n, 180n, 186
Meghem, Count of, 153n
Melanchthon, Philip, 56
Mennonites, 72, 79, 132–8, 148, 179; *see also* Simons, Menno
Merula, Ange, Reformed minister, 76, 184
Metz, Reformed church of, 48, 89–90, 103–4
Micheus, Jean, Reformed minister, 40–1, 48, 49, 85n, 86, 117, 162n, 169, 180n, 186
Michiels, Jan, Reformed minister, 20, 44, 49, 98n, 100n, 187
Micronius, Marten, Netherlands minister in London, 92, 97
Ministers, Netherlands Reformed: training and experience, chapter 4, *passim*; ordination and pastoral goals, 2, 57–60, 82, 95; and sacraments, 61–2, 64, 103, 108–9, 119–23, 135–6, 145–6; social origins of, chapter 2, *passim*; and lay preachers, 59–60, 62–3, 71–2, 81, 141, 162–7; and iconoclasm, 11–14, 21–7, 30n, 32–3, 35–8, 44–50, 132–3, 136, 174; and violence, 66–70, 81, 98–100, 156–8; and military campaigns, 9, 15, 16–20, 30, 36–7, 160–4; and politics, 2–3, 13–20, 30, 43f, 100–6, 113–17, 128–34, 136, 139, 141–2, 149, 175, 177, 181; and Anabaptism, 115–16, 133–4, 138; and charismatic authority, 3, 140f, 150–1, 167
Missuens, Jan (Cornelissen van Diest), Reformed minister, 49, 80n, 180n, 187
Moded, Herman, Reformed minister, 9, 11 & n, 12, 13, 14, 16, 17 & n, 22, 23, 24, 30, 36, 40, 42 & n, 44, 45 & n, 46, 49, 60, 80n, 85n, 91n, 95, 96, 98n, 105, 107, 114, 115, 116, 118n, 124, 125, 131–2, 143, 144, 145, 165, 169n, 170, 171, 180n, 187
Moderation of April, 1566, 1, 6, 9, 83
Moermanszone, Heyndrick (Van Beerse), lay preacher, 195
More, Thomas, 28
Morillon, Maximilien, Catholic humanist and clergyman, 32

Mostaert, Chrétien, Reformed minister, 49, 80n, 95n, 180n, 184, 187 & n
Motley, John, 21
Moyessone, Jehan, lay preacher, 162n, 194
Munt, Jan, lay preacher, 14, 162n, 165, 195

Nassau, Louis Count of, 17, 20, 101n, 104, 153
Netherlands Confession of Faith (1561), 48, 51, 64–5, 68, 69, 80, 103, 119, 122, 133, 180
Nicolas, lay preacher, 190
Nigri, Reformed minister, 184
Nobility: relations with Reformed ministers, 3, 6, 17, 36, 40–1, 47–8, 50, 70–1, 87–90, 91–4, 104–6, 116–17, 131, 161–75; and Reformed movement, 14, 15, 22, 152–5, 178; and hedgepreaching, 8, 169, 171–2; iconoclasm and military campaigns, 11–13, 18, 19, 20–1, 36, 37, 158–61, 176–7
Noircarmes, Philippe de St Aldegonde, Lord of, 16, 17, 18

Obry, Adriaan, Reformed minister, 184
Onghena, Lievyn, lay Reformer, 12, 30
Orange, William of, Count of Nassau, 11, 15, 19, 46n, 47, 48, 94, 104, 105, 116, 117, 131, 153, 154, 159, 171, 180
Orphanus, Jacques, Reformed minister, 184
Oude, Jehan, lay preacher, 191
Outreleauwe, Jehan, lay preacher, 191

Paneel, Michel, lay preacher, 191
Panquert, Nicolas, lay preacher, 91n, 93, 162n, 195
Parma, Margaret of, 6, 7, 10, 13, 14, 16, 18, 19, 21, 34, 37, 40, 43, 48n, 64, 69 & n, 72, 76, 87, 90, 149, 152–5, 172, 173, 178
Pasquier de la Barre, magistrate of Tournai, 10n, 22, 42n, 155
Perez, Marcus, lay Reformer, 17
Philip II (ruled 1555–98), 17, 18, 21, 23, 46n, 65, 87, 101–2, 111, 116, 117, 132, 149, 152–55, 157, 158, 172, 173, 177, 178 & n, 179
Pierre, lay preacher in Breda, 194
Pierre, lay preacher in Hasselt, 191

Pieters, Balthasar, Reformed minister, 46n, 187
Pinchart, lay preacher, 191
Plantin publishing house, 103, 126
Platevoet, Mahieu, Reformed minister, 49, 98n, 180n, 187
Pluquet, Nicolas, lay preacher, 162n, 191
Pocquet, Antoine, Libertine minister, 56–7
Pollon, Jean, Reformed minister, 184
Pontfort, Jacob, Reformed minister, 49, 95n, 119n, 180n, 187
Pontus Payen, Catholic administrator, 21
Poullain, lay preacher, 184
Poullain, Valerand, lay Reformer in Strasbourg, 51
Prêche, see Hedgepreaching
Protestant propaganda, 6, 23–4, 27, 29, 31, 63–4, 73–7, 81–2, 102–3, 107, 125–6, 132, 161
Pruystinck, Eloi, Libertine minister, 56
Puritanism, 2, 3, 97–8, 135, 136n, 138, 141
Puthuys, Paulus, lay preacher, 191
Pyllian, François, lay preacher, 162n, 191

Quaret, Jacques, Reformer minister, 184

Rattevangerken, lay preacher, 191 & n
René, Duchess of Ferrara, 89–90
Rhetius, Cornille, Reformed minister, 49, 95n, 131, 162n, 180n, 187
Richardot, François, Netherlands bishop, 146n
Robillart, Michel, Reformed minister, 51, 58, 61n, 78, 79, 82n, 184
Robrecht, Martin, lay preacher, 163n, 195
Rudsemelis, Jan, Reformed minister, 45n, 48, 49, 85n, 86n, 143, 144, 180n, 187
Rutgers, F. L., 94
Ruvart, lay preacher, 162n, 191
Ryckwaert, Charles, Reformed minister, 49, 91n, 113, 124, 187

St Trond, meeting (of July, 1566), 9, 19, 20–1
Saravia, Adrien, Reformed minister, 63, 117, 124, 184
Savary, Loys, lay preacher, 162n, 163n, 183n, 195
Schelins, Josse, lay preacher, 193 & n
Schoemaker, Pierre, lay preacher, 191 & n.
Schoonhove, Gilles, lay preacher, 162n, 191

Schuddematte, Adriaan, lay preacher, 162n, 193 & n

Sedan, Duke of, 40, 89, 90

Sheerlambrecht, Jan, lay Reformer, 103

Simons, Menno, 72, 115–16, 137 & n; *see also* Mennonites

Slabbaert, Godfried, lay preacher, 162n, 194

Soret, Jean, lay preacher, 193

Spiritual Libertines, 56–7, 58, 72, 74, 128, 145, 179n

Sterkenbrugge, Jakob van, Reformed minister, 49, 95n, 180n, 187

Stoffijn, lay preacher, 191

Strada, F., 20, 34

Strobbe, Jehan, Reformed minister, 49, 98n, 180n, 187

Switzerland, churches of, 1, 96

Synods, Netherlands churches, 6, 17, 44, 64–5, 71, 79

Taffin, Jacques, lay Reformer, 63

Taffin, Jean, Reformed minister, 6, 14, 40, 42n, 43, 46 & n, 48 & n, 49, 50 & n, 59n, 63, 85n, 86, 89, 90, 91n, 93, 94, 95, 96, 103, 104, 105, 107, 120n, 125, 126, 130–1, 132, 174, 179n, 180 & n, 187

Tardif, Jacob, lay preacher, 162n, 191

Theodore, lay preacher, 191

Thevelin, Walerand, lay preacher, 162n, 191 & n

Thierry, Quintin, Libertine minister, 56, 74

Titelman, Peter, Inquisitor, 72, 153

Tomas, Laurins, lay preacher, 191

Top, Erasmus, Reformed minister, 48, 49, 95n, 98, 180n, 187

Tournai, Reformed church of, 6, 7, 13, 18, 52, 53, 59, 61–3, 64n, 65, 68–70, 72, 75

Traisnel, Antoine, lay preacher, 163n, 194

Traisnel, Christophe, lay preacher, 162n, 163n, 194

Trent, Council of, 55n, 153n

Tuerlinck, Jan, lay preacher, 195

Tuny, lay preacher, 191

Tuscaens, Hans, lay Reformer, 10

Utenhove, Jan, lay Reformer in London, 92n, 103, 119n, 125n, 137n, 179n

Valenciennes: Reformed church of, 7, 15–16, 17, 65, 68, 69, 80, 82, 85n, 173; siege of, 18–20, 47n, 48n, 50, 88, 113, 160, 173

Valencijn, Reformed minister, 48n, 95n, 187 & n

Van Aken, Goert, lay preacher, 193

Van Baecx, Lambert, lay preacher, 165n, 191

Van Bombergen, Cornelis, Netherlands nobleman, 19

Van Brugghe, Hansken, Reformed minister, 61n, 184

Van Culembourg, Jacobus, Reformed minister, 46 & n, 47, 49, 91n, 93n, 94, 95n, 180n, 187

Van den Driessche, Clement, lay preacher, 162n, 195 & n

Van den Wyer, Hans, Reformed minister, 184

Van der Heyden, Gaspar, Reformed minister, 30 & n, 36, 40, 43, 45, 49, 50, 59, 67, 91 & n, 92, 93, 95, 100, 105, 119, 124–5, 126n, 142n, 149, 158 & n, 180n, 187

Van der Schuere, Nicaise, Reformed minister, 40, 49, 111, 118, 143–4 & n, 180n, 187

Van der Thomme, Mathijs, lay preacher, 162n, 191

Van Diest, Jan, lay preacher, 165n, 191

Van Haemstede, Adrien, Reformed minister, 65, 66 & n, 67, 70, 71, 72, 73, 74, 75, 81, 82, 95, 98n, 114, 135, 137n, 184

Van Hardenberg, Albert, Reformed minister, 184

Van Hatthem, Melchoir, lay preacher, 191 & n

Van Hernen, Gilles, lay preacher, 162n, 191

Van Houte, Jan., lay preacher, 163n, 196

Van Huele, Jehan, Flemish nobleman, 20

Van Kerpen, Willem, lay preacher, 196

Van Joncx, Nemaer, lay preacher, 193

Van Lommersen, Willem Florin, lay preacher, 162n, 195

Van Maeldegem, Adrien, lay preacher, 100n, 162n, 164n, 196

Van Mechelen, Jaspar, lay preacher, 196

Van Ostende, Jan, Reformed minister, 59, 184

Van Schelven, A. A., 94, 102

Van Thorn, Lem, lay preacher, 165n, 192

Van Til, Thomas, lay preacher, 112, 162n, 166n, 196

Van Vaernewijck, Marcus, magistrate of Ghent, 5, 8, 10, 15, 22, 23, 24–5 & n, 26–7, 31, 33n, 34, 36n, 38n, 40n, 115, 144, 146 & n, 148, 149n, 150 & n, 155, 158n, 159, 160n, 161, 169, 170, 172, 174

Van Vyve, Jan, Reformed minister, 49, 95n, 162n, 188

Van Wesembeke, Jacques, magistrate of Antwerp, 11n, 32n, 34, 46, 177

Van Wingen, Jan, Reformed minister, 184 & n

Van Woensel, Goert, lay preacher, 196

Varlut, François, Reformed minister, 58, 60, 68n, 76, 78, 82n, 184

Vercoye, Jan, lay preacher, 193

Verdickt, Gilles, Reformed minister, 67, 76, 82n, 184

Verrier, Gerardus Loyen, lay preacher, 192 & n

Viglius ab Aytta Svichemius, Catholic jurist, 20

Vrambout, Georges, Reformed minister, 184

Vrancq, Jerome, lay preacher, 162n, 195

Vriese, lay preacher, 192

Waels, Pieter, lay Reformer in England, 20

Waghe, Hendrick, lay preacher, 195

Wallet, Jean, Reformed minister, 184

Walraeven, Cornelis, Reformed minister, 9, 21, 158, 162n, 164n, 196

Walzer, Michael, 115, 129, 135

Watelet, Maurice (Baudewin), lay preacher, 163, 193

Watelet, Thomas, Reformed minister, 60, 75, 184

Wattrelos–Lannoy, battle of, 18, 45, 47n, 160, 165

Weber, Max, 109, 122, 124, 134, 138, 140f, 150

Wells, H. G., 151

Wille, Ambroise, Reformed minister, 7, 9, 17, 21 & n, 46n, 49, 65, 69, 80n, 85n, 86, 87 & n, 133, 144, 158, 171, 180n, 188

Wingius, Godfried, Reformed minister, 44–5, 48 & n, 49, 50, 91n, 92, 95n, 97n, 98n, 99n, 100, 103, 105, 121–2 & n, 123, 126, 128, 129, 132–3, 137, 180n, 188

Worsley, Peter, 150–1

Woudanus, Johannes, lay preacher, 162n, 192

Württemberg, Christophe, Duke of, 93

Wyart, Jacques, Reformed minister, 184

Wybo, Joris, Reformed minister, 30 & n, 45, 46n, 47, 49, 77, 80n, 98n, 122 & n, 123 & n, 180n, 188

Xhoka, Leonard, lay preacher, 163, 165, 196

Zoete, François, Reformed minister, 184

Zwingli, Ulrich, 53, 110